Mark Steel

began his route to Slight Success in 1982, after leaving his job at London Transport to become a comedian. From a first gig at the Dulwich Poetry Society, he graduated to performing his own two-hour stand-up show and now appears regularly on TV and radio.

He has written and presented several series of *The Mark Steel Solution* and *The Mark Steel Lectures* for BBC Radio Four, and the *Lectures* have been subsequently recreated and revised for BBC Television. Mark has appeared on many other programmes, including *Never Mind The Buzzcocks*, *Have I Got News For You?* and *Question Time*. He has written for a number of publications, ranging from obscure cricket magazines and *The Socialist Worker* to *The Guardian* and has a weekly column in *The Independent*.

Mark Steel lives in Crystal Palace, south London, with his partner and their two children.

It's Not A Runner Bean...

Dispatches From a Slightly Successful Comedian

Mark Steel

THE DO-NOT PRESS

This collection first Published in Great Britain in 1996 by
The Do-Not Press
16 The Woodlands
London SE13 6TY

Third edition 2004.

ISBN 1-904-316-43-3

British Library Cataloguing in Publication Data. A cata-
logue record for this book is available from the British
Library.

Printed and bound in Great Britain.

Thanks to...

Jim Driver for taking so much trouble over a project destined to make no money; to Jenny Landreth and Linda Smith for their comments; to my *Solution* collaborator, Pete Sinclair for his welcome if wonderful obsession with detail. Thanks mostly to Bindy Mellor – to live with a comedian must be difficult, to live with a writer even harder, to live with both at the same time must be a nightmare.

Bloody hell – I sound like a proper author...

Contents

Introduction to the New Edition 9
Introduction to the Original Edition 14

Part One:
Giving Up The Day Job 11
So, How Did You Get Started? 21
Why? 24
The Poet, The Owl and The Rastafarian 28
Mrs Bartlett 34

Part Two: Struggling
And Now – Richard Nixon 39
Ipswich 44
You're Shit – And You Don't Know You Are 45
Escapology 49
The Miners' Strike...50
Geordie 58
Elephant Fair 60
War Crimes in Watford 64
All The Way To Bournemouth 68
Oy, Englishman – Fuck Off 72
New Money, New Danger...76
The Early Career Porn Movie....................................80
Fallen Wimmin 86
The People Round Here 94
The Middle East Crisis and its Effect on a Comedy
Night in Manchester 97
Revolution and the Boiled Egg 102

Part Three: Established
Someone New...109
Under My Skin...112
It Looked Like A Runner Bean 114
Barbara Castle 118
Spend, Spend, Spend..123
Dual Power in Edinburgh...128
Walking Out 132
The Joy of Giving..133
Paris in Revolt...138
Sandwich of the Month...142

And the Award for Best Rebel… 145
The Joke That Brought Down Thatcher 150
A Lost Party...153
I Really Was A Milkman 157
The Case for Cows in the Street 159
I Think I Changed Somebody's Mind 165
Kilroy..169
America...170
Chicago 177
Mother 183
Saturday Night at the Movies.................................188

Part Four: Slightly Successful
The Trauma of the Slightly Successful Comedian ...195
Steel's the Name, Lady 200
Luvvies...204
Lonely 205
But…...211
Their Norman 218
'It's Only Death, Officer'...222
I Think I Changed Somebody's Mind – II 223
Can You Pay Me Less, Please? 225
Jealousy..229
Oranges Are Not The Only Joke 232
Nazis...234
William, It Really Is Nothing...................................237
Gypsy Tart..242
The Real Irish Joke 246
Belfast 252
The Great Publicity Trick 256
A Real Life Banker 261
Hattersley..264
The Girlfriend..265
The Horny-Handed Sons of Entertainment 270
Something to Look Forward to 275
Please Allow Me To Introduce Myself 277
Bosses...279
Flo...280
Mortality...284
A Message in Malvern...290
Are You Talking to Me? 292
Who's In Control Here? 296
Funny 300

Introduction to the New Edition

IN THE EIGHT years since I wrote this book, there seems to have developed a new meaning to the word 'success'. To be successful, it matters little what you've done as long as you've become well-known doing it. The modern celebrity is revered in the galaxy of specialist publications and offered countless pointless appearances on television, even if they're only known because they're an ex-criminal or the wife of a disgraced MP. If Harold Shipman had hung on for a couple more years he'd have been in *Hello* magazine, in a feature called 'Me and my Cell', with soft-focus photos of him smiling wistfully at his slopping-out bucket.

One woman, having been evicted early on from the *Big Brother* house, said that being known by so many people was 'better than sex'. She hadn't noticed – or maybe didn't care – that the reason she was being recognised was because her housemates and viewers disliked her enough to have her evicted. If she'd met Nelson Mandela she'd have said, 'Oh you're soooooo famous, what a great PR stunt to do that prison thing, I bet you could be in practically any advert you fancied.'

Chefs, gardeners and artists are considered successful only if they're well-known. A successful scientist must be a famous scientist, and there are probably science-agents advising their clients to develop a 'unique selling point', lamenting that a wheelchair would have done the trick if only that bloody Hawking hadn't already tied up the paraplegic angle.

Success is everything. I was at a radio awards ceremony recently, when the nominations for 'best documentary' were read out. The first was for a programme called *Ethiopian Famine*. At which point the *Ethiopian Famine* table yelped and cheered, and one woman gazed nervously at her *tartine aux pommes* muttering, 'Ooh my God, please, please, please...' Another nomination was for a programme called *Cot Deaths*, and a similar hubbub brewed from their table. 'And the winner... ' announced Paul Gambacinni, '...is *Ethiopian Famine*.' And the *Ethiopian Famine* table shrieked as if they'd been collectively awarded the title of Miss World. Then they all went up to collect their prize, and excitedly thanked each other, with no mention whatsoever of their subject, not even a 'thanks so much to all those who starved in agony, as without you this really wouldn't have been possible.'

This attitude has been encouraged by a government that measures success in the same way. Bands or films are congratulated when they make a decent profit, or become a 'vital addition to our exports'. If Tony Blair was asked to comment on the Mona Lisa, he'd say it was a marvellous achievement, as it showed how a small business can develop into one of the leading exporters of smiles throughout Europe.

The most pernicious side of this mentality is that it drags so many behind it. The dream of countless teenagers is not to become a good musician or writer or comedian but a famous one. Success means being everywhere. And no one is immune. I was highly flattered when someone rang to tell me that I had been an answer on the afternoon quiz show, *Fifteen-To-One*. What about that? Surely that proves a level of success, doesn't it?

And how is a subversive voice of the counter-culture supposed to react to the following incident? One afternoon, while leaving Television Centre, I noticed in the distance the familiar figure of Bob Monkhouse. Our eyes met, he strode across and said, 'Mark, I'm so pleased to meet you. I've read *Reasons to be Cheerful* three times, it was given to me on my seventy-fifth birthday by Jeremy Beadle.' I bet that never happened to Che Guevara.

And it made my day.

But, despite this cultural onslaught, there are countless examples of humanity defying the trend. Across any city are dozens of music venues, clubs and theatres hosting bands, actors and DJs that have sweated over their performances, and rehearsed in their heads all day while daydreaming through their official work. Actors and comedians perform regularly in plays and shows because they're challenging, rewarding or fun, but which would have no place in their accountant's business plan. One night, while filming for a programme, the cameraman – at the end of a fourteen hour day – insisted we all went to a certain hill to film an extra scene, because the sky there would look stunning at that particular time.

For every fool lured into auditioning for *Pop Idol*, or desperate to compile a showreel in a quest to present a banal show on morning TV, there are hundreds of talented people, eagerly in pursuit of their ambition to express something well.

Flicking back through this book, I see other examples of how little has changed, especially when I see the piece about telling lies to local reporters when asked how I first got started. I was recently asked to do a telephone interview at 9.30 one morning with a woman from the *Maidstone Advertiser*, in advance of a show at the Hazlett Theatre. But when I rang, it was clear she'd forgotten all about it, and didn't have a clue who I was, which was made more poignant because she had one of those supermarket checkout voices. 'And how can I help you, Mr Steel?' she said and it would have seemed natural if she'd followed this up with: 'Mr Jenkins to till number six, to conduct interview with comedian, interview with comedian at till number six, Mr Jenkins.'

Eventually she must have found a scribbled note about the forthcoming show, and started asking her questions.

'Have you ever been to Kent before?' she said, sounding as if her follow-up statement would be, 'Because if you have we're offering a special two-for one deal on Dairylea cheese triangles.' I told her I'd been brought up in Kent and she said, 'Oh really, whereabouts?' It occurred to me I could make up anything I liked, so I said, 'Gravesend.'

'And how did you first get started?' she asked.

'Ah,' I began, 'you see, I used to steer the Gravesend to Tilbury Ferry. And it got really dull doing the same commentary every day – "on your left is Dartford, to your right is the Isle of Grain…" and so on. So I used to make up jokes about Essex, that went down really well with the Kent people but the Essex ones would get furious and cause fights. Then the ferry was bought by a bloke from Chelmsford who sacked me, but by then I was quite famous locally so I got regular gigs from Gravesend up to Sittingbourne."

'Oh, I think our readers *will* be interested in that,' she said. Then, clearly referring to her scant notes, she asked what my first book was about. 'It's about when I stood for Parliament,' I said. 'I was in Lincoln to publicise a gig I was doing. Another ten votes and I'd have won.'

'Oh my goodness,' she said, and now I was thinking, Oh for God's sake, woman, think this through. If this was true, wouldn't it have been on the news? Wouldn't Dimbleby have been gasping, "Well, well, there's a shock result coming in where a comedian has almost gained Lincoln from the Conservatives," while Peter Snow garbled, "If this is repeated across the country Eddie Izzard could take Leicester South and Taunton could fall to Jack Dee".

'And I see you've got a*nother* book, what's that about?' she said. I said, 'It's a children's book. I wrote it because whenever I read a story to my son, he'd tell me he liked the stories but would complain that there's not enough swearing in them. So I've written a children's book full of swearing, to fill a gap in the market.'

'Oh my goodness,' she said. 'What kind of swearing?'

'Swearing swearing,' I said. 'You know, fuck, shit, piss, wank, cunt. Because, let's be honest, most stories don't cater for the modern young boy. My lad thinks Jack and the Beanstalk is tedious but he'd be much more interested if it went: "Five fucking beans, you cheating bastard? What the fuck am I supposed to do with those fuckers?" And, "Fee fi fucking fum." He'd love it.'

'Ooh, my word,' she said, 'did anyone complain?'

'The *News of the World* went mad,' I said, 'they put it on the front page.'

And then I wondered, when she realised I'd been telling her a ridiculous pack of lies, would she find it funny or not? Instead, the following week I arrived at the theatre and found a copy of the *Maidstone Advertiser*. And there it was, the whole lot, the ferry, the Essex jokes, election, a line about 'Mark is no stranger to controversy, when his children's book about swearing hit the headlines...' and a caption under the photo: 'Mark completes his journey from the Gravesend-Tilbury ferry to the Hazlett Theatre in Maidstone this Friday.' I know it's pathetic, but I'm not sure I've ever been so proud of anything in my life. And by a splendid irony, by not thinking through the implausibility of my answer about the nature of this book, she's ended up as a character in this new introduction.

Another reason for personal pride in the midst of this celebrity culture was a result of the other major change to my life over the last eight years: the arrival of two children. One of them, Elliot, was six when he sat with me watching the final of *Big Brother*. Davina announced: 'Big Brother house, we're now broadcasting *live* from the house – so *no swearing*.' And Elliot said, 'Dad, I'd love to be in that house, so I could say, 'Hello Davina, bloody hell, arse, shit.' With pride in my heart I looked in his eye, secure in the knowledge that from one generation to the next, the struggle will continue.

Introduction to the original edition

'MARK!' BELLOWED THE organiser of the Chichester Festival. 'Delighted to have you with us,' he went on, and by now it was clear that this man was so aristocratic he spoke without ever moving his lips.

'Would you care to join me for a cocktail before you do your show? Oh, I do apologise, this is Simon; he's a violinist. Have you two met?' he asked, without even a twitch on the 'm's.

On the lawn beside us was a table from which a collection of people wearing dinner jackets and bow-ties were taking bottles of Pimms and talking loudly about the unreliability of gardeners.

'Were you performing last night?' asked nature's ventriloquist. The previous night I'd been in Newcastle and my hotel arrangements had been buggered up, but two blokes from the audience had offered to put me up. A girl they'd been sharing with had just moved out and had removed most of the items that constitute a home.

'There's no spare bed,' they said.

'Don't worry,' I assured them. 'It's good of you to let me stay. I'll be quite happy on the settee.'

'There's no settee.'

'Carpet?' I enquired.

They shook their heads.

'And the gas and electricity have been cut off, as they were in the girl's name,' they warned me, adding excitedly: 'but there's water.'

As we sat in the dark, one of them suddenly stood up and announced: 'I am going to make a cup of tea,' with the same prowess I imagine Captain Scott must have shown when he stood up to announce, 'I am going to the South Pole.'

And he found a battered kettle, filled it with water and went into the backyard to collect some wood. Then he syphoned petrol out of his van and started to build a camp fire in the living room.

After succeeding in persuading him not to build this fire, I lay freezing on the bare floorboards for an hour or so before deciding to walk the streets of Newcastle until the first train back to London.

'Yes, I did a gig in Newcastle last night,' I said to the organiser in Chichester. Then I took a bottle of Pimms and walked across to the part of the cathedral known as the Bishops Theatre for a soundcheck.

This sort of experience is the first reason for writing this book. For although there are plenty of jobs that involve meeting a wide variety of people, there can't be many that tell you as much about them as when your job is to make them laugh.

Journalists or taxi drivers may, in a twenty-four hour period, meet a Geordie pyromaniac and someone from Chichester who wouldn't dream of going to the post office without a bow-tie; but I didn't just have to meet them, I also had to make them both think I was funny. And it just isn't true that if something's funny, then everyone will laugh at it.

An impressionist famous in China for doing an hysterically funny Deng Xiaoping would be a disaster on British TV. And a joke that starts, 'This thick Serb goes into a pub,' is unlikely to go well if told to a battalion of Serbian militia, even if it went down a storm the night before at a fundraiser for Croatian tank commanders. So, the way an audience reacts to a comedian says as much about the audience as it does about the comedian.

As society changes so do people and the things they laugh at. To me, the ideal position for viewing the people and events of the 1980s and 1990s – yuppies, the Miners' Strike, the birth of the satellite dish, new age travellers, roadies, cabbies, the poll tax, the peace talks in Ireland and the increasing gap between rich and poor – has been from within the world of comedy.

The latest connection between comedy and the society it comes from is the idea, prevalent in modern Britain, that to have passionate ideas and opinions about the injustices that surround us is a silly, antiquated pastime as unfashionable as The Carpenters, but without even their ironic kitsch value. Just as journalists and politicians tell us every day that to campaign for a radically different world is 'outdated' and 'unrealistic', producers and critics promote comedy that is the least opinionated; anything that tries to make a point is berated for being 'politically correct'.

Yet for me the real irony is that modern Britain seems to be a place in which more people feel passionately angry about society's inequality, and more likely to support anyone who opposes it, than at any time I can remember. Apart from which, as well as being more relevant, a comedian talking about real issues (rather than how awkward it is to find the end of a reel of Sellotape) is probably much funnier.

We can respond to the injustices of the world by supporting them, ignoring them or opposing them. The second reason for writing this book is, in its own small way, to attempt to redress the balance towards the idea that comedians can be, and are, part of the Opposition.

The third reason is to tell the story of the Slightly Successful Comedian. For no comedian could use their position to take an overall look at the world without suffering a distinct lack of personal success. After all, how much everyday life does any celebrity witness, forever meeting people who's first thought is, 'Bloody hell, there's that bloke off the telly'?

On the one hand always in work and with my own radio

show; but on the other, never remotely famous, I find that it is this, the heartwarming regularity with which people say, 'No, never heard of him', that allows me the opportunity to be the link between countless magnificent characters and situations; some of them from as far apart as a cathedral in Chichester to an icy floorboard in Newcastle, where the smell of damp is relieved only by the alarming whiff of petrol.

Part One
Giving Up
The Day Job

So, How Did You Get Started?

'NOW MARK, YOU had rather an unusual start in comedy,' said Libby Purves as we sat around a table, broadcasting live on Radio Four's *Midweek*.

The truth was that I had an exceptionally usual start in the world of comedy. 'Did I?' I replied.

And, as she continued, I remembered...

The week before, a researcher had rung me to ask how I'd first got started, so that they could convey this uninteresting information to the listeners.

'It really isn't that interesting,' I'd insisted.

'Well, go on, we'd just like to know.'

Almost every interview a comedian does, at some point reaches the question: 'So, how did you get started?'

'All right then, I'll try and make it interesting,' I said as jokingly as possible. 'Er, let's see. What about this? My father was a Polish diplomat, and when I was a boy he'd take me to Gdansk every Christmas to accompany him on his official duties. I made some friends there and wanted to learn Polish, and it's often said that one of the quickest ways to learn a language is by learning the jokes. One year, when I was about seventeen, I went with my father as usual to the Christmas function and I was asked to make a short speech, but all I could speak in Polish were these jokes. Well, what do you know, they went down particularly well and the next thing I was booked to do a whole set in Polish for officials from a vodka factory.'

'All right, Mark,' laughed the researcher and I'd got out of having to tell the boring story on the radio.

But there I was: sitting opposite Libby Purves, horribly aware that over one million people listen to *Midweek*, as she said, 'Oh Mark, you're being modest. Mark's father was a Polish diplomat, and when he was a boy he'd be taken to Gdansk every Christmas to accompany him on his official duties. He made some friends there and wanted to learn Polish, and it's often said that one of the quickest ways to learn a language is by learning the jokes. One year, when he was about seventeen, he went with his father as usual to the Christmas function and was asked to make a short speech, but all he could speak in Polish were these jokes. Well, what do you know, they went down particularly well and the next thing he was booked to do a whole set in Polish for officials from a vodka factory.'

I suppose it's imagined that there must be a fascinating story to how anyone 'got started', but the sad truth is that most comedians begin their careers by seeing other comedians and thinking they could have a go. Then they probably ring a few clubs and ask if they can go along and do five minutes, and if they show any promise, stick with it.

The interesting part is likely to be not how the comedy career began, but how every attempt at another career ended in disaster. I, for example, was a messenger who lost documents, a watch salesman who had his watches nicked, a clerk who got sacked, a petrol pump boy who got sacked and a milkman who backed his float into a BMW belonging to an ex-British light heavyweight boxing champion.

So hearing my Polish diplomat story go out on air, I decided that I would always answer the question with a tale that was interesting, but completely untrue.

I told a magazine that I'd been a dustman who'd got out of the initiation ceremony of being buried in a skip by promising to write some jokes about the depot. As a result I was booked to do a turn at the south London dustmen region annual ball, and 'it all took off from there, really.'

I once told a local newspaper that I was terrified of flying, and the only way I could get over my nerves in an aeroplane was to stand up and tell jokes to the other passengers. The captain was so impressed that he booked me to do a regular turn on the London-Dublin shuttle service.

These stories are surely so full of holes, they're utterly implausible. A captain has no authority to book comedians. Only organised criminals would bury anyone in a skip. The son of a high-up Polish diplomat wouldn't speak with a south London accent. Yet so romantic is the notion of the budding comedian that professional researchers and journalists seem to take it all in, probably because it fits the genre so much more neatly than, 'I was in a poetry group and I rang up some struggling clubs for gigs.'

I suppose journalists believe these stories because they suit what they'd like to be true. But then this is the same profession that, because it was a good story, swallowed the idea that Charles Windsor and Diana Spencer got married because they'd been swept away in a fairytale romance.

Why?

WHY WOULD SOMEONE become a comedian?

One of the most nerve-racking tasks known to humanity is to tell a joke at a social gathering, because a joke has no other purpose than to make people laugh. Tell someone you went to the bank today and you've given them information. Tell them you think Paul Gascoigne is crap and people will think: 'Well, now we know your opinion.' But a joke is a much higher risk investment.

Firstly, it requires the assembled company's complete attention. Once this is established, there's the awful feeling of having started something that will have to be seen through, no matter what; like the feeling you have as you launch yourself into one of those huge water chutes at the swimming pool. But the worst part is that jokes, unlike any other collection of words, are easily separated into successes and failures. A good joke makes everyone laugh, a bad joke makes no one laugh. It's that simple. If no one laughs, you have quite clearly tried and failed. So, as you throw yourself into the story, you have to be prepared for a verdict which, if it goes the wrong way, will leave you fumbling around in humiliation, searching for a justification for taking up people's time with such bollocks about a talking dog.

Even within professional entertainment, a drama with a dozen laughs in ninety minutes will be described as a funny play. A disc jockey's whimsical banter can make him an hilariously crazy off-the-wall genius. If someone on Open University did one funny thing per programme, they'd become the cult of the Funny Lecturer. But once you call yourself a comedian, you have no purpose other than to be funny.

So why are some people comedians in the sense that even if it was illegal to earn any money from it, they would do it for free in their tea break? It has been argued that comedy has a valuable place in society, and that this explains the need to perform. But if we wanted to provide a service we could still do that and satisfy the performing urge far more productively.

Once, after a show, someone was telling me how impressed they were that anyone could get up in front of a group of strangers and hold their attention for an hour. I smugly shrugged my shoulders with an expression of, 'Who knows how nature chooses where to bestow her gifts.'

After accepting the flattery I said, 'What do you do?' with the same condescending sense of duty as the Queen. 'Oh, I'm just a teacher,' she said.

Teaching is a job every bit as difficult as a comic's. No comedian has to do three to five shows a day, the first at nine o'clock in the morning, to an audience that's been made to attend by a combination of parent and legal pressure; with a constant threat of hecklers who can crease everyone up with ''Ere sir, Micky Tillman's farted,' with some of the audience regularly getting nose-bleeds, and throughout knowing that the father of the rowdiest person in the room owns a scrap-metal yard and a shotgun. And comedians, if they work the room sufficiently with enough material, improvisation and charm to keep the crowd happy five days a week, are not slated in reviews because at the end of the show the audience were tested and not enough of them knew the chemical symbol for mercury.

For a teacher the performance is a means to an end, so even the best teachers get no applause at the end of a lesson and go through whole careers without getting a single encore.

For similar reasons, I can sympathise with the people who do commentaries on tour buses and guide people around museums, when they feel they have to add a smattering of comedy. Like the bloke on the canal boat I went on in the Black Country who said: 'On your left is the famous collapsed house, and when it collapsed into the canal it brought a whole new meaning to the phrase, "I'm just going to drop in on somebody".'

I would imagine that he assures himself that the comedy is a tool for providing tourists with useful facts about the West Midlands' countryside. Full-time comedians have no such noble aim.

Even a barman once told me how much performance was involved in asking people to drink up and leave. 'There's an art,' he proudly explained, 'in creating the right mix of politeness and authority. I was really nervous on my first night,' he went on, 'until I became comfortable with my own style.' Who would have thought a barman could have opening night jitters?

Unlike all these other professions, stand-up comedy has no ulterior motive. It gets nothing done except itself. The answer then, is to be funny for a reason. Have something to say and not only will you be using comedy as a way of getting it across, but life will be far less risky. *Steptoe and Son* and *Catch 22* could sustain long periods without laughs because they were so wonderfully poignant. That, I sometimes convince myself, is why I always wanted to be a comedian. Because it's such a marvellous way of expressing your thoughts to the world.

But then why, at the age of fourteen on holiday with my Mum and Dad in Ventnor during a night of ballroom dancing and a bloke trying to sing like Tony Bennett, when the band leader asked if there was anyone who would like to tell some jokes while the band was having a break, did I stand up and say, 'Me'?

It can't have been a simple cry for sympathy because at fourteen you're too old to win the granny vote, unless you sing soprano. Besides which my first joke was: 'These two blokes are digging up the road. One says "Here, is that Fanny Green?" The other says "No, that's just the traffic light reflecting off that puddle."'

After carrying on in a similar vein for three or four minutes about nuns, cucumbers and constipated monkeys the band leader came across and said, 'Yes, well, thank you very much Mark, er, give him a round of applause. It's harder than it looks up here. Right?'

I never found out what my mum and dad were thinking throughout my début. I can't remember whether anybody laughed; probably not. And I'm sure some people thought, 'Who are that awful boy's parents?' But despite it all, I was hooked.

So why did I do it? Who knows? I had nothing of value to say, I didn't make myself particularly popular and wasn't even getting laughs; but what I do know is that for those four minutes, I couldn't possibly be ignored.

The Poet, The Owl and The Rastafarian

SO, HOW DID I get started in comedy? In 1980, at the age of twenty, I moved to south London, where I was unemployed, with a room in my very own squat in a street of squats, where no one went to bed before four in the morning and complete strangers would knock on the door at 2.30am and tell you they needed some peanut butter.

It was quite normal to arrive home to find a dozen people dancing in the living room because someone had given out your address for a party by mistake. The only time a party ended before two o'clock was when someone accidentally cut through the mains with an axe, and one night a bloke tapped on the window at midnight and asked if he could borrow a wardrobe as he needed it for his pet owl.

It was a new beginning and an ideal time to start pursuing the comedic ambitions that were first lit that night in Ventnor. I got a job and, during the long and tedious hours I spent gazing out of the window as an office clerk for London Transport, I was dreaming up songs and poems which I was certain would be hysterically funny if ever I got the chance to perform them. So when I spotted a notice in a magazine for a poetry group that met in Clapham, I decided to go along.

I arrived to find that the address given was also a squat, and that my fellow poets were a salesman, his sister, a teacher who'd had to leave his home town after an affair with a pupil, a Rastafarian with a black belt in karate, a painter who everyone called 'Emile' but whose name (I found out six months later) was Steve, a college graduate from a rich background who wished he was poor, a

Scotsman who got drunk and interrupted everyone else's poems, and Ian, who squatted the house.

I was to be the twenty-year-old ridiculously angry unemployed socialist who said 'bollocks' a lot. The squat had no water or heating but we did have a few beers and it was handy, being on the Wandsworth Road. And it did have a downstairs room which Ian excitedly assured us he'd almost finished turning into a theatre. He'd already got a velvet curtain and a piano.

The format for the evening was for us to sit round a table and take turns to read out our poems, while Ian's wife held their new born baby in the corner. Some were funny, some thoughtful. The Rastafarian's were too full of 'I and I' type phrases for me to understand, there not being an abundance of red, gold and green in Swanley. The Scotsman, not to be outdone, developed a comically unfathomable dialect and read a poem called *To Mary In Heaven*, which was so full of *achs*, *nays* and words like *cahoot*, I wondered whether he was reading the whole thing backwards.

My poems at this time were either attempts to be funny or angry rants against someone or other in authority, though I was so full of bile that my comical poems – like one about the relative unpopularity of green Rowntree's fruit gums – were delivered with exactly the same vitriol as the ones about the punishments I wanted to inflict on Margaret Thatcher.

Having been on the dole for some time, I'd developed the negative side of being angry, whereby the enemy weren't just heads of multinationals, but anyone who went to a restaurant or had a couple of items of furniture which hadn't come off a skip. 'Yeah well, it's all right for them with their posh flat and new suit,' I'd think about someone with a second-hand jacket and a rented place above a cycle shop.

About once a month the group would do a public performance, there hardly ever being more people in the audience than there was in the show. The first one I took part in was a recital in the back room of a pub in Dulwich Village to the Dulwich Poetry Group, a dozen or so people in their fifties who all looked like Conservative members of a parish council. 'Right,' I thought, blaming them for my own poverty and probably for the military regime in El Salvador. 'I won't do the fruit gums poem as planned, I'll do the one about unemployment, that'll teach 'em.'

For about five minutes I spat and stamped my way through my soliloquy, snarling at the audience who sat in two rows and looked like a room of applicants to become 1930's grammar school headmistresses.

I delivered the last verse, a prophecy of how Britain could look if unemployment was allowed to continue rocketing, with as much animosity as I could muster:

Will we be searching in the dustbins
When we've used our breadcrumb ration,
Killing off our families
As a last act of compassion
Millions traipsing streets, mass killings
Typhoid spreading strong
Curfews, armed policeman, looters,
Soup queues two miles long,
What will you decide then
In your new formed coalition?
Because of what we dread now
I'd rather you were dead now
If a life of unemployment
Means a death from malnutrition.

I was convinced that this would have a profound effect on every one of them. It might make them take their kids out of private school and use the money to buy arms for the Sandinistas. Or maybe they would just throw up on the spot. Instead they smiled, clapped politely, and one of them leaned over to tell me I must have a very good memory to have not forgotten the words.

Ian never attended the performances, it was all far too organised for him. Yet he had written some brilliant poems, including a heartfelt piece about the American-backed coup that had taken place in Chile. A poem about a South American coup has marvellous potential for being so horribly worthy you could start to feel sympathy for the Generals, but his was memorable not only for its sense of indignation, but also for its ability to be honest and passionately optimistic.

One night, in a drunken stupor, he told me he wanted me to do the opening show when he'd finished converting the downstairs of his squat into a theatre, which wouldn't be long as a bloke from a curry house had promised him some chairs. I walked the three miles home that night, convinced that I was on the edge of stardom.

As part of this bid for fame, I went to the Troubadour Café in Earl's Court where, on Tuesday nights, anyone could get up and do their stuff. As I arrived I noticed the drunken Scotsman, who announced that he would like to perform a poem he'd written a few years earlier called *To Mary In Heaven*.

None of it made any more sense than the last time I'd heard it. It didn't until the following week, when I flicked through an anthology of poems by Robert Burns in the local library and there in the middle was *To Mary In Heaven*, with every *ach*, *noch* and *wahoo* in its proper place.

After a while, someone had the idea of hiring a director for the shows. The result was a real life drama far more gripping than anything he could have imagined directing, as he was the campest, most effeminate luvvie imaginable and part of his job was to get the Rastafarian to perform more theatrically.

'One thing I simply can't abide,' he screamed during the first rehearsal, 'is performers standing square to the audience. That (and he demonstrated) creates a fascist relationship with an audience. This (he shuffled round to a forty-five degree angle) is a socialist way to stand.'

Then he clapped his hands quickly twice and we all had to practice standing in a socialist way. The Rasta started yelling abuse and a scene was set that could only end with one or other departing from the group. The difficulty for most of us was the classic problem encountered by anyone who gets absurdly liberal about oppressed minorities. We daren't criticise the director because he was gay, but we daren't criticise the karate expert because he was black. But they couldn't both be right, because one of them was threatening to murder the other, who was responding by calling him, 'An insensitive pig, if you don't mind.' Eventually the issue was resolved when the Rasta picked the director up with one hand and shoved him against the wall of the rehearsal room in Battersea Arts Centre.

Each of the group's performances were an indication of how most people start in entertainment, motivated not by money, centrepiece articles or the chance to host a quiz show, but by the simple excitement of getting something they've written across to other people, even if there's only five of them.

All the poets lived by that enthusiasm, getting home from a day's work to write, rehearse, design the posters, book the rooms and persuade their reluctant neighbours to come to the shows.

For Ian, even this was a sell out, and after I left the group I didn't see him again until I was driving through Brixton a few years later. He was shuffling through the market trying to sell an apparently worthless wooden object, and carrying a tin of beer which would no doubt be replaced if he made a sale.

Whether or not he was homeless I don't know, but if it's possible to look as if you are without actually being slumped in a shop doorway, he did. I've no idea what circumstances led him to this plight, or if he's now happily out of it. Still less have I the slightest idea of what happened to the baby that gurgled in the corner while we read our poems. But it's certain that many of the increasing numbers of characters who line our streets, are capable of producing something of great value; for instance, the only decent poem of the night.

Mrs Bartlett

IN 1982 I left my hideously boring job in London Transport with the aim of becoming a full-time performer. Thus ended a two year sentence, spent gazing out of the window, desperate to know what my job was supposed to be, and frequently being shouted at by Mrs Bartlett, the manager, for arriving ten minutes late when I should have known that I was employed to start gazing out of the window at half-past-eight and *not* at twenty-to-nine.

Mrs Bartlett understood terror as an art form. One day I arrived two hours late and was instantly warned by another clerk, 'Mrs Bartlett wants to see you.' Steadying myself like a soldier walking into a court martial I knocked on her door, entered and sat down, quivering while she finished her phone call.

'For two hours,' I figured, 'I'll get twelve times the bollocking I get for ten minutes.'

'Ah Mark,' she said, leaning forward with the threatening smile of a character in *The Godfather* about to garrote someone. 'I've been meaning to speak to you. Now, you're from Swanley aren't you? Well, my husband and I like to pick fresh strawberries and we've noticed that there are a number of strawberry farms in the Swanley area where you can go and pick your own. I was wondering, do you know whether the strawberries are of a high quality at these farms?'

The result was that from then onwards, whenever I was asked to go and see Mrs Bartlett I could never be sure whether I was in for a roasting or about to be asked a ludicrous question about market gardening. At least before this incident, I could brace myself, take a deep breath and accept my punishment. Now I was destined to be reduced to a bag of nerves whenever I heard the words: 'Mrs Bartlett wants to see you.'

But around this time, I was asked to do a ten minute slot of my funniest poems at a party, which went down well. So that decided it. 'I'm giving in my notice,' I told them. 'I'm going to be a comedian.'

'Well,' said Mr Wheeler the supervisor, 'I wouldn't be surprised if we end up being in his comedy sketches.'

I rang up some theatres and blagged my way into doing a slot at one or two of the early comedy clubs in rooms above pubs, little by little abandoning the poems for stand-up.

Some people revere the stark days of the early alternative scene, scornful of comedy's modern status in the same way that some football supporters moan if their team becomes a top club: 'It was more of a family atmosphere when we were in the third division.' But what is true is that early on there was no reason for anyone to decide to take part in the process unless they were passionate about what they were doing, and almost certainly a bit mad.

For why would anyone give up a regular job to earn almost nothing performing in front of a handful of people who were probably as bonkers as they were themselves? It would be quite normal in most clubs for one of the acts to go berserk and smash the pub lampshades or end the act naked.

I was by no means certain that I would qualify as good enough or mad enough for this circuit, and I set myself the test of being able to survive the notorious Comedy Store. So I turned up to do an unpaid open spot, and managed about five minutes.

Everyone seemed to laugh, and when I finished they all seemed to clap (though if it was possible to revisit that night, I'd probably find that I've remembered it being much better than it actually was, in the way that when you go back to a park or building you knew from your childhood, it's half the size you thought it was). But I'd survived, and so I considered myself ready to take my place in the world of half a dozen dodgy clubs that paid twenty quid an act and could close down at any moment because the bloke running it had run off with the plastic box that contained all the money.

It was one of the happiest days of my life.

Part Two

Struggling

And Now – Richard Nixon

ONE OF LIFE'S most compelling sights is watching a succession of people trying desperately to be entertaining and failing dismally. Whereas one bad play or one bad comedian is a disappointment, a string of truly appalling acts is wonderful, especially if some of them are completely barking.

Dreadful auditions have been the high points of films like *The Commitments* and *The Fabulous Baker Boys*, so the prospect of real life debacles was one of the attractions of being the regular compere at a tiny theatre in west London on Monday evenings in 1984. The idea was that every week anyone who responded to an advert in *The Stage* could perform there for five to ten minutes, entertaining the handful of people who'd strayed in, and my job was to introduce them.

From my point of view, this was enormously satisfying. For one of the more unpleasant sides of human behaviour is that the lower in society's pecking order you are, the more desperate you become to find someone even lower. Such logic gives us prisoners who assault sex offenders, the homeless looking down on those who are homeless *and* drunk, and the kid who shouts 'fatty' loudest at the fattest kid in the class is invariably the second fattest kid in the class.

And here I was: a comedian getting one gig a week to supplement the Giro and a recently repossessed Access card, but on Monday evenings, I could be the professional: calm and collected, while up to a dozen acts nervously bumped into each other in a five feet by eight feet dressing room, desperately hoping that someone important would spot them and give *them* one gig a week.

Luckily, in comedy it's rarely difficult to find someone doing worse than you are yourself. Whereas I know that if I try to become a carpenter, within twenty minutes I'd have snapped four chisels and sawn through the foreman's leg, loads of people believe they can become comedians because they once told a joke at Christmas.

And one of the difficulties of learning stand-up is that, as with parachuting and ski-jumping, the early failures are extremely painful. So, as with parachuting or ski-jumping, you're forced to learn the basics fairly quickly. If the first dozen attempts end in disaster you give up, unless you're completely oblivious to the derision of the rest of humanity. Some people in history who have persisted with a belief in themselves despite everybody calling them mad, have turned out, like Galileo or Copernicus, to be geniuses. But most have turned out to be mad.

Consequently, out of every dozen acts at a show like the ones on those Monday nights, one would end up doing regular gigs, one would realise they weren't very good and give up, and the rest were mad.

On a typical night, the tiny dressing room would be pulsating with panic, with acts colliding into each other as they paced around, reciting their lines; a comedy ballet dancer would be humming her breathing exercises, a mime artist spilling his face paint and someone demanding to go on seventh as it was their lucky number.

On one night, the first act was an extremely pretty woman in a short skirt who told an explicit story about snot with an expression so wild and distant that if she said, 'I've got my neighbour's head in my fridge,' it would be so unsurprising you'd probably say, 'Really, what sort of fridge have you got?'

Next came someone who'd been sitting rigidly in the corner for twenty minutes and who insisted that I announce him as: 'Clarence.' After introducing him, I came across a man in a suit with a bow-tie and watch on a chain who was getting so excited he looked as if he'd faint.

'Norwood's the name,' he said. 'Nick Norwood. Call myself Norwood cos I live in Streatham. Ha, ha. Make 'em laugh, that's what I say. Tell you what, I've got my agent in tonight. Course I've worked with the greats. Well, I say he's my agent, he's looking to sign me up. Make 'em laugh and you can't go wrong. Here, have a look at this.' And he opened up a leather combination briefcase in which the sole object was a shield bearing the inscription 'Pontin's 1981 talent contest – runner up.'

At this point the barman came rushing into the dressing room yelping, 'Get that bloke off the stage,' and it seemed that Clarence, having sat rigid for a minute or so, was now thumping the piano with his fists and wailing like a dog.

'That's all we've got time for from Clarence,' I said as I ran on to the stage. 'I'm afraid he's got to rush as he's doing a children's party later,' I added along with other pathetic attempts to ingratiate myself with the audience by distancing myself from the show.

But Clarence wouldn't go. Staring, speechless and rigid he remained until three members of the audience persuaded him to leave in the way that TV detectives get psychopaths to put down their guns.

'And now,' I said, 'Someone I'm sure you're going to love. All the way from Streatham, it's Nick Norwood.'

'Good evening ladies and gentlemen,' he began. 'I was in the garden just the other day. And who should I see leaning across the garden fence? Frank Spencer.' From inside the jacket came a beret and he was away. 'Mmmm. I've had a bit of trouble. The cat done a whoopsee in my beret. Mmmm.'

At this the whole place erupted into laughter accompanied by choruses of 'Fuck off,' to ensure there was no way he could kid himself they were laughing with, rather than at him. But he stuck out for his five minutes, and later, as he was placing his beret in the briefcase said, 'You didn't see where my agent went, did you? He seems to have gone. Maybe he had to rush off somewhere.'

On about the third or fourth week of these shows, about an hour before the public were allowed in, there was a knock at the door.

'Is this the right room for the cameras?' asked a bloke, 'Only it says here...' and he read out the address from a chit, like someone delivering a cooker. I checked with the theatre and it was indeed the right room for the cameras. An impressionist had hired a company to film his act, so cables were laid out, stands erected and cameras positioned by two blokes talking about the racing.

When the impressionist arrived, he explained that he was going to send the film to the television people. 'Oh, and can I go on first?' he asked, 'Because the camera people say they've got to go at nine o'clock.'

There was something about this chap that said if you knew nothing whatsoever about him and were asked to state one thing simply from his appearance, you'd probably have to say: 'I don't know why, but he seems to look like the sort of bloke who can't do impressions.'

And so, as the show began, it was – cameras running – action: 'Thank you. May I begin by giving you the last four presidents of the United States?'

He then followed with a series of statements roughly linked to each president; along the lines of, 'I know nothing about the burglary,' and, 'Would you like a peanut?' all in the sort of voice your dad talks in when he tries an American accent, all utterly indistinguishable from one another and barely different from his normal voice.

The film, if it ever made it to a television executive, would have shown him visibly trying to remember his words while members of the audience shouted, 'This is bollocks,' not as a heckle directed at the impressionist but as a statement of fact to their mates at the bar.

42

The camera boys duly packed up and went, and as I left for home, the impressionist joined me on the tube. 'What do you think I should do to get on the telly?' he kept asking. This to a comic who couldn't dream of signing off the dole himself. The only advice I could give him that wasn't cowardly was to give up.

'Give up? But I've paid one hundred and twenty pounds to get that film made,' he said.

I suggested he might try to perfect a couple of impressions before making films, but he persisted all the way from west London on the Bakerloo Line, through Oxford Circus underground and on to the Victoria Line. As the train pulled into Brixton, I asked him where in south London he was going? 'Oh nowhere,' he said. 'I live in Luton. I only came here because I thought you could give me some advice about how to get on the telly.'

After that I couldn't think of the dreadful acts as funny any more. Maybe the reason they seem so to audiences is why they're so therapeutic for other performers. We feel secure in knowing there's some poor sod who is sadder than us. Maybe that's why destitute Victorians liked to watch the freaks at a circus. And maybe that's why audiences laugh when a 'volunteer' is dragged on to the stage and humiliated by a comedian or magician. 'Ha ha ha, thank fuck it isn't me,' we think. But it's all the funnier because it so easily could have been. He was coming this way, but chose someone else, instead.

Ipswich

ONE DAY A hippy from Ipswich saw me at a gig in London and asked me to do half an hour supporting a band in the basement of his local pub. The pub was in Ipswich and, as a result, I had to get the coach from London and 'crash' on his floor for the night.

I doubt whether I have ever felt as important as I did over those few hours. 'I've got to go to Ipswich next week,' I told everyone in the squats and anyone I met not in the squats. The word I enjoyed most was 'got.' I wasn't going just for a party or to see some mates. 'I've *got* to go to Ipswich.'

It was my first trip out of London on account of my job in the entertainment business. I was entering a new phase of comic maturity and going on the road. The audience in the pub basement consisted of the band I was supporting and two of their friends, making a total of seven. But I didn't care; because I'd *had* to go to Ipswich.

You're Shit – And You Don't Know You Are

EVERYONE CHEERED AS he left the stage. He couldn't understand why they'd hated him. 'Lots of comedians do stuff about lads and football crowds,' he said. 'So why should they pick on me?'

There was a belief (completely unfounded by the time of the mid-eighties), that audiences for the new style of comedy were middle class and students – or both. This was the comedy version of the myth that the only people who bother with left-wing books or political films are trendy middle class types, slumming it.

So any new comedian who didn't tell stories that ended in punchlines like, 'He said: "You think that's bad, you should see the size of his arsehole",' were labelled 'alternative' and their appeal considered to be middle class.

By this time, much of the comedy club audience consisted of young office worker types. Not too many miners or canal-building navvies sitting at the back with their pigs, but plenty of civil servants and bank workers in jobs as tedious and badly paid as any.

In certain clubs however, the audience did look like the people in the workingmen's club in *Kes*. One such place was the bar of Cliff's Pavilion on Southend Pier. Every week this place was packed with lads who thought that wearing more than a T-shirt in February made them a poof, and who could fit the word 'cunt' into any conceivable sentence in the English language (eg, 'I tell yer what, I could do with a cunting cup of tea, yer cunt.').

The women were in high heels and drank Babycham, and those over the age of sixty would shriek with laughter if

45

someone said, 'Do you want some of this, or a bit of the other?' And they were as enthusiastic an audience as any that existed during these pioneering days of modern comedy. This despite the fact that 'the lads' were the butt of a huge amount of the material. From Alexei Sayle's *Ullo John, Gotta New Motor* onward, they'd become a prime target of eighties comedy.

This seemed fair enough to me, having been part of a classic group of lads who, at eighteen, spent every night down the pub, talking incessantly about cars, how brilliant it was on the night we got a lock-in and drank nine pints (remembering you always had to add two on to the total you were claiming to have drunk on any given occasion), and if any one of a list of a hundred or so local women were mentioned, you had to go, 'Wooaagh, I wouldn't mind.'

This was the behaviour that made the lads an easy target. But most of them, like the group I was part of, were not evil, just pathetic. Which is why in every group of lads there are some who do the United Nations 'No leave it, Terry,' bit whenever a fight looks likely. Some may be racist but most mean it when they say they 'know one at work and he's a really good bloke'.

I remember watching the football at Millwall one day, and seeing a particularly burly and vocal character navigate a channel through the crowd for two old people who wanted to move to a different area. As soon as he returned from this impressive humanitarian act he carried on where he'd left off, chanting, 'You're going home in a fucking ambulance.' Even this chant shows how much of the 'lads' image is just show, because they've not exactly thought through the meaning. If you were really going to be beaten up outside the ground, what sort of inexperienced ambulance driver would pick you up and dump you at home?

The Southend crowd was mostly made up of just these sorts of lads and their girlfriends. Consequently, any material aimed in that area went down especially well; at least, until this night. A young well-dressed comic with a middle-class accent began his act nervously and the audience willed him on. He got a couple of titters and, feeling a little more confident, strode into a piece about the lads. They were stupid because they were always drunk and shouted like yobs. At the football they proved their ignorance by their choice of songs. Like if the score's 1-0 they sing, 'One nil, one nil.' Maybe this was how they learned to count. And so on.

None of it was working. Ideas that in other people's hands would be working brilliantly, were creating nothing but tension. And one of the great things about audiences is that if you see enough of them, you know when they're going to turn nasty before they do.

Standing at the back, it felt like I was watching a wildlife programme, at the point where you know the lion's about to jump on the water buffalo, and the fact you can do nothing about it is horrifying but wonderfully fascinating.

The kill was about to be launched. It's not true that a good heckle can destroy a comic, any more than a single scandal can bring down a government. If a government is popular, the population will forgive the odd shady arms deal. When people feel insecure and vulnerable, every minor gaffe becomes a major embarrassment. If a comic's going down well, the most brilliantly executed heckle will be shrugged off. But if there's a general mood of, 'We don't like this bloke,' whoever takes the initiative and says so will find they've unleashed an unstoppable force.

This particular audience, which was generally extremely friendly, didn't like this bloke. And the reason was that behind his delivery was an air of contempt. When he said football fans were stupid, he didn't mean the word in the way you call someone stupid for spilling their tea. He meant they were stupid. He felt he was above them and there was no hiding it.

Unfortunately for him, there is in the English a highly developed sense of 'Them' and 'Us.' This isn't always a positive thing. It means for example that as a boy I never saw BBC2 because it was considered a channel 'toffee-nosed' people watched. But it also means that people who would consider themselves completely apolitical will refuse to speak to the woman over the road because she's a 'la-di-da type who looks down her nose at us'.

Usually this has little to do with accent or background and much more to do with attitude. Sure, this comic had a middle class accent but it was only when it was connected with a condescending attitude that the audience found it unacceptable. So, like the rumbling before an earthquake, the mumbling of quiet asides signalled the poor chap's demise. Then a loud chink from the bar-till threw him off his stride and he stopped mid sentence. 'Oh, I'll do that bit again,' he said, the sweat beginning to show.

By now the room was behaving like the lion and starting to twitch in the pre-pounce period. Unconsciously they sensed an unease in the young comic that was the signal for attack. 'I wouldn't bother mate, you're a wanker,' said somebody.

And these seven simple words caused enormous hilarity. Now the dam of silence was broken and torrents of abuse gushed forth, while the defenceless comic stood limply mouthing lines that, by now, no one could even hear.

'I just don't understand it,' he said to me afterwards. 'Lots of comics do stuff about lads and football crowds. So why should they pick on me?'

Escapology

'OY, MARK. OVER here,' wailed a muffled Geordie voice. 'Can you give me a hand.' Through the gap in the curtain I could see the good-natured crowd at Colchester University starting to giggle like someone watching a pompous TV presenter saying, 'We're trying to go live to Norwich,' while on screen, a reporter with a blank stare fiddles with his earpiece.

I was on last, after the Geordie escapologist whose last words before he'd gone on stage were: 'I finish the act with this bit where the audience tie me up in a sack, and I get out just before two minutes is up.'

Waiting behind the curtain, I was half thinking about how I'd start, and half thinking how I was sure this was a long two minutes. Then I heard the plea from inside the sack: 'I mean it, man. I'm stuck.'

So I wandered on to the stage and, together with the 'volunteer' who, as requested had 'made sure that knot's really tight now', picked and tugged at the various belts and pieces of string that bound him, until he could crawl out, to face a by now hysterical audience.

'Honestly,' he said to me as we went backstage. 'This has never happened before.' And looking at the expression on his face I realised how pitiful men look whenever they feel the need to say those words.

The Miners' Strike

AS I WALKED through the melee of about two hundred people jumping up and down to Frankie goes to Hollywood's 'Relax', I grabbed at people standing around the edge.

'Do you know Jim?'

'What?'

'Jim. Jim Tasker.'

'I can't hear yer.'

Eventually I found someone who wasn't Jim, but knew him.

'I don't think he's here, mate.'

'He must be. He rang me up and asked me to perform here.'

'What are you then, a band?'

'No. Comedy.'

'Comedy? He didn't mention nothing. Hang on a minute, I'll see if anyone knows anything about it.'

It was 1984. To many people the year of the Miners' Strike. To many comedians the year of the Miners' Strike Benefits. The incident mentioned above took place in September 1984, so by then I was used to the chaos, and decided I might as well leave. Earlier in the Strike I'd resolved a similar situation by agreeing to do ten minutes, despite the fact that dozens of people were perfectly happy and perfectly drunkenly dancing in the wonderfully uncoordinated manner practiced by those who attend fund-raising events.

'You'll have to go through the disco microphone,' I was told. The lead stretched no further than eighteen inches from the deck which meant I had to crouch down to an almost squatting position to reach it. The DJ then introduced me in the same flowing manner in which he'd been introducing the records. 'All right, that was the Beat with "Stand Down Margaret", and now we've got some more great sounds coming from a young man called Mark Steel.'

As a result, a good number of the audience were under the impression that I was indeed the next record, and with the more drunken elements amongst them unable to comprehend that my act didn't contain a beat as such, several people continued dancing while I was on.

Others took the opportunity to go to the bar, a few shouted, 'Put another record on,' three people stood near the front and laughed twice, and it's extremely doubtful whether any of it contributed very much to the miners' cause.

When arriving at a benefit, I might ask where in the room they were planning to have the microphone. Sometimes the response to this question was to show the same sort of quizzical face you put on when a clerk in some bureaucracy or other asks to see your passport when you haven't got it with you.

'Microphone,' they'd mumble in the way they might mumble 'hippopotamus,' if I'd asked where in the room they were planning to have the hippopotamus.

While many of these events were shambolic and disorganised, they were however an invigorating part of British culture for the year of the Strike.

Collecting money for the miners became such a habit for so many people that even at ordinary comedy evenings it was quite normal for collections to take place. Sometimes college gigs would be preceded by a speech from a miner. One evening at a country retreat in Surrey I did a show for the Fabian Society, a right-wing Labour Party group, and they held a collection. What was impressive was not just that these collections were held but that it seemed the most natural thing in the world that they should be.

The most memorable of the comedy events connected to the Strike however, were those which took place inside the pit villages themselves.

Towards the end of the strike I travelled to Shirebrook in Derbyshire to take part in one of these shows. The immediate effect of the Strike in areas like this was well-reported: the pickets, the battles with police, the financial problems and the consequent arguments with those wavering about whether to return to work. What was more noticeable – but far less documented – were the social changes that came about, all of which were evident on nights like the one at Shirebrook.

As I was introduced to the family who were putting me up for the night, the miner, a man in his late forties who'd never lived anywhere else whispered, 'I hope thee's got some of that wacky baccy. That's bloody marvellous stuff, that is.'

When I explained that I hadn't, he seemed astonished. He'd never touched it until the Strike, when his collecting visits to London had put him in touch with students who, true to form, all had their stashes. Everyone in London, he'd concluded, checked their pockets for a tin of the stuff before going out, in much the same way other people make sure they've got their keys.

These journeys away from their communities, and the return visits, such as the one I was making, transformed the lives of all involved. This wasn't just because of the travelling. There are plenty of English families who would find it quite possible to travel to the remotest part of Borneo, find an English pub and a chip shop and live no differently to how they do back home.

The journeys of the Miners' Strike though, were journeys made across cultures. Before the strike this miner would probably never have had cause to meet a student from London. Now he had not only met them, but understood them, respected them and smoked their dope. During the strike, many families lost their fear of foreign food, having no choice but to eat only the tins of east European vegetables and gherkins donated by various unions from abroad. And as miners mixed with gay groups, muslims, and West Indians, collecting money with them, staying with them and speaking at their meetings, all that may once have been feared, was celebrated.

But before I could ponder such philosophy, I had to do the show. Central to every mining community is the welfare club, a community hall with a bar at one end, collapsible red formica tables spread around the room, and packed on entertainment nights with all social life from every generation. Crooners, comedians from specialist agencies and husband and wife singing duos made up much of the entertainment. And just as miners found themselves in unusual surroundings as they toured the country, so did I – and this was it.

I was more used to small rooms in pubs adapted for use as comedy venues and frequented by audiences aged twenty to thirty, and they were used to being entertained by a silver-haired bloke in a frilly shirt, singing *Fly Me To The Moon*. And so when I got on stage to do my act, we were facing each other. Yet, like two tribes who know nothing about each other's customs or language meeting for the first time and managing to convey a mutual friendship by exchanging gifts, we muddled through.

They didn't really understand that I was a comedian, because I didn't tell 'jokes', and they thought it most peculiar that I swore. But most of them tried hard to like the act. I survived because they were humble enough to be grateful for every piece of support they got, when it was really the rest of us who had every reason to be grateful to them.

I also survived because although the place had the appearance of a normal club, in all essentials it was entirely different. From the age of about fifteen, I'd had arguments

53

with relatives, workmates and blokes in the pub about how the police were dishonest, corrupt and violent. Usually I was in a small minority. Yet here there people now knew the truth about the police far better than I could.

Whereas I would expect in an argument about the press someone to say something like, 'You're not telling me newspapers deliberately tell lies.' But these people had experienced attacks from the police, only to discover the next day that journalists had cynically reported the opposite.

After the show, a huge man with the broadest Derbyshire accent in Derbyshire said he'd like to tell me something. He was a pit deputy, equivalent to a foreman and therefore in a different union to most of the miners and not officially on strike. Nonetheless he'd stayed out for the whole time with the rest of them.

'During strark ot' '72,' he told me, 'I carried on working. All t' strarkers called me scab. One neet I were rart 'ere in this very bar and they kicked shite out o' me. It were then I realised strength ot' feeling, an' ah've supported every strike ot' yewnion since that day.'

Throughout the year, countless friendships were forged between the miners and their supporters, and as is one of the tragedies of humanity, the opening of new horizons and relationships entailed the closing of many old ones. Entire communities discovered a yearning for knowledge, culture and debate in ways that could only normally happen to the odd individual as in *Educating Rita*. But a glance around the social club could confirm that, above all else, the greatest change that happened to the pit villages was the upheaval in the status of the women.

At first sight that miners' club was almost identical to the working men's club I would be taken to by my dad when I was a boy; except for the women. In the club I remembered, the men dominated the conversations; they told the jokes and decided when it was time for the next round. The

54

women drank sherry or Martini from dainty glasses and if one of them got drunk they'd let out a deafening high-pitched shriek of laughter because someone had said the word 'knob.' This only happened in one of the bars however, as the other was men only.

In the miners' clubs the men had to earn their right to hold court around the tables. There was no automatic right for anyone to dictate the course of the evening, like when a couple would dance, buy the drinks, or go home. Just from the way the women sat, walked and spoke, it was clear they'd gained a confidence that power-dressing women from America would charge several hundred dollars an hour to teach. But unlike those women from America, when the mining women got drunk they would let out a deafening high-pitched shriek whenever someone used the word 'knob.'

Most of the men embracing this new regime didn't seem to think they were losing out. On the contrary, they seemed to find it as liberating to be part of a more equal relationship as it was for the women.

For many reasons then, despite the hardship, the violence and the disruption to everyday life, the Strike was an exhilarating experience for many miners and for many more of their supporters. The family I was staying with were in excellent spirits and insisted I drank some of their whisky, a luxury they'd been preserving for a special occasion. But they were also aware that by this time the saga was drawing to a close. A steady trickle of miners in the village were drifting back to work, because of a mixture of poverty and losing the belief that they could win.

The Social that night had been organised by the union and a miners' support group twinned with the pit, in an effort to boost a sagging morale. So this family, like many others were having to come to terms with the fact that, despite all the deprivation and sacrifice they'd made, they were likely to end up defeated. Yet we stayed up until two o'clock in the morning, telling jokes, swapping stories and looking at photos – without any dope.

The next day's dinner was the grandest Sunday roast they'd had for several months, but one they were determined to provide because I was their guest. Like thousands of others like them, the quality this family displayed above all others was dignity. To the national press of course, they were 'the scum of the earth'.

More than ten years on, the defeat seems in many ways even greater than it did then. A generation learned that if you confront the state over an ideal, you will lose. How many discussions about whether it would be possible to wage a campaign and win meets with the retort: 'The miners tried that and look what happened to them?' And Arthur Scargill's predictions of the extent to which the government wished to decimate the mining industry, derided as nonsense at the time, have proved inaccurate only because they underestimated the devastation that was to follow.

I've no idea what happened to the family I stayed with, and the selfless enthusiasm they and many like them showed seems to have belonged to a different era, and was buried in defeat. But when you consider what's happened to the other side...

Peter Walker is a forgotten has-been. Ian McGregor is a recluse. Kelvin Mackenzie of the *Sun* left to join an American organisation and was promptly sacked. Maxwell launched a campaign accusing Scargill of corruption, was later exposed as a fraud, before nicking sixty million quid out of pension funds and finding his way to the bottom of the sea. The police are at an all-time-low in popularity.

Of those labelled traitors from within the labour movement, Norman Willis retired into obscurity and Neil Kinnock went on to lose two elections and see his name become synonymous with failure. And Margaret herself:

deposed and bitter, she's listened to by no more than a handful of loyalists and is kept at arm's length, even by her own party. But above all, the free market 'make a profit or die' philosophy she embodied is now rejected by millions as the heartless creed it always was; no more so than by those who embraced it in the first place and who now have only worthless shares, negative equity and their own redundancy notices to show for it.

Those who took part on the miners' side will remember the excitement, the passion and the dignity of those days. Most of them may now accept the view that we should restrict our aspirations until they reach a level which is 'practical.' But deep down, most people who were at any of the miners' benefits would swap the pragmatism of today for the enthusiasm and optimism of that year.

And yet such is the ego of the comedian that whenever I think back to that night in Shirebrook the first thing I remember is: 'Hmmm, I didn't really go down that well.'

Geordie

'THIS IS MARK, he's a comedian,' the man who'd set up the comedy night in Newcastle told his four mates. They looked like the four people you would choose from thousands if you wanted extras for a film set in a Newcastle pub.

'Ar, so yoor the comadian, well ah hoop yoor funna mairt,' they chipped in. We all went to the bar and ordered a round of drinks, and the stockiest among them decided to tell me a joke.

'Ay, what do yer chuck a Paki when he's drooning? His wafe and kids.' The others laughed.

What to do? Walk away and they'd have just thought I was weird, whereas anything that might have ended in violence was hardly an option.

The tough part of these situations is that when bigotry hides behind a joke, it's so much trickier to deal with. Launching into a tirade about racism would have only made them think, 'What a stuck-up, miserable bastard'. 'All right, it's only a joke,' they'd have said. And gone off muttering, 'He's not much of a comedian.' Besides it was quite possible that he wasn't a serious racist but had never come across the idea that jokes like that are just appalling.

The one thing I decided in the two seconds after he'd finished was that I'd say something. 'What's the matter?' he said, perturbed that I wasn't laughing. 'Doon't yer get it?'

'Na, he's a comadian,' said his mate. 'He's hewered it before.'

There's probably one time in most people's lives when, instead of thinking of the perfect answer the day after the event, it comes out at the time. I don't remember thinking it but from somewhere came, 'Yeah, I have heard it before. But

I heard the funnier version. What do you chuck a Geordie when he's drowning?'

There was another silence and for a moment I was expecting to end up lying on the floor, clutching my ribs, with blood pouring from my nose, mumbling, 'I was only making a point.'

But at the end of this tense three seconds he burst out laughing and said, 'Ya can see wha he's a comadian.'

With any luck he'll now be the Equal Opportunities Officer for the Anglo-Asian Community Relations Department on Tyneside Council.

Elephant Fair

COMEDY IS NOT, nor could it ever be, the new – or any other type of – rock 'n' roll During the early 1980s I would sometimes be on with bands at colleges or festivals, in which case they would invariably go out of their way to fulfil every conceivable rock 'n' roll cliche as if it were part of their contract.

Arriving in the dressing room, I'd find them lying across armchairs with legs dangling over the side, a tin of lager in one hand and a fag in the other, skilfully holding on to both while receiving a joint, taking a drag and passing it on.

In the background the drummer would be doing his sound check, banging the bass drum once a second for a minute, stopping to suggest something like, 'Two rev higher on middle downstroke, Slimey,' and then doing it all again with no appreciable difference whatsoever to the sound.

'Hey,' someone would begin. 'Do you remember Rotterdam?'

Someone else would walk over to the table, open another tin of lager and burp loudly.

Half a minute after the Rotterdam question was posed, one of them would laugh under their breath, and half a minute later they'd go: 'Yeah, Rotterdam,' and recount how wrecked they'd been when they were there, and how they were so out-of-their-head on whiz that they'd nicked a bicycle, rode it into a canal and it had turned out to belong to the Dutch Minister for Trade and Industry.

A roadie with a T-shirt too small to cover his beer gut would strut past carrying a two feet wide spool of gaffa tape, an unfeasibly huge bunch of keys dangling from a loop in his jeans, take an exaggerated draw on a spliff and say,

'Wow, I hear there's some wild chicks here in Dudley,' and yelp like an injured dog.

Someone would start slinging pieces of dried up pizza at the bass player and the guitarist would break into one of the band's songs, accompanied by the roadie using a pair of snapped pool cues as drumsticks on the window. Then they'd all have a discussion about the filthy habits of a bloke called Oily.

Throughout this they would be so engrossed in their own world that they wouldn't notice that I was in the room, quietly nibbling sandwiches and excluded from their universe. It wouldn't be out of rudeness; they just hadn't noticed.

Nor would they notice that when they started to play, there would be only eighteen people in the audience. So that from the way each song was introduced – 'This next one's for a very good friend of ours' or 'All right, Dudley are you ready to go crazy?'– and from the way the guitarist would go down on one knee and look as if his solo was causing him extreme dental agony, you could imagine they were playing to fifty thousand in Hamburg. Until the song ended and the sorry squeals of a handful of students echoed around the enormous and largely empty hall.

Saddest of all, I'd be watching, thinking, 'Great. This looks like more fun than comedy.'

So, only once do I remember experiencing anything approaching the lifestyle of the touring rock 'n' roller. Three of us were booked to do a show on each of the three days of the Elephant Fair in Cornwall. We hired a van which broke down in Wiltshire and arrived late. We did the show as soon as we could but the organiser of the event was a hippy called Argos, who docked our money anyway, with the efficiency of a pre-war docks supervisor.

It was pouring with rain, so within hours the entire site was a sea of mud. Several people's tents blew down, including ours, which meant we spent the first night in a sleeping bag in the van. The toilets, which began as holes in the ground behind a flapping length of canvas, degenerated from such luxury into a seething cauldron of toxic bile that would have repulsed a medieval serf. Food was veggie burgers and kidney beans served three times a day, with the only variety being a change in the number of kidney beans.

If you could get into a position whereby sleep was a possibility, someone in the vicinity would play the whole of *Simon and Garfunkel's Greatest Hits* on an acoustic guitar. And if you looked up at any given moment, you would see at least one person trying desperately to learn juggling with skittles, and at least one bloke with a beard dancing naked in the mud. And everywhere there was mud. It was impossible to take the merest stroll without mud covering every inch of your clothing, getting into your hair, your shoes and at least two orifices.

So there was nothing to do but get wrecked. Become one more bumbling idiot so out-of-it that the simplest question could only be answered, 'Yeah, huh, I'm so out of it, heuugh, heuugh,' with the last 'heuugh,' going so slowly that it actually stopped before the end.

So far then, so rock 'n' roll. Now for the delivery:

It's the second day of the festival and there are about a thousand people at the tent where the comedy is scheduled. Going on first is a comedienne from our troupe who strolls on stage.

'Well,' she begins. 'I expect you're wondering what I'm doing here. Well, I'm doing what a lot of you are probably doing; getting out of a very boring dinner party.'

'Surely,' we think, 'She's not going to do the dinner party routine we've seen her perform at twee London theatres.'

'I'm just hopeless at dinner parties,' she continued, and proceeded with a piece about the drawbacks of hostess trollies.

The entire audience in this packed tent sat puzzling

through an abundance of narcotics for a minute, collectively agreed and confirmed that this woman had, in the midst of the most squalid conditions anywhere in the world without refugee camp status, walked on to the stage to talk about dinner parties and hostess trollies. As if militarily planned, a mass of projectiles made from mud were sent hurtling towards the stage, and the poor woman scuttled backstage and burst into tears.

Comedy the new rock 'n' roll? We're not fit to lick their Rizlas.

War Crimes in Watford

LABOUR CLUBS ARE fascinating places to be a guest at. An official of some sort (ie someone employed by the labour movement and as a result, not seen anywhere without a suit, tie and beer stain down their waistcoat) meets you as you enter. He is overwhelmingly friendly, forcing sandwiches and beer on you like a zealous aunty, telling you jokes with 'fuck' in the punchline, whilst chewing a mouthful of sausage roll and slapping your back like a zealous uncle.

Within seconds he has enlightened you as to the local intrigues within the club. If you're there to do a comedy show, he'll fit this in to a private briefing, told with his arm round your shoulder, the way a member of the mafia might warn a colleague there's someone in the room about to assassinate them.

'Don't worry if the table on the left doesn't laugh,' he might say. 'They're all miserable because they wanted to oust me from the Standing Orders and Finance Committee and we stuffed 'em thirteen-seven in the final ballot.'

Behind the petty squabbles of who rules which defunct body and who now lives with whose ex-wife there is a certain pride in most Labour clubs.

Around the walls are photos that serve the purpose of the pictures in ordinary pubs showing the landlord with his arm round Henry Cooper. One of the chair of the Trade Council on a march for jobs with Tony Benn; another of the chair of the Standing Orders and Finance Committee shaking hands with Jimmy Knapp. Quite possibly this room, with no heating and a tatty leaflet on the wall for a meeting about Cuba that no one will go to, has been host to organising meetings in the General Strike, fund-raising events for the

International Brigades and a centre for the great strikes of the 1970s.

In 1985, one night at such a club in Watford began typically enough. Everyone delighted in telling me how pleased they were I had come, and, with the slightly annoying regularity of an over-enthusiastic waiter in an Indian restaurant, they checked to see if there was anything I needed. I had a friendly conversation with a woman who offered to give me a lift back to the station to catch the last train. Everything was fine until someone said: 'We're so looking forward to your show; we could do with a really good laugh about how terrible the Tories are.'

Suddenly it became apparent what the main purpose of the evening was: 'therapy'. Especially as this was 1985. It was as if she was saying, 'I'm afraid the miners couldn't beat the Tories, so we're hoping you can instead.'

At this point I felt a terrible sense of responsibility. These people weren't just here for a laugh, they wanted their spirits revived. Most of the stuff I did that seemed to work down the Comedy Store would leave them dreadfully disappointed. At the end of the evening they wanted revenge on Thatcher and Tebbit for the Falklands War and the Miners' Strike, and they intended to get it by me making them laugh at them.

The first problem here is that it's incredibly difficult to be funny about someone everybody in the audience hates in the first place. You can do what kids do and be personally insulting: the 'Norman Tebbit. What a wanker,' sort of thing. But this isn't funny because everyone agrees. Getting up at Tory Conference and saying, 'Norman Tebbit, what a wanker,' would be funny. If Trevor McDonald was to start the news one night with, 'Good evening. Norman Tebbit, what a wanker,' it would be hysterical. But at a Labour club it would be pointless.

There was a second problem. The Labour movement was

itself divided in 1985 between those who thought the miners were heroes betrayed by the likes of Neil Kinnock, and those like Neil Kinnock who referred to the Miners' Strike as 'Labour's wasted year'. Most were probably somewhere in the middle, behaving as Labour Party members do so well and reconciling a passionate wish to overturn the system with a 'pragmatic' desire to run the system. My third problem was that I wasn't very good. So I started off with a few statements along the lines of: 'Norman Tebbit, what a wanker.'

No one was particularly inspired but neither was anybody outraged, so I figured I could move on and do a few unpolitical minutes from my normal act, a bit I'd just written about a trip to Yugoslavia.

'People told me how cheap it was,' I said. 'Well of course it's cheap; there's nothing there. Shopkeepers say, 'Come into my shop. See anything you like? Of course not. It's empty. Ha, ha, ha.'

Then there was a bit about this dreadful kebab type thing called cevapcici, which you could buy from takeaways where they took the pitta bread and poured hot cooking oil straight into it.

None of it went brilliantly but it wasn't a disaster either. Afterwards I got in the car for my arranged lift and decided to continue the friendly conversation I'd begun earlier with the woman driving. 'Have you any more comedy nights planned?' I asked. The grunt that served as a reply could have meant yes or no but definitely meant, 'I hope I never set eyes on you again.'

'She's a Kinnock supporter,' I thought. Or maybe she's a prospective MP and she's worrying about whether a local journalist had sneaked in and is planning to write a scoop on: 'Labour Club in Red Comic Calling Cabinet Minister W****r Shock!'

For ten minutes or so I politely asked increasingly trivial

questions until even the grunts dried up. Whatever I'd done it was clearly a major gaffe. Then, as I got out of the car resigned to never knowing my crime she yelled in a bellowing but quaking headmistress voice, 'We have enough of the capitalist press attacking the socialist countries without so-called alternative comedians adding to it, thank you,' and drove off.

Amongst the leaders of that particular socialist country at the time were Franjo Tudjmann and Slobodan Milosevic, later to become leaders of Croatia and Serbia respectively, through the years of civil war and ethnic cleansing. I'm sure that the woman genuinely believed that these people were leading socialism, and genuinely believed that the country was an alternative to the inequality of the West.

But I wonder if she ever considers now the damage done to socialism by those who tied its name to 'the socialist countries'. And I wonder if she remembers becoming so angry at my description of Yugoslavia, now that the leaders she so admired have caused their populations to look back on those 1985 days of empty shops and cevapcici, and wish life could be that good again.

All The Way To Bournemouth

BY THE TIME I'd spent a couple of years travelling once or twice a week up and down the country, Britain seemed like a neat and compact little place in which nowhere was so far away it wasn't possible to 'nip up' to in the afternoon.

Preparation for most journeys would involve slinging a spare pair of underpants, a book and a razor into a bag and glancing at the road map the first time I got stuck at the lights. It had become quite normal to arrange to meet someone at ten in the morning after 'popping back' from Newcastle on the first train.

Once I set off in the car for Bournemouth with as much preparation as you might expect before going out to buy a tin of cat food. As I arrived in the town a couple of hours later, I vaguely recognised an area, with the sort of confused half recollection that people describe feeling on weird documentaries about reincarnation. I figured it was possible my parents had brought me here on holiday when I was about nine years old.

Bournemouth, a three cassette drive into Hampshire. But what an effort would have gone into that journey twenty years earlier.

The road maps would have been studied at least three weeks in advance to plot the hundred mile route from Swanley. Friends and relatives who may have been to Bournemouth in the past would have been telephoned for advice on any potential traffic black-spots on the way. Friends of friends would have been consulted because someone had mentioned that they knew of a nice café about half way there which would be an ideal stop. Packing would have begun a full week prior to the trip. The day before departure would have been militarily planned, with my mother buying a bottle of ginger beer, sweets and headache tablets for the journey, while my father took the car to the garage to check over every part and fill up with petrol: 'So we don't have to worry about it in the morning.'

The guest house at which we were staying would have been contacted weeks before for precise instructions on how to find the place once we arrived. A map would then have been sent as well but they would have been contacted again a couple of days before departure, just in case Bournemouth had been redeveloped in the last month and had been reassembled back to front.

The house would have been circulated several times while every eventuality was checked and double-checked. Was the television unplugged? Was the airing cupboard shut? Were we sure the cat wasn't shut in it? Was the lid tightly closed on the tupperware bowl so that the cornflakes wouldn't go soggy while we were away?

We'd have left at six in the morning to 'avoid the worst of the traffic', and on getting in the car, my mother would almost certainly have repeated a poignant part of the instructions such as: 'Remember, as we get into Bournemouth it's the traffic lights before Pricerites where we turn left and not the one after, as that leads to a pig farm.'

As we pulled out of the drive, we'd have seen the people over the road who would have got up early to see us off, waving us goodbye from their bedroom window in their pyjamas. And finally, as we turned the corner into the main road, there would have been an emphatic, 'Right, we're off,' which combined the anticipation of events to unfold with a proud sense of achievement that we'd got this far; probably a bit like Columbus as he sailed for America.

Partly because it was such a performance to get there, it seemed so much further away once we arrived. Whenever I was on holiday as a child I always felt so far away. Though we'd only be in Ilfracombe, or Ventnor, or Bournemouth there'd be a sense of excitement at every moment that normal life was almost unimaginable. It seemed hardly possible that school existed, especially when separated by twenty-four hours of preparation, driving and toilet breaks.

I only experienced that sense of distance from home once as an adult when, as a nineteen year old, I hitch-hiked across Europe and found myself on a deserted beach somewhere in Italy. That in normal times there was an office, a home and a pub which shared my company three equal ways seemed inconceivable. Not because of the distance, but because getting there had taken six days of waiting by roadsides, dodging train fares, escaping from lunatics and being taken fifty miles in the wrong direction by a Dutchman who swore he was in the Red Brigade.

Consequently every moment was an adventure, because there was no possibility of changing my mind and nipping back home. Every cup of coffee or trip to the post office was an experience, as everything seemed to be so different by being so far away.

It's a feeling that's almost impossible to recapture though, as soon as you get used to travelling in aeroplanes. Because there's hardly anywhere in the world that you can be in the morning and not stand a chance of getting back to your local pub in the evening. Even in San Francisco, the reality never leaves you that at some point in the near future you're going to be walking through your front door, checking the post and messages and thanking the neighbour for feeding the cat.

Instantly accessible travel has enabled vast numbers of people to go to places they could never imagine attempting fifty years ago. But the price is a cheapening of the whole experience. Imagine the excitement one hundred years ago of sailing past the Statue of Liberty into New York Harbour. I can remember even twenty-five years ago asking my father if he'd ever been to New York and he just laughed in the way adults do when kids ask questions like: 'Can cats talk?'

Yet in 1990 I went round proudly telling people, 'I've got loads to do because next week I'm going to New York,' expecting a shriek of, 'Are you? To New York! That's fantastic!,' and instead getting, 'Oh yeah, going for the weekend?'

'No. New York,' I repeated imagining that the only reason they weren't incredulous that I was embarking on such an adventure was that they'd clearly misheard. 'New York. I have got a ticket to go to – New York.'

And I'd be looked at the same way that I'd look at someone if they said, 'Now come on Mark, there's loads to do because next week we're going to Bournemouth.'

Oy, Englishman – Fuck Off

ONE OF THE differences between being in your thirties and being in your twenties is the ability to prevent a moment's chaos from turning into complete fiasco. You learn for example that if you're five miles from home and the last bus has gone, it will probably make things worse if you break into a building site and try to drive back in a tipper truck.

As important as the fact that 'with age comes wisdom' is the likelihood that with age comes access to money. Go through the most chaotic day of your life and the chances are there will be half a dozen points at which all could have been resolved with a calm head or a credit card.

When driving up to Wrexham on the M6, a light on the dashboard that had never been on before, suddenly started flashing merrily. When you know absolutely nothing about cars, there are three courses of action you can take when something appears to be going wrong on a journey. One is to stop, open the bonnet, look at the engine for a minute, undo the radiator cap (the only bit you're sure you can remove and know how to put back) and drive off again, convincing yourself you've had a thorough check and can't see anything wrong. The second is to turn the radio up so you can't hear anything rattling. The third is to stop and call out the AA, a garage, or someone who knows which bit the carburettor is. But that requires a calm head *and* a credit card. Besides, it would be terrible to go through all that and find out it would have got to Wrexham and back anyway. So I chose the second option and kept going.

By the time I approached the army barracks-style building that is Wrexham Polytechnic, everything was fine so long as the engine kept running, but if it was turned off, it needed a push to get it started again. (I know someone reading this will be thinking: 'Well that'll be yer dynamo shorting out, that's yer problem there.').

At the Poly, the hall was packed, and a frail looking social secretary wandered on stage and introduced me in a very lacklustre way. By the time I reached the microphone, a voice had bellowed in a wonderfully baritone Welsh accent: 'Oy, Englishman. Fuck off.'

This set the tone, and for much of the gig his mates (who turned out to be the Rugby Club) and I exchanged insults. Much of this went down reasonably well with the students (who were probably used to being insulted by these boys with no opportunity to retaliate), but after half an hour or so, their insults took on a nastier edge.

At one point I mentioned death (I can't remember in what context) and the deep handsome voice that had started the exchange roared: 'You're going to die about a minute after you come off stage, see.'

I made something up about how this gig was destined to end up in the *Guinness Book of Records* for lasting twenty-three years but the faces of the students told me they were used to these characters carrying out their threats. The atmosphere for the rest of the gig was exactly what it would be if you were seeing someone who'd been advertised as 'The Man Who Promises To Die One Minute After He Comes Off Stage.'

One minute after I did come off stage, the bellowing man came over. 'Hello, mate,' I said. 'Bit of a laugh that, wasn't it?'

'I didn't find it funny,' he said. 'What time are you leaving?'

'Don't know,' I said, 'I might have a drink first.'

'I'll tell you when *we're* leaving,' he said. 'Same time as you, see.'

The one thing I learned at Swanley School was how to

tell when someone meant it if they threatened to kick your head in. And he meant it.

I asked the frail social secretary if he could gather up a posse to see me out and he ran straight out the door like the blokes in the bar in *High Noon*. One student did come to my aid and rounded up a group of a dozen or so. Then one of them found me a route out through a door behind the bar that I could slip out of without them seeing. And so, in the middle of thanking them heartily for saving my life, I had no choice but to take a breath and say: 'And can you give me a push as well, cos me motor won't start?'

When I got to the hotel it was shut and I had to wake the owner up by throwing stones at the windows, which took an hour.

The next day the car packed up altogether on the M6. I walked to a garage who wouldn't tow it off the motorway without a credit card. So I tried to ring up someone who might be able to use their's but I didn't have any change. Nor did the garage and I had to walk half a mile to a sweet shop while it poured with rain and I began to imagine what it must have been like for Captain Scott or Doctor Livingstone when they'd got to a point where they must have realised, 'I am never, ever going to get home.'

With ten pence left after the calls, I tried to hitch a lift to Hatfield Polytechnic where I was booked to do a gig that night. After an hour, I was picked up by two Rastafarians in a post office van, who zig-zagged across all three lanes and the hard shoulder on the M1 at thirty miles an hour, from Rugby to Toddington, which was where my nerves gave out and I told them I'd suddenly remembered that it was Toddington Services I was going to.

I tried to ring the college to tell them why I was going to be late, but I only got a caretaker and my last coin ran out. I begged ten pence off a passer-by and rang a taxi, who took me twenty or so miles to the college, whereupon I discovered that there were two sites of Hatfield Polytechnic and I was meant to be at the other one, fifteen miles away. When we finally did arrive, I borrowed the cab money off the student's union and was told that the gig was starting in five minutes.

And so I was in the extraordinary position of having just completed a day of utter disaster and instead of putting my feet in a bowl of water, was back on a stage talking to another bunch of students.

The social secretary had been told I would be doing a piece on the piano, but the instrument available had several keys missing so I declined. The moment I finished he threatened to hit me, as he'd gone to all the trouble of getting this piano and I hadn't even used it.

Throughout the day there were several points where the situation could have been brought under control, if only a calm head or a credit card had been available. But days like that do bring you into contact with the best and worst of human nature. The garage owner who wouldn't allow me the use of a telephone and the kind if erratic Rastafarians. The Rugby players who wanted to bash someone for a laugh, and the students who went out of their way to stop them doing it (and push the car).

But no one so nearly as irritating as the person at the end of the whole escapade who says, 'Oh well, never mind, it's all new material for you.'

New Money, New Danger

'I'LL HAVE A lager, please,' was not the answer he wanted, when John asked me what I wanted to drink.

'Lager!? We've got cocktails here that will make you fall down dead, my son. Oy, try a Banana Space Probe. We call it that cos it is rocket fuel, my son. You've got whisky, tequila, vodka – 'ere Pat, get 'im a double, you'll think you're floating; oy Pat, this one's on the 'ouse cos it's for my mate, Mark; right, get that down yer and you will be screaming, my son. Screaming.'

The odd thing was it tasted mostly of banana, and I'm sure it was less alcoholic than a lager.

I was drinking this cocktail as a result of two seemingly unconnected trends. By 1987 Thatcherism appeared to have created a new 'wide boy' sort of rebel. The 'grab what you can' prodigies of the eighties were at their most rampant, and at the same time, modern young comedy was becoming more and more popular.

So if working-class boys who'd got rich quick wanted to promote their inevitable nightclub with a bit of comedy, they weren't going to book a balding ex-Bluecoat whose motto was: 'Always leave 'em with a song.'

Two such boys who'd got rich quick were the partners of a club in the Kings Road. An establishment noted for its fine if expensive cuisine, late night licence, distinct lack of riff-raff, and of course, cocktails that are '*Fucking knockout, my son.*' How better to complement the place once a month than with a comedian on a Tuesday night.

Being new money, they were rebels. 'We're fucking mad, I tell you if you stick wiv us, we'll 'ave a fuckin' laugh. Listen…' And off they'd go, as if I was a close friend rather than someone they'd met five minutes ago and who had to do a gig in the corner in half an hour.

'Here, we 'ad a right laugh at the weekend Mark, you'd 'ave cracked up. Steve 'ere's got this 'ouse down Box'ill way, right? Well, we went out Saturday night, got so wrecked you wouldn't believe it. We was on Cherry Fireworks all night (two parts Cherry Brandy, one part Malibu and a squeeze of lemon). Well, we got up wiv a right stinkin' 'angover, I can tell yer. So we've gone down 'is local for 'air of the dog, like. Well, we've 'ad I dunno, a lot more beers. And I mean a *lot*. So anyway they've got this garden centre round his way, fuckin' massive thing it is. So we say, let's go round there, have a laugh.

'Well, they've got one o' these miniature railway fings 'n't they, right? There's loads o' kids there all waving an' what 'ave yer on one of these little trains. An' 'e says to me: "'ere, I fancy a go".

'So all these kids are waiting for the driver, Steve 'ops on the front, starts drivin' it, don't 'e? So all the kids start screamin', I was fuckin' crackin' up, I tell yer. All of a sudden wallop, the fuckin' things come off the tracks and crashed into a pile of them wooden fences you 'ave for beans, you know. So the driver's called the old bill, the guvnor's over doin' 'is fuckin' nut, 'e was. I tell yer, Mark, you should 'ave seen it.'

There's a particular social situation I've never been very good at dealing with, and that is how to behave when somebody's having enormous fun telling you an outrageous story that, (a) you don't believe, and (b) would be dreadful if it were true, telling it in a way that suggests they automatically assume that you approve. So while I stood listening to this, I was thinking, 'Regardless of whether (a) or (b) applies, these blokes are mad'. And mad in the way a doctor would mean the word, rather than as in 'I'm fuckin' mad, me.'

But I couldn't very well say that. Nor could I do the headmistress bit and say, 'Well, don't you think that was irre-sponsible – drunkenly crashing a miniature train full of chil-dren into a pile of wooden fences designed for runner beans?' So I did an unconvincing chuckle and thought of something extra to ask in order to feign interest.

'What happened when the police arrived?' I said

'Oh, we bunged 'em,' he replied with the nonchalance of someone answering, 'Oh, they were in my pocket,' when asked, 'Where did you find your keys?'

Then one of them started telling me about their plans for the club. The only reason I remember this was that in describing them he constructed one of the most amazing sentences I've ever heard. It went: 'So what we want is a nice atmosphere, cosy but somewhere you can come with your mates as well as... coo, I wouldn't mind bending that tart in the yellow hat over a dustbin and givin' 'er one ...but some-where you can come for somefing special, you know what I mean?'

He managed this without missing a single beat as he changed subject, and then changed back again. Which all left me with the same dilemma, what do you say? What on earth are you supposed to do when, bang in the middle of a sentence, someone tells you not just that they fancy 'that tart in the yellow hat' but even the precise household object they'd incorporate into their fantasy if they got the chance?

I played this club twice, and from that limited experience, would say that the two proprietors carried on like this non-stop, day and night. And with every exaggerated anecdote and every shout of, 'Go for it my son,' as they gulped another tequila slammer, they were desperate to prove two things. Firstly that they had money, and secondly that they'd made it themselves. They were definitely not old money.

Because in Britain, history has given us a distorted view of class, we seem to believe that the class we're from is deter-mined not by your position in society but by your accent and whether you slurp your soup. The two lads who ran the Kings Road club could appear as rebels because they'd raise eyebrows at the Garrick Club.

So at one and the same time they could be perfect caricatures of the modern establishment; celebrating greed, wasting money by the bucketful having dabbled in stocks, shares and housing without apparently ever doing a useful day's work; and yet still be anti-establishment because if they were at a party with Norman St John Stevas they'd probably walk straight up to him and say, ''Ere, your butler's a stuck-up cunt!'

Be funny to see them do it though, wouldn't it?

The Early Career Porn Movie

WHEN I BECAME a comedian it meant that I had now done two of the jobs perceived as the most likely to result in your being offered sex. The post of milkman has been cited in so many jokes and anecdotes as a trade in which you're expected to satisfy the carnal as well as the dairy needs of housewives, that most people must imagine it's a relief to get back to the depot with the overall in one piece.

But from my six months at the helm of a float, I can only imagine that the image of frustrated women in slinky nighties purring to 'come inside' has no basis in fact whatsoever, at least not on Swanley depot's round seven. And my round included a daily *Carry on Milkman* scenario of delivering to the residents of Hockenden Lane Nudist Camp, for whom a slinky nightie was a sell-out.

And yet the myth persists, mostly I suspect because it's self-perpetuating. Most of the milkmen from my depot reckoned they had one or two 'on the go', probably because they thought that if they admitted they hadn't, they'd be ridiculed as the only one in the yard with a celibate round. So the only way to stop the myth from continuing would be to hold a huge milkmen's convention at which the entire profession would simultaneously confess that they'd made the whole thing up.

Surely as a comedian though, the chances are much greater? Laughter is an obvious route to seduction, so a whole show must put the comic in the frame with almost the entire audience. It certainly does away with all the 'what sort of music do you like?' conversation that usually goes on between two people auditioning each other before swapping telephone numbers.

The person talking to a comedian after a show knows what sort of person they're talking to, as they've just watched them perform a presentation more comprehensive than Dateline could ever imagine.

And on the scale that awards points for open-top cars or muscles in a swimming pool, a gig that's gone well is worth a TR6 or thirteen-inch biceps. And yet the truth is, as a member of the audience you stand far more chance of ending up in bed with another member of the audience than the comedian does.

To start with, the mechanics of getting to talk to someone in the audience are quite complex. At a theatre, you come off-stage, pick some things up from the dressing room, thank the bloke who did the sound, walk back into the theatre and the place has emptied. Even if there's a bar at which a few people hang around, there'll probably only be ten minutes or so before closing in which to get into the sort of conversation that could feasibly lead to a night of passion.

It's hard enough when you're sitting inches away from each other, yawning on a settee at two in the morning, clock ticking and coffees being poured every few minutes, to fumble towards a way of saying, 'Er, I don't want you to think, er, I was wondering, look, I, um, would really like to go to bed with you.'

I've never understood how anyone could hope to get that far in ten minutes. Even at a party the first half-hour of conversation with somebody you take a shine to has to conceal the fact that you're working your way round some fundamental questions. (Are they married, are they gay, shit – who's this? It's all right, just a brother).

Anyway, there can be few sadder scenes than that of a performer coming off stage and declaring themselves 'on the pull'. The fact that there's only a few moments to establish a rapport that could lead to the sack means that the approach has to be more cynical than ever. 'Oh, this is your boyfriend? Well, I'll be off then, there's only eight and a half minutes left.'

The saddest part of this charade is that in all probability the night will end with the performer sitting on a bed in his guest house, watching a re-run of *Columbo*, and drinking coffee made with the powdered granules and tiny plastic UHT carton kept in the basket beside the fire instructions. Because, by eagerly circulating amongst people who look remotely available, you send out a signal which says: 'I want to sleep with someone. I don't care who. Just someone.' And no salesman ever closed a deal while seeming desperate.

But as well as all this, there's one more brake on the comedians' prospects for a one-night, out-of-town stand. The bigger, longer, better-attended and funnier the performance, the more impressive and possibly sexual it will be. But the bigger the performance, the more inaccessible the person performing it seems.

Do a twenty minute set to thirty people, and half a dozen of them will chat to you. But do an hour and a half to five hundred in a theatre and everybody leaves you alone. Even if someone does come over, they will probably be polite and brief, hurriedly telling you that they thought you were very funny last week on Radio Five and that you're the third favourite comedian they've seen this year, before thanking you for letting them tell you this and striding back to their friends.

The relationship in these situations is like a schoolboy who meets his headmaster in the High Street, or an office boy whose boss says 'Good morning' to him for the first time in a year. There's usually a sense of 'I know you must be very busy and probably only usually talk to someone if they've been on the telly but could I speak to you for thirty seconds?'

Either that or they'll be a bloke going: ''Ere's one for yer: this gorilla's giving this giraffe one up the arse...'

The sort of normal conversation which could lead to something further should really be a two-way affair, with each person asking about the other. But in the circumstances of a comedian talking to a member of the audience after a large theatre show, it's usually assumed that the comedian is the more interesting, which is probably untrue. When so many people are brought up with such low self-esteem, if they're asked in this situation what they do, they'll say something like, 'Oh nothing much, I'm just a hairdresser,' and look embarrassed.

The only possible sexuality in these cases would be the calculatingly miserable business of a horny comedian getting relief in exchange for a woman being able to tell her mates that she shagged that bloke who was on at the town hall. And that would destroy all the mystique, passion and romance that can grace a one-night-stand between two people who will never see each other again.

No such barrier exists however in a pub basement. It won't seem at all odd then, if the performer asks where you went for your holiday, or enquires whether the bloke you said you shared a flat with is a mate or a boyfriend?

In fact the only time I ended up going out with someone from the audience who I'd never met before, was after a show in west London to ten people. Maybe there's a rule that once in everyone's life we're granted an opportunity to live out a real life scene that could only normally happen in a soft porn movie. I was twenty-six, single and this was the night.

'Would you like to sit at the table with me?' enquired the pretty American student, who then began to brush her leg against mine under that very table and I thanked fate for not having given me a packed theatre that night.

The fact that there were so few people meant that rather than appearing as the professional entertainer, it was as if I was a bloke she'd met in a pub who she happened to find funny. Had two hundred been there, the inaccessibility factor would have come into play and I doubt if I'd ever have got to know her name.

At such a point the single life of the carefree touring comedian appears so wonderfully suave and Bohemian that the settled-down, mortgage-paying world of fidelity and settee repayments seems akin to a life wasted in a monastery. But what most of those who've trodden that path have, at some point, to admit is that the cost of being available for casual liaisons is a ninety-nine per cent rate of disappointment. Because every gig presents itself as a potential opportunity for meeting someone like the American student, when in fact once a lifetime is a reasonably average tally.

Other experiences may be different, but my guess is that most single male comedians who tour the country hoping to screw their way from one town to the next, end up watching a lot of *Columbo*. How much less stressful it is to be domesticated with a joint mortgage and settee repayments, and not having to endure the tortuous ordeal of hoping that the woman who's come up to say she enjoyed the show:— (a) doesn't have a boyfriend or husband; (b) isn't gay; (c) likes me on a personal as well as comic level; (d) likes me on a sexual as well as personal level; (e) would be prepared to sleep with someone she's only just met; (f) doesn't live in a studio flat with her mum or in a YWCA hostel with a team of axe-wielding Calvinist nuns, or in some other impregnable abode; and (g) doesn't suddenly announce that she's a practising devil-worshipper, the reincarnation of Lady Macbeth, secretary of the local Conservative Association or anything else likely to put me off as I unbutton her shirt.

Not only is the 'straight to bed on your own' option less stressful, it also allows you to imagine that you almost certainly would have been successful if you'd been available, and lets you feel smugly superior to those who behave in the same way as you once.

Most people, including most touring performers, do eventually come to the conclusion that some form of domesticity offers the greatest reward. And yet most of us spend years walking seven miles home from situations we were certain was a sure thing, or spending twenty promising minutes with someone before being introduced to her boyfriend and having to smile amiably while thinking, '*Fuck. Fuck. Bollocks. Fuck.*'

Maybe, like believing in Father Christmas, it's unhealthy not to chase promiscuity before a certain age, but pretty stupid to still be doing it at thirty-five.

But if you want to use stand-up comedy as a way of getting sex, my advice is to make sure your career never gets past those basements, or you'll never have a chance.

Fallen Wimmin

I SAW A washing powder advert in 1987 and it made me roar with laughter.

It reminded me of a night at Bristol University some years earlier, when a woman comedian was imploring everyone to sing along with the chorus, and just about everyone did. 'Now his willy's boiling in the kitchen,' they all sang. 'Boiling up with the chilli beans real fast. Now his willy's boiling in the kitchen, it's found its true consistency at last.'

There were just a couple of things that had bothered me about this scene. Firstly, as the subject of the song's culinary exercise was supposed to be her boyfriend, why hadn't she left him before it came to this? And secondly, although supporting any campaign that advances women's equality, I wondered whether an act of castration followed by boiling up the result with chilli beans (at any speed, let alone real fast) was something that ought to be celebrated quite so fervently.

That was in 1983 and the comedian concerned was Jenny Lecoat. The story of her act is the story of feminism in the 1980s

By the middle of the 1990s it was argued by many that feminism had gone too far. In particular the attempts to change language were ridiculed. Everyone knew a supposed story along the lines of: 'There's a bloke down the council who got sacked for saying manhole cover instead of person-hole road lid,' which would be told with the same conviction as someone who relates how their cousin knows a bloke who bought a rubber plant that turned out to be full of tarantulas.

Stories of PC madness, many of them invented, were

everywhere. Accusing someone of political correctness became a meaningless insult thrown into a debate in the same way in which kids losing an argument will say, 'Well anyway, you smell.' And yet somehow this tyrannical policing of words, jokes and phrases was all supposed to have taken place during fifteen years of the most right-wing government seen this century.

For some reason Margaret Thatcher, who was able to beat the Argentine Navy, the miners, Irish hunger strikers, three Labour leaders and anyone who dared oppose her within her own ranks, was powerless to stop a politically correct, semi-mafia sweeping the nation and hounding honest labouring folk from their jobs and homes for saying 'milkman' instead of 'milkbeing.'

It was true however, that an assortment of councillors, social workers and people with massive pine kitchens and enormous spice racks had won influence in some lower strata of society, and were using it to pursue aims that would later be labelled PC. Mostly these people were ex-university students who had landed fairly well-paid white-collar jobs. Many of them had been politicised by the events of 1968, and since then had retained their support for campaigns against sexism, racism and nuclear weapons. But as they'd climbed the ladder of respectability, they'd abandoned all attempts to win working-class support for their aims, because they'd given up completely on living near, working with, or having conversations with anyone who was working-class – except their cleaning persons.

The new strategy of these people was to win positions in local government, hold discussion groups, argue with each other about whether certain words were offensive or not, and often spend their free time at alternative cabaret nights.

So for this reason, many of the early alternative venues were forums for the most wretchedly smug, self-congratulatory stuck-up twaddle ever witnessed outside an art gallery.

Poets would proclaim, 'While they have the weapons it is we who have the strength,' with a ridiculously earnest face, then come out of character, give a 'thank you for sharing that beautiful moment with me' smile, and the place would erupt into applause.

A string of venues was founded under the banner of New Variety and, funded by the GLC, they soon became the heart of this circuit. One of my first professional jobs was compering at these places, and I probably made a pretty awful hash of it.

On my first night, the show ended with an all-woman band called Jam Today. After they'd come off stage they marched downstairs to where I was starting to load some equipment into the van, and screamed a marvellously eloquent tirade of abuse about how I'd deliberately given them a shit introduction because I was a man. I tried to explain that the reason I'd given them a shit introduction was because I was a shit compere, but that only made it worse.

Once I was approached in the interval by an angry white couple who demanded to know why there wasn't a black compere instead of me. Again, if they'd asked why wasn't there a half decent compere instead of me, I'd have probably thought it a fair enough enquiry.

A room above the Crown and Castle in Dalston provided the setting for a typical example of this kind of thing. Almost every week the show broke down into a debate about the political justification for something or other. One night a comedian began a poem which usually went:

I do not love my girlfriend because she is pretty.
I do not love my girlfriend because she is good in bed.
I do not love my girlfriend because I see her as a fast-food restaurant with take-away sex on the side.
I do not love my girlfriend
Because I do not have a girlfriend.

Except that on this particular night he completed the first two lines and received a barrage of abuse about how he had no right to be so sexist about his girlfriend, which made it impossible for him to carry on the act.

The audiences were like kids playing snap, eagerly anticipating each card, so anxiously ready and waiting to shout 'snap' that they'd frequently blurt it out in a fit of over keenness at the wrong moment. But at least kids then admit they're wrong and carry on with the game. This lot would try to compose an argument for why the jack of hearts and the nine of diamonds was 'snap,' and if only you weren't so macho, you'd be able to see it.

What made this all the more ridiculous was that at the same time as this scrutinising of each individual syllable for imperialist overtones was going on, mainstream comedy was genuinely sexist and remaining relatively unchallenged. At about the same time there was a new talent show on early evening weekend TV. One night a brash young club comic came on and opened with: 'I've never hit my wife in anger. It's always been a pleasure.' Had a posse of protesters followed him around barracking his act, it would have been justified.

An added problem for some of us was that the main target of the favourite acts on this circuit was the white working-class male. So if you were white, male and spoke with what seemed a working-class accent, it was assumed you were a drunken, fighting, car mechanic.

There are plenty of white working-class males who, like me at seventeen, deserve any lampooning sent their way. But there are also some who have black friends and who don't join in leering at Page Three.

Having to assert their ideas in their daily lives, they embody the opposite of the middle class bimbos at their cabaret evenings. For the most unpleasant side of these events was the smug self satisfaction shown by a layer of society that would make no effort to relate to anyone outside their own circle, but remain content that they were the minority who knew the true and only path.

Many of the faithful at New Variety would attend their weekly gatherings with the genuine ardour of cult members. So eventually I decided that if I was going to get harangued even when I was being as right-on as they were, I might as well gain some pleasure out of deliberately annoying them. One of my favourite lines from the time was: 'What I'd love to do to a middle class lefty is say I was going to come round their house with someone who worships a dictator and thinks all women are whores. So I could watch them going "Well no, oh please don't bring them, I'll be sick," and then turn up with a Rastafarian.'

Another that I was pleased with was: 'These people love feeling guilty. They feel guilty for being white, guilty for being male, guilty for being middle class. Why don't they just feel guilty for being wankers.' How therapeutic it was to feel a sea of hostility that I'd caused on purpose instead of one I'd caused because they'd misinterpreted me. One night in Cricklewood, a Scottish woman stood up in the middle of my act and said I'd been racist, sexist, misogynist, misanthropic and abusive to minorities. 'Wait till I start on the Scottish,' I told her.

One of the most popular acts on this circuit were called The Joeys. These four men would perform sketches about sexuality, like their 'male ego wrestling match'; and their roof-raiser was a poem, which all four would recite:

Men are strong, men are tough,
Men don't know when they've had enough.
Men like fights.
Men drink beer.
Men live with their mums for years and years.

This was no 'church hall and broken seats' act either. This nonsense had a run at the Festival Hall, made its way briefly on to TV and would guarantee an audience of hundreds at any New Variety or like-minded venue.

But the heroine was Jenny Lecoat. Impotent boyfriends, innocent victimised women and boiling willies would send the audience wild. 'After I split up with my boyfriend,' went one joke, 'he sent a card with a heart torn in two saying, "Look what you've done to my heart". So I sent him my appointment slip for the VD clinic with a note saying, "Look what you've done to my cunt".'

Boom, boom.

'Men are obsessed with willies,' she'd continue. 'I mean, when those missiles go launching off Greenham Common, it won't be 220-foot clitorises up there.'

With the vigour and cynicism of a record label pouncing on a teenage band, the 'Alternative' world promoted her with great enthusiasm. A London listings magazine called *City Limits*, which was a mouthpiece for the people I've been describing, hailed their new superstar. And a journalist who fitted perfectly into that mould, Carol Sarler, used her contacts with the newly formed Channel 4 to secure a TV series for Lecoat called *Watch The Woman*, which Sarler produced. *The Guardian* publicised her extensively, and Channel 4 employed her as a presenter on other programmes as well.

So what happened to all this? My theory is that two events knocked this blossoming career off course. Firstly the heartland of trendy leftydom, the Labour councils came under attack. New rulings prevented them from raising extra funds and restricted their ability to behave defiantly. Worst of all, the GLC (which funded a good deal of the venues) was abolished altogether. In addition, after the 1983 election the Labour party took a turn to the right, and began to neutralise and expel the corners of the party which provided a base camp for the fans of *Watch The Woman*.

As their influence declined, their spirit broke. But just as importantly, the beginning of 1984 saw the start of the Miners' Strike. The Strike dominated the world of political entertainment as comprehensively as it did the rest of British politics for a whole year, and anyone with a hint of resistance made it top of their oppositional priorities. Crucial to the strike was the Miners' Wives' Groups, so middle-class feminists had a problem. Many became supporters of these groups, to whom songs about boiling willies and sketches about psychoanalytical wrestling made no sense. Some, like Bea Campbell, formerly an intellectual icon of these people, condemned the Strike as a typical example of male machismo.

Middle-class feminism went into retreat, and with it went The Joeys, Jenny Lecoat and the sycophantic audiences and venues that created them. So what was their fate?

For Jenny Lecoat, 1987 brought an unexpected turn. Standing by a sink, she was telling viewers about the delights of New Ariel Automatic, the amazing washing powder that, unlike other inferior brands, leaves an extra-lasting whiteness that she wouldn't swap for anything. The princess of all those who would froth with rage at anyone who suggested that a woman's place was in the kitchen, was now in the kitchen several times a night on primetime TV, relating the virtues of a washing powder. And I for one, couldn't see any trace of a boiling member.

Jenny couldn't really be blamed for her predicament, as she was only ever the front woman for those like Sarler. And the majority of those that had comprised her fan club now rejected almost all of the ideas they'd embraced so evangelically a few years earlier. Most of them gave up political activity altogether and, if reminded of their earlier allegiances, would chuckle away their past in the way someone tuts when they're shown a photo of themselves wearing platform shoes.

Those of us who still support the idea of campaigning for

women's equality, instead of being castigated as the enemy for not being black or giving a poor introduction to a band, are sneered at by exactly these same people, but this time for bothering to mention the issue at all.

In the 1990s Carol Sarler, possibly the most influential of all the behind the scenes characters in the days of 'sexual politics' comedy, won herself a column at the *People* newspaper. There she turned her thoughts to all matters. For example, Ireland:

'We can sort out the Falklands but for some strange reason we get squeamish about asking the SAS to stroll into Ballywotsit and kick butt... It is the job of our army to fight back with all guns blazing... Even if it didn't immediately work, wouldn't we all feel so much better for trying?'

For insights like this she was awarded a regular slot as sidekick on a late night chat show with Richard Littlejohn. Formerly of *The Sun*, then the *Daily Mail*, Littlejohn, more than any other journalist, makes it his obsession to use any opportunity he's given to attack feminists, anti-racists and anyone guilty of what he sees as political correctness. A supporter of John Redwood against John Major for the 1995 prime ministerial election, for him Britain is under siege from poofs, wailing Muslims and hairy-arsed feminists.

It isn't hard to imagine the two of them joking about the sort of people who go around singing songs about boiling up willies, and just laughing, and laughing and laughing.

The People Round Here

'THE TROUBLE IS, mate, it's the people round here. They couldn't care less round here. They'd rather stay in and watch *Coronation Street*.' Those depressing words are uttered to performers in every area of the country by people who've put on a show, and seen only a handful turn up. Sometimes they're said even when quite a few people have turned up. With touching naïvety they might say, 'Well, there's twenty thousand in this town so I was reckoning that even if only a quarter of them came, that would be five thousand.'

It's an understandable reaction to blame the local population for not attending the event you've organised, but having heard it from dozens of different areas, it seems pretty daft. 'It's the Rugby people,' someone once said to me. 'They just don't go out.'

But they must do. Wouldn't we have heard about it before if the people of Rugby never went out? Wouldn't there be documentaries and newspaper articles about the strange town where everyone stayed in, and cult books claiming that it was a result of an underground earthquake, a visit from God, or that it was an alien commune; and surely by now psychologists would be describing anyone who stayed in a lot as having Rugby Early Night Syndrome?

The 'people round here' theory sadly fails the first test of logic. What could possibly make the population of one town behave in a markedly different manner to the population of any other town? And yet when someone's on a roll with this argument, there's no stopping them. 'They won't. They don't go to anything. There was a rock 'n' roll night on at the town hall last month. Twenty-two people turned up! They're a waste of time.'

Travelling around the country, I get the impression that there's only marginal differences between the level of apathy in one place and the next. The person who became more and more exasperated as he tried to convince me that, 'People in Reading are not like people anywhere else, they're all useless,' just wouldn't have it that there was someone who thought the same about Rugby. 'Well, in Rugby it's probably not true,' he insisted, 'But you don't know Reading like I do. They won't do anything.'

Sometimes I think it would be funny to get two people from different towns who thought like this to scream at each other that it was their town and not the other person's that contained the greatest percentage of useless people.

Besides, if the 'useless town' theory made any sense, surely it would mean there was a counterbalance of brilliant towns. Places where, no matter what was put on, hundreds of people would turn up on a Tuesday afternoon and performers would be told: 'It's the people round here see, they're all marvellous.'

But the argument does seem to serve two purposes. Firstly, if you can convince yourself that the people round here are hopeless, you've got a perfect excuse for never trying to initiate anything in the area ever again. Because, 'I'd love to try, but unfortunately the people round here are hopeless, so there's no point.'

Secondly it hides a certain snobbery. For implicit in the statement that everyone round here is hopeless, is that the person saying it is the exception. 'I understand the point of turning up to a cultural event, or organising a protest. But sadly the rest of the population doesn't have my foresight.'

The inescapable truth is that only a handful of people will pay money to see an entertainer they haven't heard of, no matter where they live. Coming to terms with that fact is a delicate matter for the average entertainer. Because it would have certainly helped to salvage my ego after the night in Rugby if I could have said, 'Well, it was obvious there would only be thirty in the audience; the people of Rugby are shit.'

The Middle East Crisis and its Effect on a Comedy Night in Manchester

EVENTUALLY MOST COMEDIANS get to a point where they are established enough not to have to do gigs that have any sniff of disaster attached to them. A combination of learning to sense potential chaos and not being so desperate for the fifty quid fee curtailed my need to do nutty Wrexham-type gigs. This was obviously a good line to cross, except that a bit of me enjoyed the madness of a good saga.

Life hadn't necessarily become easy. Most of the time I played clubs or colleges, often driving to somewhere like Bradford, doing the show, stopping in a damp hotel and driving home to end up with sixty quid – which is probably the same as I'd get paid if my job was to drive to Bradford and back to deliver a parcel.

And disappointments tended to come in bigger doses. When I first started, a club telling me that they wouldn't book me because I 'wasn't ready' was thoroughly disheartening but could quickly be redeemed. After all there were other clubs that would book me. Then it became more likely that BBC Radio would reject a proposal because they thought I 'wasn't ready,' and plans for the next six months would be in ruins.

But the live bookings were steady, and generally well organised. Occasionally I'd encounter a spasm of madness, like the night someone kept shouting, 'Show us yer fridge,' but nothing on the scale of the Newcastle tea-making pyromaniac. If a gig was going to end in chaos, it would need a bit of pushing to get it there. Like the night a section of the

National Union of Students were holding an annual conference at Manchester Polytechnic and three of us had been booked to do twenty minutes each for their evening's entertainment.

Many of them, being student activists, were involved in a variety of campaigning groups or political parties and there was clearly an undercurrent of hostility between some of the opposing factions. It can be extremely disheartening to watch political activists reserving their most vicious moments for each other rather than for whoever it is they're supposed to be opposing. I can only imagine that the same process takes over which leads some people in small towns to hate everyone from the next town up. The real world is ignored and the enemy becomes those who are almost the same as you but not quite.

The woman who came into the dressing room to greet us that night was a chronic sufferer of this affliction. Here she was, talking to three people who she'd never met before, having no idea of their own beliefs. And yet her opening remarks were not to ask us to support any initiatives the conference might be taking against racism, student poverty or the arms trade. Instead she launched into a tirade of abuse about every left-wing group represented at the conference, except for the one that she was a member of.

Aware of the importance of finishing on a big laugh her breathless rant ended with a joke. 'If an SWP member and a Militant member jumped off a tall building who'd land first? Who gives a fuck?!'

Even without the element of in-fighting, this was an extremely weak joke. Had she said, 'If Ronald Reagan and Henry Kissinger jumped off a tall building who'd land first? Who gives a fuck?!' it would still have not been funny. But here was a woman who presumably at some point in her life had taken up the cause of political activism in order to oppose the injustices around her, but was manically frothing at the prospect of two other activists jumping off this imaginary tall building.

I found out later that the group this woman was allied with was a supporter of the state of Israel, which had just carried out some particularly unpleasant attacks on groups of Palestinians, which included the shooting of several teenagers for throwing stones. In fact her group was linked with a Zionist student group noted for its hostility towards Arabs.

There are of course many decent people, among them a great many Jews, who agree with the idea of the Israeli state but are infuriated by what they see as that state's excesses. What her group was known for was the way in which they responded to any critics of Zionism by accusing them of being anti-Semitic. A somewhat untenable position given the millions of Jews who opposed the formation of a country which could only exist by forcibly expelling hundreds of thousands of people and agreeing to act as a highly-armed puppet for America.

The considered response to this student would have been to mutter something under my breath and forget it. The problem was the mischief gene. The gene that makes certain children tip up their father's neatly organised box of papers on to the floor, just to see what would happen. One of my earliest memories is as a two year old letting the budgie out of the cage just to see what would happen. (It flew out of the window and away.)

So just to see what would happen, half way through my set I told the story of the woman in a socialist group who'd come into the dressing room and delivered her rant, and that it seemed she was a supporter of this Zionist students society. 'No-wonder there's so few socialists around,' I said. 'If people ask what would happen in an ideal socialist state and the answer is: "Well, every couple of years we'll invade the next country along, do whatever the Americans told us to, and anyone who chucked a stone would be shot dead".'

About three-quarters of the audience began whooping and clapping and the rest began screaming abuse. By the time I came off stage, a picket line had formed across the dressing room, and a motion had been prepared that the Zionist group should be allowed a right to reply.

The mischief gene was ecstatic. A right to reply to a comedian. Surely if you stopped to think for one moment, you'd realise that this was completely silly. But all around was uproar. There were arguments about the right to reply, arguments about the dressing room picket, someone screamed that they were going to kick me down the stairs and someone else said that if he did, then he'd kick *them* down the stairs.

Eventually, despite receiving little support for the right to reply, a leading member of the offended group got on stage and began to speak. 'I can't believe we've had to sit here listening to this anti-Semitism,' she began. 'Especially not today, because today...'

There was a pause. She brought out a handkerchief and theatrically struggled for composure. What would it be? Today what? She was clearly aiming for a big sympathy number. The room went quiet with expectation the way courtrooms do on the telly just before the verdict.

'Today,' she said, 'is my birthday.'

There followed further attempts to link my act to Kristalnaacht and other outrages of the Third Reich, but the birthday line had blown it. I did ask however, if I could just deny publicly that I was quite the fascist I'd been portrayed to be. For surely if anyone was insulting Jews it was her and her performance.

Another meeting took place about whether I should be allowed to return, and a chant of 'Let him speak' began to circulate the room. The whole situation was now so wonderfully surreal that only student politics could have created it. But the comment that summed up the evening was yet to come.

I did get back on the stage but someone pulled the microphone lead out of its socket and someone else tipped over the mixing desk.

The chanting started up again and through the cacophony of stamping, screams of 'Let him speak,' and screams to the effect of 'Don't let him speak' one voice rose above the others. 'For God's sake, let him speak,' it bellowed and succeeded in quietening the whole place. Here, I thought was a major ally.

With the room at his command, he said his piece: 'I'm hard of hearing. Has no one any respect for the disabled?'

Revolution and the Boiled Egg

UP IN HULL for another University gig, again nowhere had been arranged for me to stay. The days of shivering in student squats were behind me, and I was in the league of being able to afford fifteen quid for a room. So I found some telephone numbers of guest houses and rang to book somewhere. The first one I called was a quarter of a mile from the gig, and only cost eight pounds a night. So, not only was everything quickly sorted out, I was seven quid to the good.

I was greeted by a very polite man in a string vest with thick hairy arms and a rolled-up cigarette, who showed me into the guest TV room. It was clearly a DHSS bed and breakfast 'hotel', and I suddenly felt hopelessly out of place, the way one of those politicians must feel when they get on a tube train for the first time in their lives and ask for directions to the buffet car.

A young couple were on the settee combing each other's hair, every item of their clothing in an advanced state of decay. Stuffing was pouring out of the back of the settee by the minute and forming a pile of yellow foam. Across the middle of the windows was a single curtain; brown, thoroughly frayed and hanging on a piece of wire which had bent under the weight to make a shallow U-shape, leaving the top and sides of the window exposed. A family of two adults and three kids, aged from about ten to fifteen sat in the opposite corner on the floor, half watching the black and white television which was so caked in a crusted film of dust you could barely make out the picture, and half telling each other to shut up.

Every now and then one of them would glance my way, and whisper something to the person next to them while still looking directly at me. I don't think this was supposed to be threatening or contemptuous in any way, just completely confused. A sort of 'this bloke looks as if he could afford fifteen quid for a room so what the bloody hell's he doing here?' sort of look.

The following morning, having got through the 'bed' side of the deal I went downstairs for the breakfast. The family that had been watching television was sitting around a table, still telling each other to shut up and to 'Shut up, yourself'. This was followed by a whole array of: 'Don't tell me to shut up', 'I'll shut up when I want to shut up', and, 'Shut up or I'll shut you up', type sentences. At one point two of these exchanges were going on at the same time across each diagonal of the table so that it was hardly possible to tell the 'shuts' from the 'ups'.

Every now and then the yelling would stop and they would all start giggling. This was obviously one of those families that was so used to conflict that shouting at each other no longer expressed any anger but was just a way of life.

Polite table manners and respect for the rules of society could hardly be expected for a society who had given them a DHSS dump as their way of life. For the saddest part of this place, worse than any of the filthy surroundings and 'out of the skip' furniture, was the lack of control the residents had over any aspect of their lives. Breakfast was a regimented ordeal, with the guy in the string vest dictating what the meal was, when it should be served and how it should be cooked. A lie-in would mean no breakfast at all. After breakfast there was only the shared TV room or the squalid bedroom to go to, in which even the choice of ripped wallpaper was not their own.

Poverty-stricken families in their own surroundings can at least maintain their dignity by improving tiny aspects of their environment, and making their own breakfasts. But these families are denied even the pride of cooking a decent boiled egg.

As breakfast progressed it became clear that for this particular family the nature of the boiled egg was a source of conflict which had been brewing for some time, and today it would come to a head.

'Is that my bloody egg?' screamed the fifteen year old from the Shut-up Family, holding it as close as he could to the face of the bloke in the string vest.

'What's wrong with it?'

'What d'yer mean, what's wrong with it? It gets smaller every bloody day.'

'Shut up, Neil,' said the mother quietly but obviously starting to enjoy the scene.

'I won't shut up. Look at the bloody size of it.'

'There's nowt wrong with it,' said the manager and returned to the kitchen.

Then the youngest of the children started shouting abuse into the kitchen, and the parents stopped pretending to be neutral and started giggling. Back came the manager, spatula in hand to tell the entire family to shut up.

Now the family was united.

'You shut up.'

'Yeah, shut up yourself.'

'Where'd thee find a hen small enough to lay an egg like that,' said the lad, and everyone agreed except the manager.

The first victims of the Russian Revolution, I was reminded by all this, were not the Tsar and his generals but the foremen who'd been forcing metal workers to work unpaid overtime for the war effort. In Zola's *Germinal* the first victims of the miners' strike were not the mine owners but the shopkeepers who'd been filling the miners' bread with sawdust. And if a revolution ever happens in Hull the first victim will not be the secretary of Hull's chamber of commerce but the guy in a string vest who makes a few extra coppers by feeding the residents of his Social Security guest house the oldest, smallest and most miserable boiled eggs in all Humberside.

'Eat yer bloody boiled egg,' he said. 'It's all yer getting.'

And at that the lad raised his hand and brought it down at a ferocious rate, flat on to the egg which splattered to all corners of the room and brought the whole clientele, myself included into hysterical laughter.

All comedy, it is said, is tragedy. And that place had piles of both. As for the show I'd done the night before, I honestly can't remember a thing about it.

Part Three

Established

POPULAR PRODUCTIONS
PRESENT

EDINBURGH
FESTIVAL
CRITICS AWARD
WINNER

YELTSIN, TROTSKY
& THE BETTING SHOP

MARK STEEL

goes Russian

Someone New

THERE COMES A time in the career of many comedians when they're suddenly noticed as someone new. It usually comes about three or four years after they first start, so that they just become accomplished at what they're doing when they find themselves surrounded by producers, journalists, agents and people who just hang out at comedy clubs, comedy parties and comedy festivals for no apparent reason.

Entertainment to these people is of course a product so, as with any other product, if someone wants to make their name they have to find a new and exciting brand. Young ambitious designers in the chocolate industry wouldn't further their careers by jumping into the boss's office and saying, 'I've got a great idea. A caramely sort of thing we can market as the chocolate that helps you work, rest and play.'

So in comedy the search for the next big thing is a continuous battle for those who have an interest in 'discovering' someone. As a result there is a string of performers who at one time were snapped up by agents and TV executives and slung in front of cameras before they knew what they were doing, while millions of viewers mutter: 'What's this bollocks?'

In 1987 I went to the Edinburgh Festival and put on my own hour-long show, which at that time, only a handful of other comedians from the cabaret circuit had done. My target for the three week run, as far as audience numbers were concerned, was simply to win enough popularity not to have to cancel any performance by having fewer in than six. In fact I did much better than that (the lowest was fifteen) and a variety of people who you're supposed to be excited about if they come along, began to turn up with their note-pads.

Suddenly I was on the invisible list of comics asked to go on things. *Sunday Sunday*, with Gloria Hunniford, *Wogan* (which was subsequently cancelled), and *Des O'Connor Tonight* all asked me to appear. There's no conspiracy or official policy behind this invisible list, but a list there is, because there comes a point when someone is invited on to programmes in the automatic way you write certain people down first when you're organising a party.

At this time I was also finding a number of agents hovering around, telling me how marvellous I was. Nobody in senior media circles had a clue who I was, so if I was going to be the next big thing there would certainly be a few points for whoever it was that got the credit for alerting the world to my existence. However, as you probably realise with this not being a work of fiction, I wasn't the next big thing. The Des O'Connor show went well and was great fun, but the following week I was asked to appear as a guest on *Tarbuck*.

There are plenty of good, principled reasons for avoiding Jimmy Tarbuck and people like him. The sleazy demeanour of false showbiz camaraderie, the avid campaigning for Margaret Thatcher, and let's face it, most of them are shit. It seemed that the logical progression from doing all right as an unknown guest on different programmes was that I'd be asked to be a guest on loads more programmes until I became one of those people who pop up on things like *Celebrity Squares*, or *That's Showbusiness*. I could then aspire to get my own afternoon game show and introduce each programme with an amusing anecdote about playing golf with Ronnie Corbett. But though I would like to believe that my brief period on the invisible list came to a close because I chose a pure and righteous road, the truth is that I just wasn't asked to go on anything like that again.

It's not that I was struck off for refusing to do *Tarbuck*. It's more that to venture into the world of mainstream telly you have to do it wholeheartedly, waving fervently into the camera at the end of the show with the other guests, clapping enthusiastically when Jim Davidson says he's going to add fifty pounds of his own money to a children's charity, pulling a silly face when Brigitte Nielsen's chest comes near, looking excited when Noel Edmonds introduces you to Mr Blobby. Like catching a cricket ball, the only safe approach is to do it with complete conviction. Half dabble at it and you'll break your fingers.

The silliest-looking people on TV are those that recite puns and innuendos written by ageing hacks, but do it with a look on their face that tells you they know it's rubbish. Like Winston Smith in *1984*, it's not enough to pretend the inquisitor is holding up four fingers when he's holding up three. The only way to survive is to believe it.

So really the choice was made for me. The peculiar thing is that when I look back at the sort of stuff I was doing then, it mostly seems quite poor. I'd only just started doing full length shows, I'd never written a half hour programme, far more people come to the shows now than in those days and I would have to be a complete mess not to be 'better' now than I was in 1987.

But the agents, producers, journalists and hangers on have moved on to other pastures; praising acts that are finding their feet as geniuses and coining nonsensical quotes like 'a Tony Hancock of the nineties'.

None of this makes me or most of the other comedians who are in the same boat sad or bitter. For every year sees hundreds of newly-marketed brands of chocolate, some of which are successful for a few months because of their novelty. But everyone knows, in the long run, you'd be hard-pressed to beat a Mars Bar.

Under My Skin

ONE OF THE television programmes I was asked to appear on during a temporary flurry of media requests was a weekly programme about entertainment in the London region.

The producer of this new programme was keen on me doing a character on his show he'd seen me do live. The parody was of an old fashioned dinner and dance singer/pianist. The sort of chap who would be at the Holiday Inn in every seaside resort in Britain in the 1960s (especially Ventnor), and who my parents would seek out so that they could spend every evening of their holiday listening to him.

I'd do a version of *I've Got You Under My Skin* on the piano, played and sung in the smarmiest sickliest way I could recall those characters doing themselves, and it seemed to be recognised by most audiences.

'I'd just love you to do that on the programme,' said the producer, and though I thought it was an odd choice out of all the bits I could have done, I agreed to go along and record it.

Getting ready at the studio I was trying to make polite conversation with the producer. 'Do you have to make any payments to the writers of songs in situations like this?' I asked.

'Well, usually, yes,' he said. 'But obviously not in this case.'

I asked why not.

'Well, I'm assuming you wrote it yourself.'

'Er, no. It was Cole Porter.'

'Oh,' he said a little confused. 'I thought you wrote your own material.'

Sometimes somebody says something that is so astonishingly stupid that you feel dreadfully embarrassed in correcting them. I'm sure I've said some myself, but then I'm not head of entertainment in a production company making television programmes.

'I do write my own material,' I explained gingerly. 'But the original song was by Cole Porter.'

'Oh,' he said. 'Well, we'd better make the necessary arrangements. Is he someone you know?'

It Looked Like A Runner Bean

MOZART DEPENDED ON the patronage of the Austrian Emperor. Art galleries are full of paintings that painters painted because the royal courts told them to.

I was telling myself these things on the way to Leicester Square one night in 1987, when I was part of a package booked to entertain a club full of graphic designers and their clients from various advertising companies. The show would start after the main course but during dessert, and would take place in front of several hundred suits and Rolexes.

'Just grit your teeth and get through it,' I kept telling myself. 'I shouldn't have much trouble finding twenty minutes of material so innocuous even the most greasy-haired twenty-five-year old covered in gold cuff-links could tolerate.'

As I arrived, two seven-foot bouncers with black bow-ties glanced down a list of names on a clipboard in that way that sends your heart racing while you await the verdict of acceptance or rejection with the same anxiety as in the moments before the cashpoint tells you whether you can have money or not.

'Yeah, in yer go, mate,' one said eventually and I wandered through a door, found a table and sat down. Within seconds a queue of people had gathered around to give me things.

'Champagne, sir?' said the first, and poured a glass.

'Cold meats, sir?' said the second, and began delicately serving paper thin slices of the stuff from a silver tray on to a plate with the grace of the demonstrators who do things like that on *The Generation Game*.

'Salad, sir?' said the third. 'Pickles, sir?' said another.

The moment my champagne glass was one third empty it was refilled by a waiter with the eagerness of an aunty topping up your teacup.

Sitting there stuffing my face, I pondered how one clerical error spelling my name wrong on that bouncers' list would have resulted in a curt, 'Not on 'ere, mate,' and left me appealing with the hopelessness of someone rejected at the Pearly Gates. But the paperwork had obviously been done, so the queue continued.

'Smoked salmon, sir?'

'Chocolate mints, sir?'

'Some more napkins, sir?'

One of the difficulties the affluent have when it comes to food is that no matter how rich they are, they're prevented from eating quantities that relate to their true wealth by the awkward fact that the human body can only eat a certain amount. For instance Rupert Murdoch is perhaps one million times richer than a teacher, but whereas he can have houses, cars and jewellery that correspond to that statistic he can't possibly eat a million times more than Mr. Wilkins in the language lab.

So they try to compensate by laying on such ridiculously extravagant spreads that no matter how much people stuff their faces, indulge in food fights or drunkenly tip up entire tables festooned with cheese, there will be plenty left at the end of the night to throw away. And what sort of a host are you if you don't end the evening with whole trays covered in untouched salmon that are heading straight for the bin?

I teamed up with the other performers and tried to get in the right frame of mind for the show. Even without the Borgia-style decadence it would be a difficult gig to control. Life is always made more tricky when the performer is in the territory of the audience rather than the other way around. And especially difficult when everybody's drunk, seeing mates they want to talk to and planning to squash a chocolate mousse down the back of the girl at the table in front.

Those problems aside, I got ready and conditioned myself into thinking that lots of these people were perfectly all right, and that there was no reason why it shouldn't go well. But sometimes, no matter how diluted you become, it's never enough.

So five minutes in, I'm getting a general buzzing of drunken chatter, glasses being smashed, girls screaming as balloons are burst in their ear and trifles being lobbed out of windows. At this point a piece of food was launched, and landed next to my feet. 'There,' I said losing control, 'is the reason you people are considered the backbone of modern Britain. Because only you have the necessary talent to know that the correct use for a runner bean is to chuck it across the room.'

'It's not a runner bean,' the chucker shouted. 'It's a *mangetout.*'

Later I discovered the purpose of the whole event. It seems that the company staging this party was celebrating on account of having won a coveted contract to design a new crisp packet. All the beef, stilton and prawns being trodden into the carpet, all the subservience of the caterers and waiters, the surly bouncers, the lace invitations, a close-up magician and the out-of-place comedians. All the mountains of food, drink and decadence; all this was to celebrate the design of a packet of crisps. Not even the crisps themselves, just the fucking packet.

Of all the things that take place in society that might possibly be worth celebrating, the design of a crisp packet is quite possibly in the bottom half dozen along with drawing a game of noughts and crosses, stubbing your toe and sneezing.

But there it was. Another comedian and I decided to play Robin Hood and steal some wine and food in order to give it to people sleeping on the street. For half an hour we walked around Leicester Square trying to give away fifteen quid bottles of wine to the homeless, and none of them wanted it. Maybe they didn't trust us, maybe they thought we were being patronising or maybe it would just have spoilt the taste of their Special Brew.

So we went back home and drank it ourselves, assuring our consciences that Mozart would have done exactly the same.

Barbara Castle

PUBS BECAME WINE bars, clerks became yuppies, and dockyards became office units and luxury apartments. Complete strangers would delight in relating how, 'We bought it six months ago for sixty thou and last week the one next door, which is exactly the same, went for eighty-five.' 1987 was one of those years, perhaps *the* year in which naked greed ruled the earth. And, as a perfect symbol for the times, in the middle of the year Margaret Thatcher won her third election, an event which many saw in retrospect as inevitable.

But at the time of the Labour Party's Red Wedge banner-waving, morale-boosting comedy show in Bolton Town Hall, we didn't know it was going to end that way.

Eight hundred people crammed into the hall for the electioneering show. It is of course, quite possible that a number of other events in Bolton could attract a similar number of people: a rave, a football train to a Wanderer's away match, a local celebrity's funeral. But the eight hundred there that night weren't just out to see a gig, but to express a passion that was stirred by the possibility (for it was only slight) that Thatcher's reign could meet its end.

We now know that Thatcher herself considered this possibility and, as a result, cabled a variety of shady characters with requests for donations because she genuinely believed she could end up losing the election.

At the town hall, the first job of the day was to meet the candidates. Dressed in white shirts and black suits, they stood in a line like dignitaries at a banquet and limply shook our hands, affording each of us an 'Hello, nice to meet you' that sounded as convincing as the 'I'm being treated very well' of a captured pilot on Iraqi TV.

The candidates left and a dozen or so people remained (performers, promoters and the sort of people who are always around but you never find out why) in the dressing room. We all mooched about, ate the odd sandwich we didn't want and hung about in the way performers hang when there's still two hours before the show.

Then the door opened. And in walked a frail-looking woman helped along by someone who seemed extremely honoured to be doing so. The woman stopped, made a couple of slight gestures with her hand to indicate 'Enough, I can stand on my own now,' and adopted a pose like that of a Shakespearian actor about to deliver a soliloquy.

It was Barbara Castle, minister in the Labour governments of 1964-70 and 1974-79. A woman as prominent in those days as Michael Heseltine or Kenneth Clarke in the 1990s. And almost as disliked in her day as they are in theirs. And there she was.

How long you stare at a celebrity is almost certainly in proportion to how famous they are. Maybe this is because a piece of you can't believe it really is them. So if you saw a bloke you thought was on *Pebble Mill* yesterday, he'd warrant just a glance. John Thaw would merit a whole two seconds while you puzzled out what he was doing there. But if Boris Yeltsin wandered into the public bar (an example not altogether unlikely if he was in the area) everyone would stare for hours.

So I stared. Then I composed myself, and began to recall why it was so many people had disliked Barbara Castle at the peak of her high office. The betrayal many people felt when, as the most radical member of Harold Wilson's cabinet, she'd introduced an anti-union bill, the support she gave to the government on every issue from cuts in hospitals to supporting the Vietnam war.

And there she was. As Labour Party officials came and went they all afforded her the reverence usually reserved for the Queen Mother. She had quite clearly attained an untouchable status, being not only a great figure but a great old figure and she loved it. The slightest request (eg, 'Could you pass a teaspoon?') was met with fawning compliance that all but vocalised, 'Of course, your majesty.'

The merest statement about the weather or the traffic created a hush as if she were a kung fu master preaching wisdom to his pupils. On the other hand, some of the performers, technicians and people who nobody knew what they did, were not at all sure who she was.

'And where have you been today, Mrs Castle?' asked a local Labour member.

Mrs Castle took a breath before answering, in a way that only people who are used to being treated as she was could do. For only someone of her standing could be sure that no one would butt in, answer in her place, suddenly arrive with a round of drinks or interrupt her in any way.

'I've been speaking to groups of pensioners,' she said. 'I very much enjoy speaking to them, though one has to be extremely sensitive.'

Now it just so happened that in that very week a leaked letter from Neil Kinnock's press secretary intended for Labour Party campaign managers had found its way to the media. The letter had advised, 'We should not appear as if we support the rights of gays as this will lose us votes among the pensioners.'

This was my chance. I had to be polite but firm. 'When you say "sensitive", Mrs Castle, do you mean abandoning principles as "supporting the rights of gays might lose us votes"?'

'Well, look,' she replied. 'I've been in politics a long time and one learns to be... cautious.'

Now she was being infuriating. 'Cautious,' I said. 'Do you think it was being cautious to send in troops to break the Firemen's Strike?'

The room became even more silent than it had been before; and it had already been silent.

There are a great many arguments which take place not with any hope of one or other party convincing the other, but because both sides know there is an audience watching. And though the audience in this case was some officials with red rosettes, a couple of comedians, some technicians and someone nicking sandwiches, this was one of those occasions. Aware that to some of these people Mrs Castle was just a frail old lady, I knew I shouldn't overstep the mark.

What would she say? I'd introduced the subject of the Firemen's Strike and felt like a chess player who'd confounded his opponent by unexpectedly bringing his queen into the middle of the board.

'Firemen's strike?' she said in a quizzical Lady Bracknell-type voice.

'Yes, the Firemen's Strike. Would you say that was being cautious?'

'Which firemen's strike?'

This I wasn't expecting. 'The Firemen's Strike. The Firemen's Strike of 1977.'

'Which firemen's strike of 1977?'

'The Firemen's Strike, you know. The firemen's Firemen's Strike. Green Goddesses, toot if you support us. The *Firemen's Strike.*'

'I'm afraid I've no idea what you're talking about. I don't recall a firemen's strike.' And she carried on sipping her tea.

At this point, I concluded that either she was completely batty and had genuinely forgotten the whole thing, or I was completely batty and there really never had been a firemen's strike. Or maybe it was just her way of dealing with this type of question. Whichever of the three it was, there seemed little point in carrying on. If I persisted I would clearly look like nothing more than an arrogant upstart haranguing a sweet old woman.

The show that evening had a brilliant atmosphere which came from a feeling that whatever happened in the election there were many people who hadn't swallowed the 'get rich quick' mentality of the times. Later in the hotel several of the people who'd been in the room at the time of my aborted confrontation with an ex-minister came across to say how much they'd enjoyed the few prickly moments I'd given her.

'Why should everyone take notice of her just because of who she is?' they all demanded. 'But,' they agreed, 'we were so disappointed that you stopped just as it was getting interesting.'

And they clearly were disappointed. As a result I learned two things from the experience. Firstly, unless you're in a court, the boss' office or being kidnapped by a terrorist, it is definitely best to have a go and while remaining polite, say what you think, as even if people watching don't agree, you win their respect.

Secondly, if anyone asks me about the time I had a crap gig in say, Birmingham, I'll say 'Birmingham? Which crap gig in Birmingham? I've never been to Birmingham,' and carry on sipping my tea.

Spend, Spend, Spend

WHEN I WAS about eleven, I heard my dad say he had a hundred quid in the bank, and thought, 'Wow, if I ever have that much money, I'll never have to work and I'll live on an island, or maybe I'll buy every record in the world.' It was a sum I just couldn't comprehend. Now, if I receive a cheque for that amount, even after allowing for twenty years inflation, I just think, 'Oh, that'll pay for the boiler to be fixed.'

In a similar way, politicians play a trick on the public by mentioning large sums of money. So a government may boast that it's spent five hundred million quid looking after us all, and we're impressed because we forget that when you're talking about such huge sums it's an entirely different language and that five hundred million spread over the whole country is just a curry each.

Alternatively, they try to frighten us with tales of how the 'party opposite' wasted ten thousand pounds on decorating dole offices and people go up the wall thinking, 'Ten grand! I could have bought a BMW if they'd given it to me.' Yet to a local authority, this is loose change.

But because it's hard to differentiate between the money these people talk about in massive sums and the twenty quid we get out of the cashpoint, it's completely numbing to watch at first hand huge companies proudly blowing tens of thousands of pounds, with no one in the slightest bit bothered.

Nowhere can such extravagance have been more in evidence than in the TV world I was a small part of in the late 1980s. In response to Rupert Murdoch's multi-million pound venture into satellite telly, a company called BSB set up their own network, which to watch, you needed an object called a 'squariel' on your roof.

I was asked to write and perform for some of the programmes, and found myself among teams of producers, cameramen, sound technicians, directors, people with headphones, people with mobile phones at a time when they still attracted astonished onlookers, and people looking anxious whilst holding a clipboard. About once a week, whole crews of us went out to film something, doing as decent a job as we could, but always thinking, 'There's not one person I know of who's got one of these bloody squariels.'

Now and then I might be in an office or studio and hear somebody say something along the lines of how the plan was to go into profit in three or four years, so it didn't matter if they were losing tens of thousands of pounds a week. And I would think, 'Tens of thousands of pounds a week! If I ever have that much money I'd just give up work and live on an island, or maybe buy every record in the world.'

At first the programmes I worked on were not for transmission but for dummy runs to see how the network would come together. Then the launch date was put back, and then the programmes did go out, but because of a problem with something or other, the squariels weren't in the shops. So for several months, enormous amounts of effort went into writing, performing, filming and producing things that no one in the world would ever see.

Eventually the squariels became available but it didn't make any difference because no one bought any. Then I would occasionally ask if there were any viewing figures for the shows we were doing and the answer would always be 'a million'. I've never quite worked out how to deal with people who tell you something which is clearly daft. For instance if I'm in a pub and someone informs me that their brother invented peanuts, I usually just say, 'Oh, really?' for an easy life. But a bit of me wants to shout: 'No he bloody didn't, you lying bastard.'

And when this figure of 'a million' was chucked around

by people responsible for hundreds of thousands of pounds worth of equipment, labour and satellites I wanted to say, 'How can it bloody well be a million? That's one in fifty-six of the population including babies, prisoners, blind people and the criminally insane, none of whom watch telly; and yet I don't know a single person who's even considering buying a share in a squariel, even if they win the bloody pools. Not once have I heard anyone at all make any comment whatsoever about absolutely anything with regard to a programme on BSB, so how can there possibly be a million people watching?'

But instead I said, 'Oh, really?'

Yet on and on they went, pouring seemingly endless resources into a project that everybody from producer to cameraman to actor to security guard knew was failing miserably. Everybody in fact except for the people whose job it was to know, and therefore were in charge of this vast pool of dosh.

A sense of professional pride meant that all those who were working for the network tried to perform to the best of their ability, although subconsciously we probably didn't manage it, as it's hard to force yourself to agonise over the right phrasing of every sketch of a programme no one will ever know exists.

And so, like office workers who resignedly get on with a new filing system worked out by management they all know is twice as cumbersome as the old one, everyone continued with their business. Though we all knew that sooner or later it would come to the attention of whoever was responsible that spending millions of pounds on a TV network with viewing figures of nought was not a viable business proposition.

At that time even Murdoch's Sky was losing vast sums, despite the enormous publicity his venture had created, his ability to give endless plugs in his own newspapers, his teams of salesmen parading through the housing estates of Britain and his plans to buy up every major sporting event in the country.

In many ways I shouldn't complain, as it kept a number of us in employment for quite a while and we learned a fair bit about working with cameras and it was always enjoyable. But throughout I just couldn't help wondering how anyone could chuck so much money away and not seem to care. For most people, if they lost twenty quid, their whole day would be in ruins. The directors of BSB were losing that every minute and didn't even have the decency to go around looking miserable.

It was the only time I've ever seen the other, extravagant side of television. Most of the time TV, like schools and hospitals, is beset with accountants tutting and grumbling that the budget won't allow for development money, two people doing two people's work or sandwiches in the afternoon. But sometimes the opposite devil takes over and waste is glorified with the decadence of a Roman banquet.

One day I was asked to write and recite a two minute journalistic piece on an issue of the day for a BSB show. The poll tax was a major story at the time, so I wrote something on the Labour Party's response to the campaign against it.

I turned up at Regents Park to film the piece and was met by the crew, who proudly informed me that they'd brought with them dozens and dozens of boxes, each containing about thirty fresh red roses which they'd bought from a shop in Camden.

'What are they for?' I asked.

'Well, as your bit's on the Labour Party, we thought they might come in handy,' they said. So I stood gazing into the back of a van at about a thousand pounds worth of red roses, all of which had arrived there because 'they might come in handy'.

When those poor sods come round pubs on a Saturday

night embarrassing women by trying to get the bloke opposite (who's probably a cousin or a neighbour), to buy a single rose, wouldn't it be brilliant if you could make their day by saying, 'I tell you what mate, I'll take a thousand. Well, they might come in handy.'

But on this particular afternoon they didn't come in at all handy. Someone thought it might look all right if the roses were falling behind me as I spoke. So the junior member of the crew climbed up a tree while being handed box upon box of the bloody things. Then he dropped them around me while I was trying to do this piece, and of course as it was a close-up shot the stems whizzing past my cheek just looked like interference. Except for the odd one that landed on me.

'I know,' said somebody, 'we'll try it with just the flowers.' So for ten minutes or so we all sat round snapping the flowers off the stems; all except the lad up the tree, who was stuck. So to get the flowers back up to him, we had to throw them as he leaned off a branch trying to catch them in one of the boxes he'd taken with him, so that for all the world the scene looked like a game from *It's a Knockout*, and I honestly expected Eddie Waring to pop out from behind the tree and tell us that the Belgians were going to play their joker.

In the end it was filmed the only way it could have been, with no roses at all. In terms of TV money, the expense of that episode was not very great. When BSB went bust shortly afterwards and was bought up by Murdoch for a song, it was probably not the deciding factor. But to think like that only makes sense if you think of money in corporate terms. In human terms it could have paid for a holiday for a family that couldn't afford one, or bought a car for someone stuck indoors without one, or even a bloody great piss-up for people who'd already had one the night before.

I doubt if there is anyone, anywhere in the world, who ever thinks, 'If only I had a thousand pounds. I'd buy a van load of roses, snap the flowers off and chuck them up a tree.'

Dual Power in Edinburgh

BY THE LATE 1980s the Edinburgh Fringe Festival was becoming a serious business, with grandiose marketing strategies, executive decisions, poster wars and the Perrier Award beginning to dominate. But the event's spontaneous tradition was hard to defeat, and for a while the corporate media circus ran the festival in a sort of power-sharing deal with the carefree anarchy of old.

Agents and directors of production companies with filofaxes would sit frowning through shows, occasionally consulting each other to ask, 'Could we use this?' But then the show might be disrupted by a double act who'd just finished their performance next door running on to the stage. Venues would draw up detailed clauses in the contract concerning the correct procedure for the allocation of complimentary tickets, but if fifteen mates turned up having hitched from Leicester with no money, it would be easy to find an usher who would slip them through a back door.

The two ideals, which could loosely be summarised as 'fun versus profit' existed side by side in an uneasy coalition for some time. But like any case of dual power, eventually one would win at the expense of the other.

Leading the charge for military efficiency and ruthless elimination of any outbreak of non-money-making enjoyment was the venue known as the Assembly Rooms. Run by a junior member of a famous banking family, it created a prestige value around the complex, which ensured that no matter how unpleasant the place was to perform in, there would always be a queue of agents and promoters eager to get their prodigy into the Assembly Rooms brochure.

And unpleasant it certainly was. In 1988, after much

negotiation and dealing worthy of a city takeover bid, my agent secured me a three week run for the Edinburgh Suite, one of the five theatres that make up the Assembly building. From the opening moment of the soundcheck on the afternoon before the first show, the rules were laid out. 'If you like we could give you a bit of blue,' said the lad operating the lights as he waved the thin blue plastic which would make that possible, 'but that will cost you extra.'

I took a mic-stand from the dressing room and placed it by the piano. 'Oh, we charge extra for mic-stand hire,' I was informed. As time went on, I realised that the performer gets charged for such things as the fee paid to Access and Barclaycard for allowing people to pay by credit card. Each performer was allowed six complimentary tickets for their own show, for the whole of the three week run. Only the staff, who were students paid ridiculously low wages, were allowed to see the shows free. For complementary ticket the performer was charged sixty per cent of the ticket price, as this was the percentage that went to the management from paid-for tickets.

The audience was ushered in at the last possible moment and herded out the moment the show ended, so as to allow the greatest possible number of performances per day. And in each of the theatres the noise from the other shows blared through so loudly that quite often the audience thought it a surreal soundtrack to the one they were watching.

Every night in the Edinburgh Suite, about ten minutes into the show an African drumming band would start playing upstairs and bash out such a distinct beat that it was hard not to start doing my act in rhythm with them. Every night I would try and find a novel way of making a joke out of the whole business, for instance by banging on the ceiling with the mic-stand and pretending to be a neighbour wanting to get some sleep.

Even without the other shows, the sound travels so freely

that if you're watching a play there it's quite likely that you'll hear a couple of blokes from the brewery rolling a barrel outside and shouting 'Got it up your end, Stan?' just as the main character drops dead.

At the Edinburgh Suite the audience has to walk around the stage to get to the seats, so anyone arriving after the show has started (and the shows have to start exactly on time) was faced with the prospect of clambering past the performer. I could hardly ignore the fact that halfway through a story three people had marched past me at a distance of nine inches, so the first twenty minutes of every show was an enforced chat with late-comers that made me feel like a game show host.

To one side of the theatre was a fire exit door, which rattled so loudly that in the odd gap between audience members crossing the stage and the pounding of giant bongos, the metal bars of the door clattered as if the SAS were trying to storm in. I mentioned this repeatedly to the management but nothing was done to repair it. On the last night the door did indeed fly open, revealing two tramps on the street who then wandered inside and probably still spend many hours puzzling out how they got so tanked up that they imagined they ended up in front of eighty people as part of a comedy show.

The only way I felt I could respond to the perpetual mean treatment of performers, audience and staff alike, was to refer to it in the show. So by the time the run was half way through, I had a fine rant worked out, which invariably won the approval of the audience. I started reading out the more elaborate penny pinching elements of the contract, and said I felt like a peasant who'd received a demand from the landlord for a payment of tithes, and that I was expecting that soon I'd be asked to help lay a road to the lord's house, and spend Sundays looking after his chickens.

So then I started getting whispered messages from the

staff. 'Just a word of advice: I wouldn't carry on saying those things, the boss doesn't like it.'

On the last Sunday of the Festival, the Edinburgh Playhouse staged a fund-raising event which sold three thousand tickets, and I was invited to do a ten minute slot, so I used it to deliver my piece about the Assembly Rooms. Again it seemed to meet with complete approval, except that one of the other performers was a personal friend of the Assembly Rooms' lord and master and was watching from the wings. Suddenly he ran on stage, pounced full length in my direction and rugby tackled me so that the pair of us tussled our way across the floor, the microphone shooting out of the stand and crashing on to the ground, before he eventually Sumo-wrestled me into the wings on the opposite side.

I've since spoken to people who were there that night, and asked them what they thought was happening. 'Was it part of the act?' most have suggested. Well, no, it was as it seemed. The friend was outraged that someone should publicly say what was clearly obvious about this living symbol of meanness. And the result was that at last the man who made a fortune and a reputation out of comedy was finally responsible for something funny happening.

Walking Out

ONE YEAR IN Edinburgh, there was a story in *The Observer* about a fringe play a critic had been sent to review. 'The lights went down,' it began, 'and three men walked on to the stage, stark naked. For some time they walked round and round in circles until eventually one of them stood still, his back to the audience and defecated.'

'At this point,' it continued, 'twelve of the audience walked out.'

What interests me here, I thought as I read this piece, is the people who stayed. Did they sit there and whisper to the person next to them: 'We'll give it another five minutes'?

The Joy of Giving

THERE IS A GENERAL rule that the less money someone is paid for a performance, the worse they are treated when they arrive to do it. At the best paid shows I've done, when I would have been quite happy to buy rounds of drinks for the organisers and find a local restaurant for a meal, there is someone who seems to be on duty to go to the bar, buy drinks and food and periodically come into the dressing room to ask if I need anything.

It's easy to see how prima donnas can be created in this atmosphere. It's tempting to say something like, 'I wouldn't mind a box of Lego,' just to see if they'd set off to find one.

At the other end of the scale is the 'benefit', a show for which you're paid absolutely nothing. And here you may well be asked to set up the speakers, rewire the broken microphone, make out a standing order to whoever the gig is for, and afterwards help stack the chairs and give the care-taker a lift back to Bethnal Green.

Benefits seem to come in three categories. At the bottom end comes the disorganised shambles, as I learned back in the days of the Miners' Strike. These are usually put on by someone in a trade union branch or campaigning group who is a personal fan but who doesn't realise that no one else in his organisation has heard of you. So five minutes before the gig's due to start, everyone apart from him is standing next to the pasta salad and chicken legs, discussing what slogan to shout at tomorrow's demonstration.

The fan will then walk across to this gathering and urge them to come and watch. But it's the same predicament as the person who wants everyone to watch a video when a crowd has come back with a few beers after the pub. No matter how brilliant the film, or how urgent the cries of: 'No, there's a really good bit in a minute,' if people aren't in the mood to watch, then there's no reason why they should.

So in these situations, there's usually a brief crisis. 'Look,' I usually say to the frantic organiser, 'everyone's got loads to talk about and I'm just going to get in the way, so wouldn't it be better just not to do it?'

But in the face of all the evidence they insist with a passion that once I start it will all be fine. It's a touching sentiment but comedy is one form of entertainment that simply doesn't work if no one wants to listen. Music can float along in the background; a painting doesn't fall off the wall if no one's looking at it; but a comedian rattling through his act while everyone else carries on their business, is a distressing thing to be.

Usually though it's less of a hassle to do the show than to let down the fan, so it goes ahead. While the fan does his introduction, someone will quite possibly come up to say, 'I haven't seen you at any of our meetings before, which branch of UNISON are you in?'

'I'm here to do the gig,' I explain as I walk to the front. Within the first minute a row will break out between someone trying to count the money they've made from selling badges, and the fan who is going 'shhh' to everyone in the whole room, one by one.

Someone responds to something I say by yelling, 'What, do you mean like Teddy Boswitch?' and everybody laughs except me, because I'm the only one who doesn't have a clue who Teddy Boswitch is.

Two or three tables are now telling the fan he's got no right in a democratic organisation to tell them to shut up, and I have a dreadful vision that as a result of the gig, the entire group will split into four hostile factions and cause a split in the Labour movement that keeps the Tories in power for the next seventy years.

'Maybe we should break the whole thing into workshops,' I say, before wishing them well and finishing before any more damage is done.

Another type of benefit at the bottom of the scale is the fund-losing event. A dedicated but clueless follower of a cause decides to put on a show, and as an impresario is excellent. They book the acts, get a special set made for the stage, have an intricate poster with fourteen colours designed and printed, hire a saxophonist to play as people are coming in, and get professional caterers to make a huge trifle in the shape of a dove, reflecting the logo of the campaign.

As a result, even if every ticket is sold, the evening will run up a loss of three hundred quid. Unfortunately though, no one can read the expert calligraphy in tiny print on the posters, so nine people turn up and the campaign is forced to file for bankruptcy.

At the other end of the scale are the huge events headlined by celebrity names that receive plenty of media publicity and are sold out weeks before they happen. The problem with these shows though, is that they can't help but take on a momentum of their own. So whatever it is that the show is raising money for becomes lost in the glitz of showbiz.

It's not just a cynical view to suggest that the first thoughts of the performer on these occasions are of how the show will benefit themselves. It's an inevitability of something sold on the names and the grandiose nature of the event rather than on the issue.

So just as the Live Aid Concert became a battleground for managers arguing about who went on during peak viewing times in America, and release dates of albums were shifted to coincide with the worldwide publicity, a West End show for an AIDS charity or for Amnesty International can't help but make the performers think about how it might affect their careers.

Agents, TV researchers, reviewers and an array of media types attend these events, for there they can see a dozen or more leading acts at a time. I've been asked to do a variety of shows, including some on radio and television as a result of being seen at one of these functions. On nights like this I've gone home extremely pleased with myself, knowing in all honesty that going down well in such settings has done me no harm, and whatever we were raising money for has come a poor second in my thoughts. So the problem is not the cynicism of the acts but the momentum of an event hurtling itself out of the realms of fund-raising and into showbiz's grubby pocket.

Somewhere in the middle of these two levels of benefit, it is possible for there to be an occasion which is both down to earth and successful. One of the most noticeable aspects of hitting the right balance is that although the venue, the publicity and the bill are important the most crucial point of all is the issue. Cynics often claim that most people who attend concerts or carnivals linked to a campaign do so just to see the acts. But my experience is that a Saturday night benefit with well-known people in a central theatre can easily end up half empty if the campaign is for something which hasn't connected with public emotion.

If the issue is right however, the atmosphere is at a higher level than for any other type of show. Because the event is sold on the issue rather than the names, there is a sense of unity in a common cause which must sound corny to anyone who's not experienced it. The famous people involved are looked on in a different light than in a glitzy 'Night of the Stars' do, because it's obvious that they're taking part because of a genuine commitment to the campaign.

So the luvvies, journalists and media types tend to stay away. For if two thousand tickets have been sold on the basis of the money going to, for example the Anti-Nazi League, even though there may be well-known people on the bill, it would hardly be appropriate to swan up to them in the foyer and tell them that we simply must do a photo shoot for our magazine, darling.

It would be easy to dismiss the positive sides to a successful benefit, but apart from the obvious gain of the funds raised, there is the overcoming of the biggest enemy of any campaign: the feeling people have of being on their own. To be part of a large crowd, passionately supporting an issue that they previously thought no one else was bothered about, is in many ways more valuable to people than the money raised.

For example, during the winter of 1989, Jeremy Hardy, Kit Hollerbach and myself were offered a night at the Hackney Empire to raise money for whatever cause we wanted. The obvious choice was the ambulance dispute, but the others wanted to pick the campaign to free the Birmingham Six.

In the event, against my vote, the Birmingham Six campaign was chosen, and the result was one of the most memorable atmospheres I can ever recall at a comedy show. The thousand tickets were all sold and a speech by a daughter of one of the imprisoned men was extraordinarily moving. By the end of the evening there was a tremendous sense of purpose among the whole audience for an issue which was only just beginning to capture people's imaginations.

Maybe it's pompous and self-congratulatory, but most performers would probably say that the best of these events are the most enjoyable shows they've ever done, for however much like the vicar it sounds, there's no better feeling than that of doing something for somebody else's benefit.

Paris in Revolt

KENNETH CLARKE'S NAME is periodically mentioned as a potential leader of the Conservative Party, and as the most competent of the post-Thatcher Tory ministers. Whenever that happens, I remind myself what happened at the Paris Studios.

For many years the studio was the setting for almost every radio light entertainment recording made in London. *The Goons* was recorded there, and *Round the Horne*, and *The Clitheroe Kid*. Its heyday was during the peak of radio's popularity, from about 1950 until the domination of television.

It was still an extremely popular venue for radio recordings up until being sold off in 1995, but strangely the building and the atmosphere within it remained as 1955 as ever, so that you'd come out after a show and expect everything to be in black and white, and Anthony Eden to ride past wearing a bowler hat.

Security guards dressed in immaculate uniforms, peaked caps and a medal or two would greet you with a wonderfully clipped, 'Morning, sir,' that made you think they were going to follow it up with: 'Ah tell you what, sir, it's mighty nippy aht tonight right enough, ah shall be looking forward to getting home and having a fresh bowl of the wife's delicious hot soup.' As you descended towards the studio itself, you passed a series of black and white photos of Tommy Handley, Kenneth Horne, Kenneth Williams and Peter Sellers, all pictured performing on the stage ahead of you.

The recording itself would be as charmingly simplistic as a television recording is tediously complicated. Sound effects were (and still are) mostly made by the improvisation of specialists who had spent years perfecting the art of recreating every possible noise that might ever be needed in a sketch. There is a metal cup of beans, that when turned forwards and backwards makes a sound exactly like that of a marching army. The noise of a telephone would be made by rattling a huge old black thing that future generations will hold delicately on *Antiques Roadshow*, saying, 'Was it an Edwardian device for killing rats?'

One night I was in a sketch which included the sound of splashing water. So Colin the soundman filled a bowl with water, and at the appropriate moment took off his shoes and socks and paddled in the bowl, holding a microphone near his feet as he did so. Consequently this got the biggest cheer of the show, to the bemusement of anybody listening when it went out.

A two-foot-high cracked and decaying wooden door sat on a table to be opened and closed whenever the script demanded, and was almost certainly the same door 'opened' by Spike Milligan, Tony Hancock and Sid James.

During the recording, each performer read off the script, and at the end of each page had to carefully turn away from the enormous old microphone so as not to create an audible rustle. In front of the performers was an art deco wooden stand with an oval green light at the top, which came on at certain points as a cue to start speaking. Because of all this, there was a regular audience which loved going to the Paris Studios, regardless of what was on, which suited the general atmosphere.

Many of them were sixty and over, and would arrive wearing two overcoats and thick scarves, which they would keep on throughout the recording, probably because the time it would take to unravel would be longer than the show. Although certain programmes would attract their own following, these people made up a good section of the audience, loving the gentle puns of the panel games and not understanding why in modern comedy everyone seemed to say words like 'bollocks.' On one occasion, the producer had to stop a recording half way through because the sound of snoring was drifting through on to the tape.

One night in 1990, amid the quaint and marvellously English charm of this building, an argument had to be settled. Four of us had been writing a programme to be recorded there, and at one point we had to have a discussion about how to end it. One of us came up with the idea of finishing with, 'Next week we'll be asking the question: Kenneth Clarke, is he a man or a bag of shit?'

Clearly this was not intellectual satire. But it was four months into the ambulance dispute, and Kenneth Clarke was the then Minister for Health. So popular was the dispute that everyone who was used to supporting campaigns had a story along the lines of: 'My old aunty who's always voted Conservative has been collecting money for the ambulance drivers at her Methodist church.'

On the other hand, to call anyone a bag of shit in the setting of the Paris Studios was liable to cause uproar. After an unhealthily lengthy argument we were split two-two on whether to include the line, but somehow it made its way into the script.

On the night of the recording, there were only about fifty people in the audience, and the thick scarf fraternity were a fairly high proportion. The show was about to finish, up went the performer: 'Next week we'll be asking the question – Kenneth Clarke...'

The two of us who had stuck out for the line looked at each other in a moment of tension, '...is he a man or a bag of shit?'

'Hooah,' coughed all the older people who up until then had been unable to make sense of anything we'd been doing, and began clapping with an enthusiasm that they hadn't seemed capable of, as they clasped their plastic bags of shopping tightly to their laps.

It was the best response we'd had all evening, and in the lace tablecloth and cream tea atmosphere of the Paris Studios, it had a touching and genteel quality. Had Kenneth Clarke been there in person and we'd called him a bag of shit to his face, the oldest of the women with the thickest of scarves might have turned to her friend and said, 'That's rude, dear. They should say: "You're a bag of shit, *sir*."'

Sandwich of the Month

IT SEEMS TO me that there are two types of occasions on which surreal Monty Python type things can happen and seem perfectly normal. The first is when you're drunk, and the oddest thing can seem quite natural. Until the next morning when you think, 'How did we end up in the bowling alley with that horse?'

The other is when you're half asleep. For example, I was on the 6.00am train from Hull and, still half asleep, I strolled to the buffet. As I handed over the money for my tea, I noticed a large sign: '*We will be pleased to serve you Sandwich of the Month.*' And underneath, '*Please ask the steward for details.*'

Groggily slurping the tea and checking I hadn't misread the sign I asked the steward, 'What's sandwich of the month, then? Only it says there I'm supposed to ask you for details.'

'It's corned beef, sir,' he replied.

'How did it win that, then?' I croaked. 'And was cheese and tomato really upset? Was there an awards ceremony?' I was making myself laugh, though not the steward. 'Did the corned beef make a speech and say "I'd like to accept this award not just for myself but for the margarine and the pickle"?'

Now I don't expect public service employees to be so subservient as to laugh at every tinpot joke made by a member of the public, even though we've since been promoted to customers. But I was reckoning on a: 'I know, it is a bit daft.' Or even: 'If you don't bloody want one, don't have one, mate.'

But instead came: 'I'm afraid we haven't got any at the moment.'

This surrealism actually made sense, but only because I was half asleep, so I decided to play my part: 'Haven't got one? But it's Sandwich of the Month!'

'We've got tuna and cucumber, sir,' he said. 'Or bacon, lettuce and tomato.'

'Where did tuna and cucumber come this month?' I asked.

'I don't know, sir,' he replied with the professionalism of a nineteenth century butler. So I gave up, though I really should have have stamped my foot and said, 'Don't take it seriously, for Christ's sake. Don't you see? You can't have sandwich of the month, it's mental.'

I don't hold it against this steward for failing to see the absurdity in awarding an honour to an over-priced slice of bread with tinned meat. Especially as he probably earns just enough on a trip to Hull and back to buy a handful of the wretched bacon and tomato rolls on the shelf behind him. But there do seem to be a growing number of jobs that entail learning a standard politeness which can only be described as rudeness.

Staff are made to repeat phrases like: 'Good morning, sir. Howard speaking, how can we help you with one of our delicious pizzas?' As if we then think 'What a pleasant chap. He wants to help me with a delicious pizza.' And you know they don't mean it because they only learn the first line. If you say, 'Uh, I'm not quite sure yet', they go: 'Well, hurry up and make yer bloody mind up.'

Maybe the managers that dream up these soundbites are following the rules of the class they belong to, which doesn't make anyone appear warm and friendly because they're warm and friendly, but because they've learned the correct place to say their: 'pleases', 'thank yous' and the odd 'my word, you look ravishing'.

So the staff they employ are expected to drain themselves of all humanity and reply to enquiries with robotic answers.

Like the air stewardess who smiles at the end of each flight, going, 'Thank you for flying with us. We hope you enjoy your stay. Thank you for flying with us. We hope you enjoy your stay. Thank you for flying with us. We hope you enjoy your stay.'

Wouldn't it be so much more genuinely friendly and personal if they said something human – like, 'Bet you crapped yourself in the turbulence.'

And the Award for Best Rebel...

IT WAS THE last night of a three week run at the 1990 Edinburgh Festival, and there was a bit of a 'We're going home tomorrow, so let's muck about' atmosphere, as if the audience were not obliged to listen to the show and were allowed to bring in games instead.

About ten minutes after the start, the door at the back opened and a burly middle-aged man with a huge Victorian grey beard marched confidently between the chairs and tables to the one seat available, right at the front. He took out a note-pad and pen from his jacket, every action containing a defiant flamboyance. He was the complete opposite of the typical British late-comer at a public event, who tiptoes one step at a time to the back of the room, grimacing at every squeak of their shoes, to sit on a broken table rather than risk further embarrassment by walking past people to a chair.

Later on, when he had made copious notes and was still the centre of attention for a good deal of the room I swiped his note-pad and tried to read out what he'd written. But like all good note-takers his scribblings made no sense to anyone but himself. So I initiated a game with the audience in which we all tried to decipher what they meant. The man sat still, undaunted and without flinching, with the air of a captured British general showing no sign of weakness to his captor.

The next morning I was told that I'd won the *Scotland on Sunday* Festival Award, and was supposed to go to a hotel to receive the thing. I arrived just in time for the ceremony to begin. A few journalists, executives from *Scotland on Sunday*, and award winners from other categories were in the room, and a formal introduction was made to, 'Your host for this afternoon's proceedings, Owen Dudley-Edwards.' And in classic sitcom style, up stepped the man with the grey beard.

It seemed he was a theatre critic with a number of Scottish and Irish newspapers, including *Scotland on Sunday*. He began his speech, and spoke with a musical middle class Irish accent in which every word was pronounced with great precision as if he was reading a poem, but with a delicacy that I felt could easily be abandoned at any moment in exchange for a fearful roar of booming wrath.

In his speech he described in great detail how the previous evening he'd arrived late at a comedy show, having rushed from a play, and sat in the seat he'd previously reserved. Then, he recounted with a sterner tone how he'd had his notebook snatched and read out while the audience puzzled over the meaning.

Was he aware, I wondered, that I, the notebook-snatcher was going to be receiving an award. If so, would he conclude his speech with a condemnation of the decision that gave the award to someone so lacking in Victorian ethics that they had the affront to behave in such a disrespectful manner to their elders?

I felt the quivering sensation I remembered from a school assembly when the headmaster had bellowed, 'And some of you know which boy is responsible for this dreadful act,' and it was me.

At this point, he leaned forward to make his crucial point, paused to create a hush of expectation and with the same defiance with which he'd strode through the audience the previous evening, said in the roar I'd been half expecting: 'And it is this instinct of rebellion and challenge to authority which makes the Edinburgh Festival the magnificent spectacle we've come to love.'

At the lunch following the presentations, I sat next to

Owen Dudley-Edwards, and began to realise that he spoke in this wistful manner the whole time. At one point in the conversation I mentioned the Castle in passing, and he gently put out his hand to stop me and said in his most poetic Irish voice: 'Ah, the Castle. Built to prevent an invasion of the English; and now the only reason the buggers come here.'

While the rest of the table indulged in the familiar Edinburgh-speak about the shows they'd seen, with the polite formality that's forced upon people compelled to have lunch with a group of people they've never met before, Owen Dudley-Edwards employed his robust and poetic language to vent fury about the poll tax, Scotland's domination by England, a dreadful mime show he'd seen and Margaret Thatcher.

What was marvellous about this man was that although he was an academic, a respected journalist and a man of the theatre, for him rebellion was a virtue and a necessity. There are plenty of liberal-minded people from such backgrounds who are genuinely outraged by the world's injustices, but who still see confronting authority as: 'a last resort', or a situation, 'we clearly want to avoid at all costs'.

He, on the other hand, revelled in it. In the 1960s he'd lived in America and undergone training in the art of non-violent action. He'd then participated in many marches and protests of the civil rights era and the movement against the Vietnam War. Far from dismissing these actions as youthful exuberance, he was clearly proud of his past, and this combination of respectability and rebellion made him fascinating company. For instance, he castigated me for being an atheist, and then implored me to look up two priests he knew who had been arrested for throwing paint over a South African minister.

Gradually his passion, his language and his presence began to dominate the room and more and more people

147

became sucked into the conversation we were having. Stage by stage, the tittle-tattle of who'd got what review was subsiding, and replaced with fiery statements from differing viewpoints on whether Scotland should be independent and how to defeat the poll tax.

After a while, an American – who it turned out was on the editorial board of the exceedingly uncontroversial *Scotland on Sunday* – decided to say something. He began to tell a story completely unconnected to anything that had gone before:

'As a young man on a local newspaper in New York, I once saved up for several months so that I could take my girlfriend to a particularly pricey restaurant in Manhattan on her birthday. Well, the day arrived and we went along, took our seats and she was just thrilled. Then half way through the starter I noticed that two tables along was Henry Kissinger.

'So my girlfriend starts to ask, "What are you looking at?"

'"I can't believe it," I tell her. "Right there is Henry Kissinger."

'So I keep looking over and my girlfriend starts to get a little agitated and telling me to stop and not to let it ruin the evening, but I just couldn't get it out of my mind that just a few yards away was the man responsible for countless deaths in Vietnam and Cambodia.

'So she keeps saying that I shouldn't allow it to ruin the evening and that tonight was her birthday, and I'm getting more worked up you know. Like this guy dropped napalm! But she insists that I drop the subject and I agree. But a couple of minutes later, without thinking I find myself walking over to his table and saying "Mr Kissinger, I want you to know that as far as I'm concerned you are a murderer and an insult to humanity, and I can't allow you to sit here without telling you... " and then these big guys appear from nowhere, pick me up and dump me straight outside on the sidewalk.'

During the course of the story he had become more and more animated, as if he was reliving the emotions of that night so that by the end he was actually sweating. It seemed as if he hadn't told this to anyone for a long time, maybe because although he was proud of his actions (which at the very least sound as if they cost him his girlfriend), this would not be the sort of image which he felt would endear him to his executive colleagues.

There was a brief pause after he finished, at which point Owen Dudley-Edwards got out of his seat, hugged the American, banged his considerable fist on to the table causing twenty plates of salad to be lifted off it and bellowed with the purpose of a general leading his troops into battle: 'I tell you, as long as there are men prepared to act as this man did that day, my God we have a world in which to live.'

Later on, Owen and I spent a couple of hours wandering around Edinburgh, debating various matters, and occasionally he'd break off to make a whimsical comment on the origins of the Scott Monument or the nature of cats. But as we parted, he said, 'We re-awakened the rebel in that man today, Mark, and of that we should be proud.'

He was wrong, because he had done it by himself.

It would be hard to imagine, looking at the American, that inside him lurked a pocket of rebellion, but it did. There must be huge numbers of people, who, however subservient and 'straight' they seem on the surface, have a rebellious side tucked away somewhere. Age, circumstance or despair can dilute it or bury it, but rarely does it go away completely.

If you're in any doubt about whether someone's lost theirs, try snatching their note-pad. If they punch you in the face, you've probably found a dud.

The Joke That Brought Down Thatcher

ONE OF THE shows I'd done for BSB was a live music and comedy night called *The Happening*. They were recorded at a rock venue called The Astoria in London's Charing Cross Road. As the show started at around six o'clock, this thousand seat theatre was packed, mostly with white-collar workers. Normally in the moments before going on stage, my mind is frantically concentrated on running through the order of whatever it is I'm going to be talking about, especially when there are cameras, directors and blokes running around with headphones making the whole business seem important.

But on this particular night I was pondering two views of history. One is that history progresses gradually and smoothly, with technology and reforms improving our lives bit by bit. The other is that while society seems to remain much the same for long periods, underneath the surface, changes in attitudes, social movements and the material interests of massive numbers of people come to a head to produce apparently sudden eruptions.

These thoughts were a result of watching the brilliantly anarchistic comedian Mark Thomas, who had just come off stage. Earlier, when he'd arrived he'd told me with great enthusiasm what his opening line for the show would be. He'd done this on previous occasions when we'd been on the same bill, often exclaiming with delight a new joke which managed to incorporate multinationals forcing peasants to grow cash crops, a desire to drown a right-wing Tory MP and anal sex, and yet still manage to be funny. Usually I would suggest that although it was a fine joke, tactically it might be better to get established with the audience first, and then hit them with the Ethiopian coffee/Teresa Gorman/buggery routine.

The date of the recording was April 2nd, 1990, two days after the Trafalgar Square poll tax riot, and his favoured opening line was: 'What's all this fuss about the Poll Tax Riot? We pay the police's wages; we're entitled to knock 'em about a bit.'

I suggested that it was probably best to get established first, etc, etc. There was no guarantee that the audience would be at all sympathetic to the anti-poll tax movement, (and certainly no guarantee that they would approve of advocating the random 'kicking about a bit' of the old bill), and I was simply following a rule that once you've got people on your side with stuff that's less controversial, you're in a much better position to launch into the bits they won't approve of. Surely this is not surrendering to the forces of reaction any more than being careful not to say 'fuck' within the first minute of meeting a new girlfriend's mother.

After this discussion, I'd got involved in a debate with a cameraman about the meaning of the riot which had taken place forty-eight hours earlier in the streets outside the theatre. The mood told me, I put it to him, that the event signalled the end of Thatcher and the death of Thatcherism. For the poll tax was not just an issue on its own, but a focal point for all the rage against the Thatcher years, mobilising crusties and women's institutes alike.

What's more, most people were blaming the government and the police for the riot, which had to be a sign of a general distrust of Thatcherite ideals. The poll tax riot was a sharp break in history; Britain was a different place to the country of just three days before.

The poll tax, he replied, was an issue on its own which would soon die away. Only a minority cared about the issue, and Thatcherite values were as strong as ever.

We stopped our argument as the producer finished his introduction to the audience and the recording began. A few moments later Mark Thomas walked on to the stage and without as much as a 'good evening' said, 'What's all this fuss about the Poll Tax Riot? We pay the police's wages, we're entitled to knock them about a bit.'

It was impossible not to admire the audacity, and I prepared for the inevitable 'Whhhhh' sucking noises that would mean: 'He didn't really say that, did he?' But virtually the whole place, from the T-shirted bar staff to the suited executives that had rushed from their computers to get there, clapped, cheered and yelled with delight like a packed courtroom at the end of a bad Hollywood legal drama.

'There's a difference at McDonalds,' he continued, singing the jingle. 'Yeah, no fucking windows.'

And once again the place erupted. The cameraman leaned across and said, 'Looks like you were right, mate.'

I was, but only sort of right. Because despite what I'd been saying, if I'd really believed it why did I doubt that Mark should open the show the way he did?

It was the moment that I became convinced that society had turned a corner. I've no idea where Margaret Thatcher was at that precise moment, but from that joke on, the only way was out.

A Lost Party

WHEN THE DAY finally came when Margaret Thatcher resigned, I had what seemed to be the good fortune to be doing a show in Nottingham for the Trades Council. What a perfect night to be doing a gig for the Labour movement, and what a celebration it would be.

Travelling up on the train, I felt as ecstatic as I ever had, and as English as I ever had. For no one seemed to be taking any notice of the news which had come a few hours earlier. People were doing their crosswords, queuing up for their coffees and listening to their Walkmans as if it was just a normal day.

Surely if this were Italy or Spain, there'd be groups of drunken communists letting off fireworks in the carriage, or a massive punch-up between those who loved her and those who despised her. But here no one seemed to give a toss.

So I sat there, inwardly celebrating, but outwardly doing the crossword and queueing for a coffee. Tonight was certain to be brilliant. The apparently invincible woman who'd blighted our lives for eleven years had gone, so there was bound to be a huge party.

I pieced together a string of ideas about the events of the day, and was able to make these the bulk of my hour-long set. On a day when there was obviously only one issue dominating people's minds, it would just seem daft to go on as normal and talk about my old English teacher or something, especially at a do put on by a Trades Council.

The show went well enough, and I prepared myself for the inevitable festivities which would provide an outlet for the euphoria so many people felt. At the bar a bloke covered in badges came up to me and said, 'I don't know why you're so pleased about Thatcher going. They'll only put someone else in her place.'

There was no denying this, of course. The Conservative Party was not going to close down and sell off its furniture as a result of the day's event. But some people on the left are just completely incapable of being happy for even a moment. When Nelson Mandela was released that bloke probably moaned that it didn't mean anything because, 'What about the people who haven't been released, eh?' Which is a game you can carry on playing until everything in the universe is utterly perfect. But I was in too good a mood to argue, so I walked away.

But while nobody else was quite as miserable as that, several people were worried that it made it more likely that the Tories would get back in again and the mood was strangely flat.

Rarely have I felt so cheated. For years loads of people had been chanting: 'Maggie, Maggie, Maggie – out, out, out' to no avail. Now she'd gone and the people who'd done the chanting were moaning. For years I'd imagined what it would be like on the day she finally went, and had terrible visions that at the age of ninety-five she would still be there while I marched along as a sixty-year old shouting: 'Maggie, Maggie, Maggie – out, out, out – or at least die.' But she'd gone. And gone at least partly because people wouldn't do as they were told, for if everyone had merrily paid their poll tax she would still be there. So surely I was entitled to a few pints.

Someone did throw a party but it was one of those affairs where everyone goes back with a few tins and starts rowing about who's to blame for Simon and Lorraine splitting up, and a girl who was completely smashed threw a glass of wine over me because she thought I was somebody else.

The next day I wandered round Nottingham and everything seemed exactly as normal. In many ways life does carry on as normal in the midst of great events, I thought. On the night of the fall of the Bastille there were probably some French blokes drinking wine in a bar and complaining about the miserable weather. On the night Charles I was executed there would have been people in London who tutted, saying, 'Well, let's see if this lot's any better,' and got on with tidying the kitchen.

I made my way to Bristol where I was doing a show at the Waterside Theatre. If a crowd connected to the Labour Party couldn't find reason to celebrate, what chance a normal venue where some of the audience may even have voted for the woman?

And so the normality went on. Arriving at the theatre the sound crew were setting up the PA and asked if I needed any special lights. Surely someone somewhere was going to say, 'Wahoo, I tell you what, bollocks to the sound. The old bag's gone so let's put balloons up round the street and drive round the town in an open top car swilling champagne and singing revolutionary songs in Italian.' Instead it was: 'We've put a plate of sandwiches in your dressing room.'

There were about three hundred people at the show, and no indication that any of them were radical in any way. The act on before me did his normal routine about the peculiarities of dogs, *Star Trek* and his old English teacher.

Eventually I was introduced, and I was unsure exactly how to begin so I went to the microphone and said, 'Well, she's fucking gone.' A large section of the audience cheered as if to say, 'Yeah, and why has no one else mentioned it,' and the following hour became a virtual rally.

I finished off by saying, 'Wouldn't it be brilliant if somewhere in the audience there's a couple of Tories who earlier tonight were going, "Oh well, let's try not to get too upset. I tell you what, why don't we go down to a comedy show, have a good laugh and try to forget about it?"'

The mood continued afterwards and was the complete

opposite of the previous night's gloom. The Labour Party, embroiled in a quagmire of opinion polls and parliamentary arithmetic denied themselves their moment of euphoria. A random collection of punters at a Bristol comedy evening had no such qualms and were happy to celebrate, once they were given the go ahead.

How many other people, on the train, in Nottingham city centre and in the Pizza Hut I'd been to, had been privately overjoyed? There were probably people in all those places wanting to raise a glass to the events of the day, who looked over at me as I did at them and thought, 'That bloke doesn't seem bothered, must be a Tory.'

Maybe if someone had got up in each of those places and shouted, 'Well, she's fucking gone,' lots of others would have joined in. So, the next time a Tory prime minister resigns after eleven years, that's exactly what I'm going to do.

I Really Was A Milkman

SOMETIMES I'VE STOOD in a room with someone from the world of entertainment so used to being surrounded by actors, artists, designers and lawyers that the fact that I've got a London accent and haven't been to Cambridge clearly makes them feel uneasy. They shuffle from one foot to the other, look at their watches and say things like, 'Well, I see that er, that West Ham are having rather a good season,' in an effort to be accommodating. In the same way that someone in their fifties meeting a black person for the first time might think they're being polite if they say, 'So, you're probably used to hot summers are you?'

The body language is like someone stuck in a room with a wild dog that's being friendly. As if they're thinking, 'Well, he seems fine at the moment; but I expect that at any time he's likely to revert to normal and go "Oy, shitface, do you want a kick in the bollocks or what?".'

Once, in the canteen at Broadcasting House I was standing next to a writer who'd been to Cambridge University. We struck up a canteen queue sort of conversation about the ropy looking custard, and then in a genuine attempt to be friendly, he asked me if I'd got into comedy by my knowing someone at the BBC. I told him I hadn't and he said, 'Oh, so drama school then, was that it?'

Then another go. 'So, university and then on to the boards as such, eh?'

When I told him I hadn't been to university he actually seemed astonished, as if I'd told him I'd never been in a house.

'Oh, I see,' he said. 'So it's an old fashioned story of one day a barrow boy, next day the stage.'

There is however, a breed who are way beyond the level of feeling uneasy with anybody who doesn't have a BBC accent. There are some who have surrounded themselves so much by graphic artists, travel writers and parties where some poor bloke comes round in a bow tie carrying a tray of vol-au-vents, they don't seem to believe that any other sort of person actually exists. I was talking to an actress once and began a sentence with the apparently innocent words, 'I know this postman...'

Clasping her hands and rocking backwards she burst into haughty laughter and said, 'Oh, Mark, you do it deliberately. Listen to you, saying that you know a postman.'

It was a similar sort of character, unwilling to accept that there are real postmen in this world and people who know them, who interviewed me for an article in the actors' newspaper, *The Stage*.

Having come to a show I was doing in London, she taped the interview during an interval. She asked the usual questions: how did I get started, which jobs had I had before, what were my plans? And then she wrote a whole piece about how I deliberately faked a London accent to appear more street-wise, that I'd claimed I'd been brought up in an area where everyone carries a flick-knife and that I'd tried to convince her that I'd been a milkman when I'd quite obviously never been any such thing.

Who, I wondered, does she imagine delivers the milk? Are all milkmen middle-class lefty actors pretending to be proletarian? Do they get back to the yard, throw down their crates and scream: 'Derek love, saw you on round fourteen delivering Mrs Osmond's yoghurt, you were a revelation darling'?

Maybe then they'd get reviewers following them on their rounds and writing pieces in *The Float* that said, 'He tried to convince me he'd been an actor but he'd clearly never been any such thing.'

The Case for Cows in the Street

THERE ARE TWO fascinating aspects to travelling around Britain so regularly. One is noticing the differences between areas. The other is noticing the similarities.

Two of the first questions usually asked by local radio station and newspaper interviewers are: 'How do you find a (Chesterfield or wherever it happens to be) audience?' and, 'Are the people of Taunton difficult to make laugh?'

The mistake with this line of questioning is to assume that where you come from is the issue that most determines what makes you laugh. A check-out girl from Swindon is much more likely to laugh at the same things as a check-out girl from Aberdeen, than at something a chartered accountant from around the corner finds amusing. Even more important is the setting in which people are being asked to laugh. A theatre audience will be relatively polite, a club with tables and a bar will more be more conducive to raucous cackling and banter, and playing support to a heavy metal metal band while local bikers ride through the audience on Triumph 850s will be a disaster, whether in Peckham or Wick.

On top of this, the cultural differences that give a distinctive air to people from certain areas are gradually being eroded, as every town centre develops its identical corporate image. A wander around the shops while you're away is becoming an increasingly predictable trudge through a pedestrianised precinct past the inevitable River Island, Our Price, Clinton Cards, Abbey National, Thornton's Chocolates, Waterstone's, K Shoes, Top Man, Marks and Spencer, WH Smith, Currys, Woolworth's, Blockbuster Video and Body Shop. And in the middle of the square, a bloke selling roses in an unromantic plastic wrapping competes with a bloke selling chocolate-covered almonds and probably a bloke in an AA uniform, cheerfully seeking recruits.

Far from being comforting, this makes travelling thoroughly miserable and functional. If I go to New York I want burger bars with customers shouting: 'Hey, you trying to fuck with me?' If I go to Morocco I want to be woken at four in the morning by wailing Muslims. So in Barnsley I want a game of skittles with a bloke who says, ''appen as like,' and in Norwich I want cows walking through the street.

The uniform modern facades of British towns can drive the touring performer mad. Stuck for several hours in Coventry or Dundee you need something different to look at so that there's some purpose to your day. Surely Cardiff city centre's Our Price could have a male voice choir selection in the window, or Glasgow's Marks and Spencer could employ someone to stand outside shouting, 'Ye can bring back yur wee items yer'll not want, by the way.'

The demands of big business have thwarted local eccentricities. They have not however succeeded in destroying them. Sensing the local air has become a pleasure that has to be worked at, rather than something which you experience naturally but each area does still retain its own distinct character.

The most obvious and identifiable feature of each town is its accent. Despite enormous influences from TV, cinema, commuting and instant travel, it's astonishing that it's still possible to instantly judge where someone comes from by listening to them speak for about twenty seconds. One of the fascinating points about Reading is that despite it being fifteen minutes on a train from Paddington people speak with a definite west country accent. As they do in Maidenhead. But not in Slough. Maybe I'm easily amused but to me that makes doing the gig in Reading worthwhile.

But not only does Britain contain a plethora of regional accents, each area becomes jealously precious of its very own, quick to assert, 'No mate, you're doing Dudley, not Wolverhampton.'

So while audiences appreciate it if you mimic the local dialect with some accuracy, there will always be someone who complains with religious fervour that no one can ever get it right. I've heard northerners do perfect south London accents that would pass without question if you didn't know they weren't from the area, only for friends to shout, 'no mate, that's bleeding Australian.' Equally I find it fascinating that in St Helens most of the population is obsessed with rugby league but in Brixton the most famous player in Britain could walk around a supermarket without anybody noticing.

What makes travelling to do shows a continuous pleasure is that in Manchester the most appreciated part of the performance will be the ten minutes about trams that wouldn't make the slightest sense in Glasgow. Or that everybody in Sheffield knows the local council wasted millions of pounds on the ridiculous 'Student Olympics'. Or that most people in Cork feel that their city should be considered the capital of Ireland, creating a rivalry with Dublin which to anyone not from either town seems completely daft.

At a show in Leicester I did ten minutes about a curry house called the Akash, in which the five pound special means that they keep bringing more and more plates of food until you have to beg them to stop. In Edinburgh there's a newspaper-seller who stands all day behind his piles of the *Evening News* shouting, 'E, E, E, E, E, E, E.' In Oxford they can't stand students, in Aldershot they can't stand the army and in Colchester everyone reckons they went to school with Damon from Blur.

Gigs can stand or fall on how well a comedian spots the local nuances of the town they're in. To ignore them completely is not just a wasted opportunity, but an insult. I once saw an American comedian at the Comedy Store say 'Hey, I went into the post office this morning to buy a stamp, and like I handed over my fifty cents...' He couldn't even be bothered to adapt the bloody currency. Watching him I just thought: for all your American schmaltz and 'Hey you're a really special crowd', we're just any other audience to you, no different from last night's, or tomorrow's. I felt how a woman must feel when a bloke tells her how beautiful she is and then forgets her name.

One adjustment that almost always has to be made is for small towns, which are generally much more defiantly proud of their parochial claims to fame.

In my town of upbringing, Swanley in Kent, there can't have been a single week in which a scout's fete, church jumble or whist drive wasn't formally started by Henry Cooper's brother because he lived in nearby Farningham and because he was the brother of Henry Cooper.

In Swanley the TV moment that stopped the town in my youth was not the moon landing or the 1966 World Cup, but the time a two minute piece of *Softly, Softly* was filmed near the White Oak Library. Thousands flocked to see someone or other chased by an actor I can't remember (not Stratford Johns) round the High Street. On the night it was shown the entire town sat in anxious anticipation and yelled: 'there it is,' 'there's Woolworth's,' and 'isn't that Maureen from the cake shop in the corner?' at appropriate moments. This was almost superseded in the year that the Walker family from nearby Dartford reached the final of *Ask The Family*.

Small towns are so defiantly proud that a single mistake about the area can destroy an entire show. An otherwise brilliant ninety minutes can be remembered for years as a disgrace if you go to Buckinghamshire and mention the 'H' in Thame; or in Cheshire pronounce Altrincham as Altrincham instead of 'Altringam'.

Local peculiarities condition us to accept certain things as perfectly normal which anywhere else would be thought of as utterly mad. Do people in Newcastle have any idea that the practice of running from bouncer-protected pub to bouncer-protected pub in packs of thirty, dressed in the flimsiest clothing (in January) at ferocious speeds is, to a Londoner, just weird?

It's also easy to see how people get used to living without something that to others is an absolute right. Historians have puzzled over how entire populations have put up with dictatorial regimes that deny basic rights. Well, how have Londoners put up for so long without being able to get a drink after eleven o'clock? Most other cities have at least one club, at which it's only a pound or two to get in. Belfast has its Barfly, Hull its Silhouette, Liverpool its Casablanca. It's only when visiting such establishments that you realise how hard done by is the Londoner, harangued out of bars from 11.01 with deafening shrieks, doors jammed open in mid winter and tribes of bar staff stood over you ready to snatch your glass like an over-eager child playing Mousetrap.

If travel is to be tolerated and no more, then the job of the hotel managers, high street stores and restaurant chains is to do everything possible to eliminate the twists and oddities of each locality. Seeing it as purely functional, their reasoning is that, despite being away from home, you needn't feel out of place because the room at Copthornes' Hotel in Aberdeen is identical to the one you were in last night in Plymouth, with the trouser-press behind the cupboard on the left with the fixed coat-hangers that you can't take out and steal. You might be two hundred miles from home but Pizza Hut have ensured that life remains unaltered with the same salad bar, uniforms and aluminium jars of parmesan cheese that you get in Folkestone or Torquay.

Harvester restaurants apparently now have a national Muzak tape that is played simultaneously in all their establishments at once, so you might be in Luton or Dundee but *The Girl From Ipanema* will come on at exactly the same time during your exactly-the-same tomato soup.

But if travel is to be enjoyed we want to know that people will talk, eat and do things differently to anywhere else. Which is why comedy routines about work, sex and school mean the same in one town as the next, but the most gratifying is the stuff that audiences only appreciate because they know you're talking just to them.

And it's supposed to be communism that would make us all the same.

I Think I Changed Somebody's Mind

ONE OF THE most depressing things a political comedian can be described as, is as a political comedian. For in Britain the word 'political' means ministers squabbling on *Newsnight*, old boys groaning, 'Hear, hear,' MPs on TV at one in the morning claiming that although they got thrashed, they're delighted with the result, and the bits of the budget that aren't about beer, fags and petrol.

Politics is a peculiar minority hobby for people who somehow get excited about a proposed act to curb the sale of undersized apples, and who can tell you what the Maastricht Treaty is all about. It's a pastime as dull and distant to the average person as model aeroplanes or matchbox collecting. And if I looked in a local newspaper and saw my show advertised as, 'Comedy from the hilarious matchbox-collecting comedian, Mark Steel,' I wouldn't expect a huge audience.

Most people are not interested in politics because politics means the House of Commons, and the House of Commons has very little apparent effect on our lives. So to be described as a Political Comedian not only narrows the number of people who will listen, but also means that those who do turn up are likely to go home disappointed because I didn't make any references to the proposed act on undersized apples.

So when asked if I'm a Political Comedian I don't deny it, but I do try to explain that I'm political in the same way that it's political to complain about a boring job, or to be able to hear every cough in the block on a housing estate, or think that things should be different from how they are. In that sense, the term Political Comedian is as misleading as describing a television programme as a 'sociological study of class and power in Britain during the 1940s', when you're talking about *Dad's Army*.

In addition, the British seem less inclined to call themselves 'political' than many other nationalities, because there's less evidence of politics directly affecting our lives. 'There they go, arguing about politics,' my mother would say if a couple of people in the house said they didn't like Ted Heath, for in Britain being interested in politics appears to be an option. You can be interested, if you like, in the same way that you can be interested in matchbox-collecting, if you like.

In Russia during the Glasnost days, comedy clubs sprang up everywhere, and almost all the comedians were considered political. For the connection between government corruption and a freezing afternoon in a queue for fish was obvious, so the audience could accept that the comics were talking about politics and everyday life at the same time.

There are people who grumble about the British for not being more interested in the news, and believe it to be because we're an apathetic nation. But more likely is that the news just makes most of us feel impotent. Most people do care about the events they see portrayed but don't have the slightest idea what they can do about it. When I was a child almost every news bulletin would provoke a response from my mother of, 'Ooh, isn't it terrible.'

There's no doubt that she genuinely meant it, but what could she do? So the best thing seemed to be to say, 'Ooh, isn't it terrible,' while watching film of a napalmed village, and then tell anyone that brought the subject up at meal times that they'd only start an argument.

Very occasionally though, an issue arises which captivates the nation, every newsagent's shop is crammed with people exchanging views on a single subject, and the first conversation in every pub is about that issue. An event so compelling that it would seem ridiculous to chat to someone on a bus for two minutes without mentioning it. The time this happened most that I can remember, was during the Gulf War. It was a huge and dramatic event; there was a great deal of unease about how far it could escalate, and it was the most enormous media extravaganza ever.

As a result, for about ten weeks any audience was happy to listen to a show that was almost exclusively about the news. Two nights after the war started I was at a theatre in Crawley and began with a rant about the ridiculous experts filling the screens with graphs and arrows, jumping out of their seats with excitement at the accuracy of these bombs (it's now admitted that almost all missed their targets), and clearly loving every second of their glorious moment.

Instead of the laugh I was hoping for, there was a cheer, almost of relief, for this was the first time they'd heard someone contradict the relentless media tirade that the war was going perfectly to plan and was killing no one but those who deserved it. Over the weeks, as the claims of the television pundits became increasingly bizarre, so did the enthusiasm for anyone putting an opposing point of view.

It's often the Political Comedian who is accused of not having a genuine sense of humour, and yet only the most fervent nationalist could listen to the nonsense of these experts and not find it darkly funny. For instance, the outrage on the odd occasion that Saddam managed to fire back a wayward scud was as crazy as any Monty Python sketch. Respectable presenters would shake their heads as if in disbelief at the level that he'd now sunk to; for firing back one missile in response to a three day bombardment of every major city in the country. It was as ridiculous as a football commentator demanding that an entire team is sent off because after half an hour's play they kick the ball for the first time in the match.

In the many shows I did during this time, I can't remember a single instance of anybody being troubled by any of the material. And yet it's inconceivable that there were only opponents of the war present. So surely, although most people said they supported the war, deep down they were extremely sceptical about it. Far from it proving how susceptible the population is, the episode suggested that despite the most rampant propaganda onslaught many people were discerning enough to withstand it.

From the response at the gigs I would say that it's the only time I've ever done shows that have changed anyone's mind, which became possible because of the large numbers of people who were ready to have their minds changed.

During this time I did a three night run at a club in north London, and found that the two biggest fans were these huge West Indian bouncers who'd been listening at the door.

'This is the stuff we want to hear, man,' they greeted me after the show, thumping their palms into mine. 'You've got to get out there and tell the people what's going on,' they implored me.

Two weeks later I was back at the club having a late drink, when a drunk lad came across and started a 'what are you looking at' type conversation. Within seconds the two bouncers had scuttled across the room, picked the bloke up, yelled, 'You don't start on him, he tells it like it is about the war,' and as they escorted him out of the building with perfect grace, I noticed that each had a *Stop The Gulf War* pamphlet sticking out of his back pocket.

It was the one period when overtly political comedy related to the whole population, and the proof was the dumping of this drunk on to the pavement, with an accuracy Norman Schwarzkopf would have been proud of.

Kilroy

I ONCE HAD the peculiar experience of being involved in an argument with Jim Bowen at ten o'clock in the morning. It was on a *Kilroy* programme, and the subject was racism in comedy.

'People have got to be able to laugh at themselves,' said one comedian justifying jokes about Asians. 'I mean I'm bald and I don't mind if people take the piss for that.'

'The difference,' I suggested, 'is that bald people don't get attacked or have slogans painted on their house for being bald, and nobody claims that there'd be more jobs and houses if bald people didn't take them off us.'

'I'd like to come and see your show, mate,' said Jim Bowen, 'because I don't think you've got a funny bone in your body.'

'Well, why don't you see if you can do a show to my audience,' I yelled back, 'and I'll see if I can tell people where to sling a dart.'

But after the show he was as friendly as could be. Until he said, 'You know what though, you're right about racialism. I mean there's been that many attacks on Asians in Manchester lately that if I'm doing a show there now, I don't do me Paki stories.'

America

'IN A FEW minutes we shall be landing at John F Kennedy Airport,' said the captain, and I doubt whether I had ever been so excited in my life. What was the matter with everyone else that they weren't all screaming: 'I don't believe it, I'm in New York!'

And the marvellous thing about the place, I was soon to discover, is that it's exactly as it's meant to be. Claustrophobic streets stinking of urine, nutcases bellowing chunks of the bible to themselves, constant sirens, constant horns, waiters yelling, 'Hold the mayo', skyscrapers, beggars, the filthy subway covered in graffiti, someone rocking on a bench muttering that you've got to have a gun these days, and thousands of characters acting out their stereotype like extras in a modern musical, as if the whole performance was put on especially because they knew I was coming.

For a city that's supposed to encourage individuality, it's astonishing how so many seem determined to play up to their own caricature. Cabbies bang their fists on other cars and shout, 'Muthafucka!', the armed police eat doughnuts, queens in leather caps blow whistles and everyone tells you to have a nice day.

In the first comedy club I went to, the first act wore a string vest and did stuff about being a truck driver; then a camp comedian talked about his clothes, and a black comedian said 'shit' a lot. The compere tried to engage the audience in conversation, but this was proving tricky as there were only fifteen of us. Then one by one the rest of the audience left their seat, got on stage to do ten minutes, and it became clear that I was the only person there who wasn't doing an act.

At least half of them depended on banter with the audience, so seven times I was told, 'So you're from England, huh? How about that?' and I felt the pompous satisfaction that could only come from the knowledge that there were people in the comedy business doing even worse than I was.

What a crack it would be to do a couple of spots at these clubs. There would be no pressure, simply a social experiment to see what worked, but it surely wouldn't be difficult to look good compared to these misfits. And coolest of all, no one would know who the strange Englishmen was who rode into town, reeled off his act and disappeared again.

So I found the manager of the club and offered to do ten minutes one evening. He told me I'd have to ring the next day, arrange an appointment, bring some publicity leaflets, talk to him about my act and see about getting booked in at some point in the future. Just to try out a few minutes of material in front of no one at all except the other acts, in return for nothing.

It was one of those situations where, if the other person didn't understand that what he was saying was mad, there was no point in trying to explain it. Like when someone in a café tells you that they can do bacon and egg, or bacon and beans, but can't possibly let you have egg and beans because it isn't on the menu.

So the next day I rang round a few other clubs and each in turn launched into a spiel about the enormous portfolio I would need in order to get on to the list of hopefuls who might be allowed to do a small spot on their stage. There's a certain tone that people adopt when their job entails explaining to someone who's desperate for something, that in order to get it they have to follow an endless list of instructions. It's a sort of concise, confident, smug, patronising way of speaking that comes from knowing that your life will hardly be affected by the outcome of the conversation, but the poor bastard at the other end could be devastated by it. It's the sort of superiority expressed by personnel officers when they're interviewing you for a job and ask why you want to come and work for British Telecom, knowing that you're going to have to concoct some bullshit about admiring the firm and its go-ahead principles, when inside your stomach's in a knot and you're screaming: 'Please, please give me the job, I'm fucking skint.' And in the city where everyone can make it if only they'd try hard enough and are prepared to grovel low enough, there's no shortage of people willing to believe that they can be a great comedian if only someone will give them a break and let them do ten minutes in their shit-hole to no one.

So every time I had this spiel fired at me, I tried to correct the person at the other end as to the nature of our relationship. 'Well, I'm only here for a few days, so if you can't fit me in this week there's no point,' I'd say, with the self-satisfaction of someone telling a bank manager that they don't really need a loan any more because they found a pile of diamonds under the bed. But even if I'd said, 'If you refuse me a booking I'm really not that bothered because I'm English and you're just jealous that you haven't got a Royal Family, so fuck you,' they'd have just gone, 'Well, if you ring back Wednesday between three and three-thirty you can make an appointment.'

One man, Lewis from a place called Catch a Rising Star, did buck the trend and asked me to do a short spot (no money of course). The address he gave me was a tatty bar full of broken chairs, with a room at the back which I presumed was where the show took place. The bar was packed with comedians so I had to conduct the tricky business of interrupting a crowd of blokes all joking and laughing loudly to ask, "Er, is Lewis about at all?'

'I think he'll be back in a half hour,' someone told me.

So for half an hour I sat on my own in the corner while this group of lads exchanged stories of who'd gone down well or badly at which club, in exactly the same way that I must have done sometimes in London, maybe ignoring some poor bastard from New York sitting on his own in the corner.

Every now and then the volume of noise would go down and I was certain they were saying something like, 'Who's that weird guy in the corner?'

'What, that Australian?'

'He's not Australian, dickhead, he's from Kansas.'

Eventually Lewis arrived. Like excitable children all the comics surrounded him, making jokes about him and each other as they did so. Then with the control of a dog-handler, he simply lifted his hands, told them quietly not to get so excited and they all calmed down. From a distance it was clear that he was the man with the power. He was smaller than the rest, slightly camp and without any of the energy or banter of the others; but he ran the club and they all looked up to him.

He was their mate, because every jocular insult and play-ful slap on the back they gave him was a reminder of how they were a part of his gang, and there were loads that would love to be but can only get through to the reception-ist when they call.

If, I discovered later, you were fortunate enough to win a coveted place in Lewis' affections and earn a regular slot, you were paid an amount equal to the cab fare to your next gig. Most of the comedians were doing four or five gigs a night and going home with nothing but the hope that some-one important had been at one of them, and thought their face cute enough for a commercial.

I introduced myself to Lewis, and was particularly look-ing forward to the point where he knew that I was the English comic who he'd given the booking to. For then he would probably introduce me to the others, and at last there would be someone to talk to instead of being stuck in a cor-ner on my own.

'Mark what?' he said worryingly. 'Look I'm real busy at the moment, we have a show here tonight.'

'I know you do, Lewis – that's why I'm here. You asked me to come along tonight, and here I am.'

'Well, give me your video and I'll take a look, and get back to you next week,' he said and turned to walk away.

'Lewis,' I said in that way you speak when you feel you can't possibly leave it at that but know there's no hope of getting any further: 'There was no mention of a video, you said...'

'No video?' he said getting more camp and more irritated at the same time, 'But I don't let anyone perform here without seeing a video.'

He then uttered the phrase that should be acceptable as an admission of guilt in a court of law: 'Look, there's obviously been a breakdown in communication here.'

No one ever says that unless they've told someone something which was complete bollocks and then try to make out it's all a silly mix up – just one of those things.

By now the other comics had seen the fracas and were coming across. There wasn't much chance of a fair trial and Lewis was starting to yell, 'Stop hassling me, I just feel that you're hassling me here and I can't operate when I'm being hassled. Look,' he added. 'You get me a video and I promise I'll get back to you and see if I can give you a date in a couple of months.'

'Lewis,' I said. 'Have you any idea where England is? It's not across the river in New Jersey, it's three thousand miles away.'

And then I realised that the bar I was sitting in was the club itself. This argument was about whether I had the right to perform for free in a bar full of broken chairs. In a matter of minutes I'd become a New Yorker, or at least one type – the unknown person with nothing, trying to sell himself as worth being given at least a try, and not even managing that.

New York prides itself on being a city in which anyone can make it to the 'top of the heap'. So thousands of Lewises own thousands of comedy clubs, acting classes, strip joints, bars and restaurants that thrive on people believing that these places are the first step on a road to glory.

But the other side of a place that believes that anyone can make it, is that if you're one of those that hasn't, it's your own fault. So even a dirty old comedy club can routinely humiliate the enormous number of people desperately trying to claw their way into entertainment as an escape from their everyday drudgery, with only a marginally better chance than if they did the lottery.

And yet, despite this, New York is a magnificent place. Even if, from my experience, its beauty comes not so much from the sirens, the irate cabbies, the yelling waiters and the creeps of the comedy business, but from the fact that despite its cut-throat 'every man for himself' ethic, there is a tremendous humanity which manages to shine through.

They shout, but they do it across the street to ask if you're lost. They confront you in the poorer areas, but to make sure you can find your way out without getting robbed. On a subway train one afternoon, a beggar got on and began a speech about how he had no money, and was nearly blind. Everyone looked down and wished he'd go away. But then his story took an unexpected turn.

'So I appealed to you good people for some money to save my arse. And because of the generosity of you good folk I was able to buy myself some glasses, and once I could see I could get myself a job, and a small apartment. and so I'd just like to say thank you to all you folk who help the needy.'

'What's the scam?' we all thought.

'So thank you,' he said, followed by, 'Merci beaucoup, Danke schoen,' and he went on to say 'thank you' in about fifty different languages. At one point a Chinese woman looked up startled from her newspaper and said, 'That was my dialect,' and off he got.

There were more people on that subway carriage than I'd seen in any of the comedy clubs. And the show was far better than any of the acts I'd witnessed. And I doubt he had to show the driver a video before he started.

Chicago

CHICAGO IS NOT a village. It hosts the tallest building in the world, a population of three million, a railway network built above the ground and the setting for the pile-up scene at the end of *The Blues Brothers*. And yet after New York it feels like a suburban outpost, the sort of place that has residents' meetings about untidy hedges. Someone actually said to me, in the shadow of the gigantic diamond-shaped Amoco skyscraper, 'I wouldn't live in New York, that's a rat race.'

He meant it as sincerely as someone in Aylesbury explaining why they couldn't live in London, or someone in Chipping Norton explaining why they couldn't live in Aylesbury.

Unlike New York, in Chicago people don't think you're weird for standing still for two minutes; but unlike New York, if you're twenty-one stone and go skateboarding down the main road wearing nothing but pink fluorescent swimming trunks people do think you're weird. So I renewed my enthusiasm for doing a turn at an American club.

But once again bookers for comedy clubs housed in damp basements had set up bureaucracies fronted by chillingly polite secretaries who informed me that I should send a parcelful of material for them to look at, and allow three weeks before expecting a reply, making me wonder whether I'd rung United Airlines by mistake and asked if I could have a go flying one of their jumbos.

Some simply said that they would ring back but didn't, and I accepted that it wasn't to be.

Chicago is laid out entirely on a grid system, so that a

map of the town is divided into perfect squares, just as if you're looking at a London *A-Z*, but instead the lines of the squares are roads. Each road across is numbered, and only those going up and down have names.

As a result whenever you ask where something is, the reply will be a grid reference. For example:

'Can you tell me where the nearest bar is, please?'

'On Michigan and Ninth.'

This struck me as odd, and rather soulless. It's certainly efficient but I quite missed the useless but well meaning lists of instructions like, 'Go left up the alley by the third set of lights past the library (not including the new ones by the shop with a stuffed otter in the window).'

And despite its efficiency, one afternoon I got completely lost. Wandering aimlessly about, I noticed I was standing by a club, and that it was one that had promised to ring me back but hadn't. At that moment an extremely tidy man came out of the door, and I remembered that the name of the man that you had to send your parcel to at this place was Chuck.

'Excuse me, but is Chuck around?' I asked.

'Who wants to know?' said the tidy person as if he should have been in a bar in a western, staring straight ahead at his whisky rather than turning round to face the stranger who had asked the question.

'Well, I do, I suppose,' I told him. And I said that I was a comedian from England on holiday, and that I'd rung earlier in the week and that nobody had got back to me.

'Then I'm Chuck,' he said and shook my hand.

We went upstairs into his office, and he said, 'We have a policy of not returning calls.'

This is the sort of thing that makes America brilliant. In Britain it would be, 'Well, I've no record of you ringing,' or, 'I know, I'm sorry, we've been so busy – it's like a madhouse.' But Chuck cut through all that and admitted that there was a deliberate policy of telling people that he would ring back, and never having any intention of doing it.

The 'not ringing back' policy had worked in my favour, for it seemed that only if you were dedicated enough to hunt him down personally were you considered worthy of a booking. If he'd know that I'd stumbled across the place by accident he would probably have told me, 'Chuck's not here, but I'll get him to ring you back.' But he didn't, and so I was booked to do the last show on Sunday night.

When I arrived on the Sunday, a bouncer looked down a sheet of paper on his clipboard, nodded his head about a quarter of an inch and I went in. It was far bigger and plusher than the dumps I'd seen up to then, and everything about the place was unashamedly businesslike. Because the comedy business is relatively young in Britain, sharp businessmen haven't yet perfected the corporate comedy clubs with quite the same precision as the Americans. For instance, at the weekend this place did three shows a night, each lasting exactly ninety minutes. The audience was kept outside behind a rope until one minute before the show began, then ushered in and shoved in their seats by waitresses who took their orders for drinks, which everyone had to agree to buy three of or they weren't allowed in.

Looking around the place, I felt like being a new boy on his first day in the office, for everyone was familiar with the format, the way you ordered drinks, and what they were supposed to shout.

The role of an audience is entirely different in America to Britain. If a performer tries to drag someone on to the stage in London, the rest of the audience shrieks with laughter at the unfortunate victim, who will probably stand there nervously giggling, holding their face in their hands and going, 'Ahabe prrr, oh God,' when they're asked what their name is. In America, the slightest request for a volunteer will result in someone striding on to the stage, holding both arms

179

up, screaming, 'Hi, I'm Bob and I sell Crunchynuts, the dog biscuit for the All-American pooch.' Then the rest of the audience whoop with delight.

And so on came the compere. There were whoops of delight. And these were American kingsize whoops, not the pathetic attempts that a workmate's colleagues bark at the beginning of *Gladiators*. These were cult-status whoops, not seen in England since Beatlemania, and all the bastard had done was walk over to the microphone.

'Okay, okay, welcome to another comedy night,' he began. There were some smaller, regular-size whoops.

'Hey, I'm really happy today; because today is one month that I've been drug-free.'

Now the place went berserk. They were standing up, cheering with every possible ounce of emotion, necks tightening with the strain like in the ferocious unrestrainable joy of a football supporter after a goal.

Eventually I was introduced, feeling like part of an alien culture; like I was one of these characters in *Star Trek* who finds himself surrounded by creatures who are expecting him to do something, but he has no idea what.

A minute or so went by, and although there wasn't a single laugh there wasn't any hostility either. What there was, was confusion. For I hadn't thanked the compere.

Suddenly I remembered that in that dingy bar in New York, every single act had begun by saying, 'Hey, what about a round of applause for the compere.' It was clearly something that had to be said, otherwise nothing else counted. Like if an entire country adopted the habit of not having to do anything anybody tells them unless they start with: 'Simon says…'

'Oh, er what about a round of applause for the compere,' I said, and there was a round of applause. Hmm, I thought, like a shipwrecked sailor coming across a tribe for the first time, I'm beginning to communicate.

I then mentioned the grid system and the Chicago method of giving directions. 'When someone's in your house and asks for the toilet do you say, "It's on Hall and Third"?' I said. More confusion.

I had been fascinated by Chicago's TV station dedicated to weather for twenty-four hours a day. I did some jokes about that, and only sowed more confusion. This went on for five minutes or so, none of my thoughts about Chicago that I had convinced myself were funny were producing any laughing or whooping; only confusion. There was no question of them feeling insulted, they just didn't get what I was talking about. So I reverted to some bits from my normal act in England, and it went down fine, even provoking the odd whoop.

What I hadn't understood is the extent to which Americans are incredibly parochial. Their television stations deal almost exclusively with their own city, their newspapers mention nothing that's happened more than ten miles away. The lottery is local, the politics are local and there are plenty of celebrities in one town, who are unknown in the next.

In that context, there was no point in trying to make anyone laugh by being surprised at how they go about their business. For most of the people of Chicago have no idea that anyone else goes about it differently. An Italian can laugh at someone unable to work out how to eat spaghetti. A Norwegian can laugh at someone who comes to Norway and is amazed to see everyone skiing. Because they recognise that what seems familiar in their environment is fascinating to others. But most Americans from the big cities give hardly a thought to other cities, and even fewer to other countries. Their reaction to my comments was, 'Well, don't you have a grid system then?' and, 'Well, surely England's got a twenty-four hour weather channel.'

Parochialism can be a result of power, or of isolation. America is the most powerful nation on earth, so less of its citizens trouble themselves with nations that don't directly affect them. But its cities are like states in themselves. So Americans can claim both reasons for never having to put themselves in the mind of someone from outside their own vicinity.

That's not to say that Chicago is unfriendly. On the contrary, it's as welcoming as a city can be. But don't expect many people to know very much about what happens outside its borders; still less to understand that, from your point of view, their customs are odd. Because in that sense this magnificent city is exactly like a village.

Mother

ONE OF THE things I am fortunate to have been blessed with is a proper mum. I don't mean it in the way that Donny Osmond would, or the way that adverts mean it, with the mum in question gladly serving a steaming dinner to dad (who's come inside after failing to build a garden shed).

I mean a proper mum who says 'Eric Toncona' because she can't say 'Cantona,' and thinks you're clever if you know the German for thank you. A mum that rings up three weeks before you visit to make sure that you still like carrots, and rings again a week later to warn you to be careful because the weatherman said it might be windy. A mum that worries that you're going to New York only six months after 'those riots in Los Angeles', as if a riot could travel, (a) three thousand miles east; and (b) six months backwards in time.

A mum like that is of great value in this job, whereas it would be a terrible handicap to have one of those modern mums that smokes dope and goes to Thailand.

The amusement to be had between a comedian and a proper mum begins as soon as you start in the job. For the first year after I packed in my job at London Transport it was obvious from every phone call that my mum was finding it very difficult not to say, 'You're bloody mad, you were good at maths, got four O-levels, had a steady job and now you think you're going to make a living telling jokes. Well, you're too bloody scruffy for a start. I know what's going to happen; you'll end up owing so much money that you'll have to start robbing banks and end up in prison. Well, don't think I'm going to come and visit you, because I won't. Why can't you be like your friend Michael, he's got a proper job selling photocopiers?' But she didn't.

As she gradually got used to the idea, instead of every conversation finding its way round to whether I could pay my electricity bill, every conversation found its way round to the possibility of me getting on one of these cruises and being paid to go all round the world, like that Bobby Crush – if I was lucky.

For years my mum must have been completely confused as to what on earth I did once I was on stage. To that generation entertainment meant holiday camps and pantomimes. It was hard enough at that time for me to explain to anyone from the older generation how I could be a comedian but not tell jokes like the frilly-shirted blokes off the telly. So my mum must have got in all sorts of tangles trying to tell neighbours and relatives what it was that I did. 'Is he clean or blue?' they must have asked, and she must have wished I was selling photocopiers.

But then the time came for my brief flurry into the world of mainstream TV. An appearance or two on ITV, and regular slots on the radio, and suddenly the whole thing was legitimate. For, to someone like my mum, telling someone that her son's a comedian was saying one of two things. Either that I'd been on the telly and was therefore doing incredibly well, or else I'd never been on the telly and was therefore doing incredibly badly, introducing bingo at the British Legion, and on income support. Now I was in the 'had been on telly' category – even though I was still in need of income support. Furthermore, I'd met people who everyone had heard of. So everyone in the street would hear about how apparently the woman who plays Vera Duckworth is just like that in real life, and that Lenny Henry's much taller than you'd think.

After she'd moved up to the midlands, I was doing a show in Birmingham, and for the first time she said she'd like to come. Though it was nine years since I'd started performing for a living, this was the first time this had happened, but the instant she said she was coming I was filled with one fearful thought: what would she think when I said 'fuck'?

The show I was doing in Birmingham was the one-person play I'd written, and there were several points at which the word 'fuck' would be pretty difficult to replace. Being the son of a proper mum, I had never even said 'fuck' in front of her when I was driving. Sons of proper mums develop a mechanism that stops them from saying 'fuck' within their mum's earshot, no matter what the circumstances are, or how drunk they are. For instance, if my mum was nearby while I was attacked by a swarm of bees, my first thought would be to make sure I only said, 'Blimey.'

Luckily the show was in a proper theatre and was sold out, which would mean that from now on if I told her that I'd been to say, Derby, she would imagine that I'd been to a proper theatre and that the show was sold out. Though it would have been far more representative of a normal night's work if she'd seen me at a place where I had to get changed in the toilets and the bloke at the door insisted I paid to get in because he didn't believe I was the act.

So the show began and all I had to worry about was the 'fuck' bits. What sort of mums do these actors have who appear in films and plays stark naked? Of course it's right that theatre should be able to portray nudity as provocatively as possible. But a proper mum would surely march straight on to the stage, cover their son or daughter with a blanket and tell them that apart from anything else they'll catch their death of cold.

Up came the first 'fuck' and I said it in the way a schoolboy says, 'I haven't done it sir,' when asked why he hasn't handed in his homework. As the show went on I got more and more confident about the issue, so that by the interval the 'fucks' were coming out at about eighty per cent of the volume of the other words.

At the interval I spoke to an actress I knew who was in the audience, and she told me that she'd missed large sections of the show because my mum was sitting in the row behind her and had spent the whole of the first half telling everyone in the vicinity that I was her son and that I used to be a milkman.

The brilliant thing, I realised, was that being a proper mum, she wasn't going to offer any dramatic criticism or bother about the insignificant fact that she didn't have a clue what half of the show was about. She wasn't even bothered about 'fuck,' probably dismissing the word as something the local council insists on you saying if you're going to do a play these days. For the other side of the bemused despair that she'd shown when she first knew I was taking up comedy for a living, was embarrassingly blind pride once it seemed real.

So now she reports every person who hears anything I do on the radio, adding, 'And she said she thought it was very good,' as if the woman in the chemists is likely to say, 'I heard your son on the radio this morning and he was shit, Mrs Steel.'

With great pride she sent me a review from a local free newspaper, calling me first to tell me that she was doing so. When it arrived I read it and discovered that the reviewer had thought the second half was 'scrappy,' 'over-long,' and 'badly-written.' To my mum it simply read: 'Mark must be doing well; he's in the paper again.'

Once, I spoke to her just after I'd recorded a radio play. 'Jill Gascoine was in it,' I told her, 'and Jennifer Saunders, and Ade Edmondson...'

'Oh, were they, dear?' she said, quite clearly unimpressed.

'...And also the bloke who used to play Jim Baines in *Crossroads*.'

Suddenly there was a shriek. 'Ooooo, did you hear that?

Mark's done a play with him who was Jim Baines in *Crossroads*. What's he like? Is he tall in real life? He must be getting on now.'

A proper mum is essential in this business for maintaining a proper perspective on how the world sees you. For at one and the same time they can make you realise how someone who's on the front cover of every magazine in London has not necessarily done all that brilliantly, but that by getting your picture in the *Bromsgrove Gazette*, you really haven't done that badly.

Saturday Night at the Movies

THE STAGEHAND FOR the play was a lad from Sheffield called Elb, and he was looking most perturbed when I met him outside the hall in Hammersmith. It was the hall in which the play was supposed to be performed, and he'd driven down from Sheffield with the lights, props and tapes. But he'd got there slightly ahead of me, and walked into the hall to be told that no one there knew about any play, because tonight was Filipino night, at which lots of blokes were hoping to buy themselves a Filipino bride.

There's a procedure to follow when you find yourself in a predicament like this. It begins with self-blame. 'Maybe we've both got it wrong and it's next week. Maybe we didn't make it clear that it was this year's March 14th.' Then comes the ludicrous explanations. 'Maybe there's another hall in Hammersmith with the same name and the same address, but somewhere else.' I once arranged to meet someone under the Eiffel Tower at one o'clock, and when they hadn't arrived by twenty to two I started to wonder, 'Maybe there's another Eiffel Tower in Paris?'

Having realised that you've got the right time and date, bravado temporarily sets in. 'Oy mate, this is definitely where I'm supposed to be doing my play, all right. So you must have the wrong hall.' As if a group of thirty blokes intent on ending the evening by buying a wife were likely to go, 'Oh all right then,' and spend the night playing table tennis instead.

Finally there's the standing hopelessly around and waiting for someone to turn up who will make everything clear. In this case I assured myself that all would be explained when Charlie arrived. Charlie was the name of the bloke who'd booked the play through the theatre company that had arranged the tour. He'd booked the hall, received the tickets and the posters, liaised with the company about the ticket price, cost of the show, and all other arrangements, and it would all be explained as soon as he got there.

Then bit by bit the audience started arriving. Though it was becoming decreasingly likely that the show would take place, such is the performers' ego that I couldn't help being pleased with the turnout. There were now over one hundred people spilling on to the road, mingling with people waiting for buses and offering conflicting advice; ringing up their mate who knows a bloke who used to be something to do with the hall; suggesting that their sister-in-law might let us set up the show in her pub; wondering if it was worth offering a compromise and incorporating the Filipino brides-to-be into the show.

But where was Charlie? If only Charlie was here we might have some idea what to do. 'Did you say "Where's Charlie?"' someone asked. 'Charlie Macbride?'

'Yeah, that's his name.'

'He's not coming. He said he didn't fancy it. Gone to the pictures instead.'

'He can't have,' I blustered. 'He's organising it. It was Charlie who put the whole thing on.'

'No he can't be, he didn't even know it was on until we told him,' said a group of people claiming to be his best mates.

At that point someone shouted, 'Sod this, let's go to the pub,' and almost the whole crowd, including someone who'd come from Luton and someone who'd cycled from West Ham set off to spend their Saturday evening in a way not one of them had intended.

I tried to ring Charlie the next day but he was engaged. So I tried again, and again until it was clear that he'd left the phone off the hook. So it became an obsession to confront him. Any twenty second period that wasn't accounted for I would use to try and ring him; waiting for a kettle to boil or for baked beans to heat up or for someone to put their coat on before we went out were all ideal times to slot in an attempted call. Eventually I was able to lift the receiver and dial his number each time I walked past the telephone without interrupting my stride.

At the start of the third week I got a ringing tone. After two weeks he must have considered himself safe, so he cheerfully answered. Who knows what he was thinking as he said, 'Oh hello, Mark, how are you?' when I told him who it was. He told me that several months ago he'd booked the show without actually checking to see if the hall was available. But when he tried to book the hall, the owners said it was already taken, and it was no more complicated than that.

Except that when the theatre company asked the following week whether everything was going fine, he couldn't face the embarrassment of saying that there was no hall because he'd never checked its availability. So he just said that everything was going to plan.

This meant that the following week when he was asked if he'd got the publicity leaflets he'd been sent, it was even more difficult to say, 'Well, yes, I did get them, but er, I lied about there being anywhere to do the show.' So he just said, 'Yes, I got the leaflets and they're just fine.'

And so it went on, with the theatre company ringing to ask how many tickets he'd sold and him replying that they were going very well, thank you. With each enquiry as to whether everything was going to plan he would have to make up more stories, knowing all along that this was making it even harder to say, 'Actually there's something I ought to tell you...'

By this time there was an advert in the newspaper of the union sponsoring the play, announcements being made on the radio and details of the show were in local newspapers and listings magazines. As the event which he'd set in motion with a couple of foolhardy telephone calls gained a momentum he could no longer halt, he must have watched each new development with mounting horror.

His friends (the ones that turned up on the night) must have seen the publicity and asked if he was going, and he must have stood there as calmly as he could and told them he was going to the pictures because he didn't fancy it. None of this lying and deceit was in any way for his own gain, just a result of his complete inability to confront the reality growing around him.

He was called up the day before the show and asked, 'What time should we arrive to set up the props?' and he went through the procedure of saying that half-past seven would be fine and that he was really looking forward to it and lots of people he knew were going. By this time his first thought each morning as he woke up must have been, 'What's going to happen when they all turn up at that hall?' And yet he traded the calamity to come for the moment's peace. To own up might make next week better, but the next five minutes would be much easier if he carried on pretending.

Who knows what farcical situations Charlie found himself in as a result. Were his friends nearby when he was on the phone telling the theatre company that all was going well? What did he tell them? How did he explain the posters when they arrived on the doorstep?

Where I can relate to Charlie's dilemma is that I think most of us have a tendency to put awkward admissions off to the last minute, even though by doing so we make the admission even worse. If we inadvertently book ourselves up to do two things on the same night, rather than face the discomfort of causing disappointment by letting someone know as soon as we find out, we think, 'I'll do it later, once I've had a bath.'

It's probably the same condition that makes people stay in jobs or even marriages they can't stand. Better to go through twenty years of slowly stifling torture than a relatively short period of mayhem that would sort the problem out.

What was admirable about Charlie was that he carried the cowardice to its limit. By wanting to put something on, he wished only that it would be nice to organise an event that others might enjoy. As he realised what was involved, he wanted only to not be thought of as a berk. Several times each day he must have thought, 'What am I going to do about that bloody play?' Every time he heard a mention of it he must have frozen inside. By the time he was in that cinema he must have spent the whole film wondering how many people had gathered as a crowd on the pavement, and how loudly I was shouting: 'Well, where the fuck is Charlie?'

At any point the furore caused by him owning up, or even making up a story as to why the show would have to be cancelled, would be less than the furore caused by leaving it another day.

As a result of the episode, all sorts of people changed their lives in a modest way. From the one original telephone call that Charlie could never retreat from, vans were hired and loaded, printers contacted and probably moaned at for delivering things late, a stagehand drove from Sheffield to London, someone may have run to the postbox to make sure leaflets were sent on time, and at least one hundred people planned their Saturday night around it, and trekked from wherever they were to Hammersmith.

I just hope that as a result of him not booking the hall properly, a happy, loving couple exists: comprising a bloke from west London and a Filipino maid.

Part Four

Slightly Successful

Mr. Mark Steel and Guest

London Weekend Television

INVITES YOU TO

an AUDIENCE with JIMMY tarbuck

ON SUNDAY 16TH OCTOBER 1994
AT THE *London Television Centre*
AND TO A PARTY AFTER THE SHOW

Champagne RECEPTION AT 6.30PM
Show STARTS AT 7.30PM

R S V P
Production OFFICE
071 ████████

ADMITTANCE BY INVITATION ONLY

The Trauma of the Slightly Successful Comedian

THE TORTURED SOUL of the successful comedian has been analysed through the centuries – the tragic tears behind the face of the clown, the internal agonies of Hancock or Lenny Bruce. On the other hand, the failed comedian is the subject of many a study: *The King of Comedy*, *The Entertainer*. But supposing you do the occasional slot on the telly, have your own Radio Four series, acquire a following of about two hundred in the larger cities of Britain, or seventy in smaller places, like Kettering. Suppose you're always in work but are unknown to more than a tiny fraction of the population. You will be in the undignified and tormented plight of playing a role with no identity; the Slightly Successful Comedian.

The Slightly Successful Comedian no longer trucks round the clubs on a bill with jugglers and people with stage names like Sir Laughalot, but plays to a group of fans in the smaller of the two rooms in the smaller of the two theatres in the average town, as he arrives passing a bustling queue for *Murder at the Tennis Club*, starring a bloke who was in one series of *London's Burning*, in the four-hundred seat auditorium upstairs.

The struggling comedian can look forward to an appearance on TV that will change his life forever. The Slightly Successful Comedian has been on TV and the next morning had to go to the launderette.

The marvellous thing about being a struggling comedian is that you know where you stand. Once in Norwich I went on stage at a miniature rock festival in front of three hundred students who were screaming for a band called

Fuzzbox who had been due on an hour before, but who were running behind schedule. Forty seconds later the promoter was delicately wiping a pulsating globule of gob from my shirt and ordering a roadie to sweep a glistening path of smashed Thunderbird wine and cider bottles from the stage. Later, as I tried to get to sleep sharing a settee with a St Bernard in the promoter's squat, I felt proudly part of a living tradition, the struggling comedian on the road.

Compare that to the mind-twisting experience some years later of getting two encores after a ninety-minute show to two hundred people in Leicester, then ten minutes later waiting outside for a bus to the bed and breakfast while two blokes growled, 'You'd better not be pushing in, mate,' while their girlfriends protested, 'Oh leave 'im Kev, 'e's all on 'is own.'

Or what about the emotional turmoil of the night I appeared on a programme with Barry McGuigan, Jan Francis and John Alderton. For an hour or so after the show we chatted, drank and joked together. 'Good luck with the new telly series,' I said to Jan as we parted. 'And good luck with that gig you're doing in a pub in Bradford,' she replied. Less than an hour later, I was dragging a mattress into the living room of my Tulse Hill council flat because water was dripping through the ceiling in the bedroom.

There are two crushing insults you can make to the Slightly Successful Comedian. The first is to go up straight after a storming show and say, 'That was really good, mate. So do you actually make a living out of this, then?' This is the equivalent of getting a plumber round and as he's reaching behind the washing machine, asking, 'So what do you do as a day job then?' The correct response to this question is to tell them you earn between twenty and thirty thousand pounds a week.

The other insult is to say, 'Oh, you're a comedian are you? Well, who knows? One day you might be famous.'

This approach supposes that: (a) all comedians crave fame above all else, and (b) you clearly haven't got it because I've never heard of you, mate. Therefore you are, so far at least, a failure.

To this you must reply that fame is the most appalling possible yardstick to measure success by. David Mellor, after all, is famous. So is Keith Chegwin. And Myra Hindley and Jeremy Beadle and Alan Titchmarsh and Reggie Kray and that irritating twat who introduces *Countdown*.

Bamber Gascoigne is famous. I know because I once saw him arrive at a theatre and as he was collecting his tickets a security guard shouted at him: 'Oy mate, here's your starter for ten. Haah haah.' Whether it annoys him or not that every time he goes to a shop he has to expect the assistant to say something like: 'What would you like? No conferring, I'll have to hurry you...' I don't know. But it surely can't have been his life's ambition.

I was fascinated by a television advert for toothpaste, in which three actors play dancing teeth singing something along the lines of: 'We're all smiling because now we get smothered twice a day in new oxygenated Crest. Mmmm.' At one and the same time those actors had attained the height of their fame and the peak of their failure.

So I can reassure myself that semi-obscurity is healthy. That a project such as writing a radio play that will go out on Radio Four at 10.45pm to twenty thousand retired antiques dealers dotted around the home counties is far more worthwhile than going on a BBC1 panel show and scoring two extra points for singing the theme to *The Wombles* with Robin Asquith.

It's also a complete myth that appearing on any old day-time cack is going to bring in the crowds to your live show. If being on telly was all that was required to build a live following, the weatherman would be doing sell out runs at the Albert Hall.

So Slightly Successful Comedians know full well the limitations of fame as a gauge of value to society. But they also know that if they look out of the window and see the postman they think, 'Ah, there's the postman,' whereas if they looked out of the window and saw Des Lynam they'd shout: 'Fuck me, there's that bloke off *Grandstand*.' Which is why it does feel awkward, and slightly depressing when I come out of Broadcasting House after doing a radio show such as *Loose Ends*, and I'm almost pushed over by a heaving throng of autograph hunters reaching over my shoulder desperately waving their pens at Diana Rigg.

It's also why there's nothing more flattering than being invited to something you would never take part in on principle. For example I'm extremely proud of an invitation I received to be in the audience for *An Audience With Jimmy Tarbuck*.

Tarbuck is the latest in a line of buffoons who saw the way the wind was blowing towards comedians like Eddie Izzard and Jo Brand. These types of performers have been attracting a young mainstream audience, which the likes of Tarbuck must tap into if they're to remain stars. So they're desperately trying to re-invent themselves with a kitsch image by surrounding themselves with younger comics. The only stand to take was not to go. But on the other hand I'd have been well fucked off if someone I knew had got an invitation and I hadn't.

The Slightly Successful Comedian understands that a comic's real ambition should be to wish to be funny by being passionate about things you love and vitriolic about things you hate, and that to convey that to a small number means far more than being a guest on *Win, Lose or Draw*.

But if you are half satisfied with something you've written or performed in, you must want it to go out to as many people as possible. In other words, be more famous. And more successful. The egomaniac wants fame no matter how it comes. The Slightly Successful Comedian craves respectability and fame. That's real megalomania.

At this point the person who said, 'Well, who knows. One day you might be famous,' will probably say, 'All right mate, I was only being polite.'

Steel's The Name, Lady

THERE IT WAS again: 'At the Gilded Balloon, chirpy cockney backchat from the former milkman'. Every day during the 1991 Edinburgh Festival, *The Independent* would include a list and brief description of comedy shows playing that evening. And for the fourth day in a row my description was 'chirpy cockney backchat'.

The arrival of newspapers at a flat occupied by performers during the Festival is not a heartwarming moment. Wars, famines and coups are rapidly dispensed with in the frantic hunt for the reviews page, before eyes scurry from review to review along with mutterings of, 'Where is it?' and, 'It must be in today's, for Christ's sake, they came on Tuesday.'

Once found, every syllable is dissected as if it were a German war document needing decoding. A generally favourable piece will still cause uproar for including a phrase like: 'despite a slow beginning…'

'It's meant to be bloody slow! That's the whole bloody point, can't she see that, stupid bloody cow!'

After a few years of this agonising, it tends to become less of an issue what the motoring correspondent from the *Edinburgh Evening News* who's been drafted in to the entertainments section to cover the Festival wrote about your show. Besides, unless you're talking about something as influential as the *New York Post*'s review of a new show on Broadway, one account in one newspaper has a limited effect.

I've sometimes heard performers that are being interviewed scream in anger about an article which didn't please them, and it only sounds bitter and twisted. It's unlikely that many people listening will have paid any attention to the original article; and anyway, it's appallingly self indulgent to admit that out of all the dreadful events in the world, the one that puts you in a seething rage is the theatre critic of *The Scotsman* calling you an unattractive oaf. Still less does it matter when the offending piece is a one line comment. But this 'chirpy cockney backchat' thing was bugging me.

For one thing, the term 'chirpy cockney backchat' could only be composed by someone so utterly pompous that they deemed it a novelty to hear someone with a London accent. And apart from the accent (which is far more south London than east London, anyway), there was nothing in my show which could remotely be described as 'cockney'. Besides, if there was a comedian who had a middle class accent the journalist wouldn't have written 'toffee-nosed comedy'.

So I decided to start the show by warning the audience that if anyone had come as a result of this description they were probably thinking that I was going to wheel out a market stall and yell, 'Here you go, ladies, bathroom scales, twenty quid in the shops, I'm not asking twenty, fifteen, twelve, ten, nine, eight or six, here y'are girls, I must be crazy, stick yer 'ands up, fiver each.'

I then did a bit about how you would have to be completely divorced from the real world to consider it note-worthy that somebody had a London accent, as after all there are eight million of us. But presumably this journalist was so used to mixing with Cambridge graduates, he'd watched my show one day and was forced to ask: 'I say, Tristram, what dialect is this chap speaking in? I mean, nobody at lunch spoke like that at all. Must be cockney, I suppose.'

So one night in the bar, a colleague of the journalist responsible for the 'cockney' line told me that he'd heard I wasn't happy with their description. 'What would you rather be called?' he asked.

I replied that it was up to him to write whatever he thought, and that he was well within his rights to say if he thought I was shit, but 'cockney', was pure snobbery. So the next day, under the heading of 'Tonight's Edinburgh Comedy', was my name, and 'Backchat from the chirpy cockney who'd sooner be called a "crap comedian".'

That night, as was the normal procedure, one of the staff leaned into the dressing room shortly before I was to begin my show, to tell me which of the press were in the audience. 'Only one tonight,' she said, '*The Independent*'.

Maybe it was a coincidence, or maybe it was because I knew he was there and gave it an extra boost of vigour but that night the opening piece about the 'chirpy cockney' remarks went down better than they ever had. As a result I added some extra lines, and kept on the theme a while longer, enjoying the secret that there were only two people present who knew that the butt of the routine was in the audience: him and me.

There are a few nights when a show goes particularly well, when the performer and the whole audience seem to be in the right mood, when a series of incidents take place which add to the atmosphere, and which you wish you could recreate over the next six months. That night was in this category, so I looked forward to his review.

Often when objections are made of a review the complaint is that the show went down really well, so therefore the journalist must be in the wrong. This is clearly nonsense, as by this criteria it would be impossible to knock *Neighbours*, Michael Bolton, or *Noel's House Party*. What any half decent journalist must surely do though, is to acknowledge the popularity of something they're reviewing, and try to explain the appeal.

How, I wondered, would this reviewer deal with the fact that on the night he'd attended the show, it had been undeniably well-received. Well, he didn't. The entire show 'fell to bits', he wrote. And he continued on the 'chirpy cockney' theme by claiming that the workingmen's club pianist character I portrayed was meant to be a genuine attempt at a singalong. As if I was from London so just couldn't help it. Which if he really believed it, was as daft as these people who believe the characters in *Coronation Street* are real.

He was quite within his rights to detest the show, of course. But it was clear that he had sat through the whole performance seething about the fact that (for once) his remarks had been replied to, and that the bulk of the audience seemed to agree. Having spent hours dismally failing to persuade people to calm down after reading unfavourable articles about themselves, I found myself boiling with anger. It was impossible to forget the review: I would put it out of my mind, start cooking dinner and find myself shouting: '*Bastard!*' and banging wooden spoons on the cooker.

Only a few people will ever have read the review. Most would not have cared that much about it, but there it was: in print in a national newspaper and written out of pure malice and with deliberate disregard to the truth.

To see three column inches of lies about yourself does provide one worthwhile thought. If I find a piece like that infuriating, how must Arthur Scargill have felt when he read, on the front page of the *Daily Mirror*, that he'd stolen vast sums of money, which in reality he'd never seen? How on earth did the Birmingham Six feel when for years the newspapers reported that they'd callously murdered people? What can possibly have gone through the mind of Winston Silcott when he saw the tabloids carrying a picture of him alongside the words 'the face of evil', for committing a murder he was innocent of?

There must be plenty of people who have never done the things the vast majority of people assume they have, because of loathsome journalists who concoct stories when it suits them. In which case I should be grateful that this arrogant and conceited man at *The Independent* remains a jobbing part-time theatre critic, and hasn't been promoted to a position where he could do the damage he no doubt aspires to.

Luvvies

IAN MCKELLEN IS a principled man and a fine actor. He is also so wonderfully typical of the acting profession's estrangement from the rest of the planet. The first time I met him was in Glasgow, and we were discussing the Miners' Strike. During our conversation I used the term 'shop stewards'.

'I'm sorry,' he said. 'I didn't quite catch that.'

'Catch what?'

'That thing you just said.'

'Sorry, which thing?'

'That shop-something.'

'Oh, shop stewards.'

'Yes, that's it. I'm awfully sorry, I haven't come across this phrase before. What exactly is a – shop – steward?'

Several years later he and I were guests on a radio discussion programme, along with Rosie Boycott, editor of *Esquire* magazine and a selfless campaigner for a number of social issues.

'I don't know if you all know each other,' said the presenter of the programme as we arrived at the studio.

'Ah,' said Rosie and Ian to each other, and at exactly the same time said, 'I believe we met at the Follett's.'

Which phrase, I wondered, did people imagine summarised the Labour Party when it was founded. 'Justice for the working man' perhaps, or, 'Fair wages for a fair day's work.' Well, it now seems summed up quite simply by words which should be on every party membership card: 'Didn't we meet at the Follett's?'

Lonely

THE SLIGHTLY SUCCESSFUL Comedian on tour has to overcome a potentially lethal obstacle: the blight of loneliness. As a struggling comedian I would have travelled with somewhere between one and three other acts, and the successful comedian has a driver and stage manager. But the Slightly Successful Comedian does his or her own show, but can't afford an entourage, even of one.

Driving to the theatre, the first reminder of how utterly alone I am is arriving in the town and getting lost. Asking for directions is fraught with danger, for human beings have a design fault which prevents them from being able to comprehend that somebody doesn't know the area as well as the person they're asking.

'Oh that's easy,' they say. 'You go past the Kingsdale warehouse, turn left where they hold the craft fair, go straight along the road that went to Britwitch before the bypass was built... '

'Stop. Look, I don't know the area. I've never been here before in my life.'

'Well, you must know where the Kingsdale warehouse is. Everybody knows the Kingsdale warehouse.'

'Well, I'm sorry but this is my first time here. Ever.'

'Oh I see. You don't know the area at all. Well, then you're better off going up to the first roundabout, and you know Barclays Bank... ?'

Another brand of the same disease is to sound helpful but actually be incredibly vague, so that you drive off thinking you now know where you're heading. But then you remember they've said, 'Follow the road round and at the end turn sort of left and then right and go straight along by some grass and then it's either left or right and you can't miss it.'

Equally frustrating is 'The Shadcroft Theatre?' said with the air of disbelief with which Lady Bracknell said, 'A *hand-bag*?'

'Well, I've lived here thirty-six years and I've never heard of the Shadcroft Theatre,' they go on.

'Are you sure you don't mean the City Zoo? I know where that is. Or maybe you're supposed to be in Halifax. There's a theatre there.'

Apart from being exhausting, this process is also thoroughly depressing, as it reinforces the idea that you don't belong.

On arrival, the theatre staff are often reassuringly pleasant, but if they're not, or are too busy to talk, there follows another hour and a half of sitting in a dressing room on my own. At certain points I might wander outside, then over to the bar for a lemonade I don't want but which breaks the monotony, the way that unnecessarily sharpening a pencil does for bored office workers. Then into the theatre, across the road to sit in the corner of a pub reading the free local newspaper I found at the box office. Then put a couple of quid in the fruit machine and back to the dressing room.

In fact, one night in Wolverhampton, I worked out that the first complete sentence I'd constructed all day was my opening line on stage.

Later, twenty minutes after the show, the scenario usually includes me standing amongst the fag-ash and plastic glasses while a bloke who used to be a roadie is packing up the speakers. 'See ya then, mate,' I'll shout to him, because it would seem odd to leave after doing a two hour show without saying goodbye to anyone. 'Yeah, see ya,' he'll mumble in reply without looking up or taking the cigarette out of his mouth.'

Is that it, I think? I've come all this way and done a show

and there were all those people; doesn't something happen now? Surely I just can't go. But not only can I – I have to.

In these circumstances, finding a friendly face is heavenly, as the whole experience can be transformed from a nightmare of solitude into a brilliant evening. Like the night one of the bar staff in Oldham took me to a club with a late licence, where a heavy metal outfit played tributes to Alice Cooper at a spectacularly deafening volume to him, his wife, me and three blokes in leather jackets playing imaginary guitars.

Even a ten minute conversation provides such solace that it remains unforgettable.

The alternative to these memorable pearls of experience is to be driven by rudeness into a chasm of gloom. 'Yer cannna get a drink at this time, it's five past eleven, man,' a bar manager told me at a club in Newcastle, although I'd been performing all evening five yards from his bar.

'Well, I've only just finished,' I pleaded and he must have been able to hear my voice start to crack with tragedy.

'Notten to do with me, it's after-hours, you should have asked before eleven, we've stopped serving,' he insisted, as if I was likely to have got off the stage and wandered across to the bar in the middle of the show, purely out of respect for the licensing laws.

It's not so much a love of being surrounded by people that makes life so difficult in these circumstances, it's the contrast between the two extremes that confuses the emotions. One minute you're the focus of attention in a room full of people who have planned their evening around you; the next, a soulful stroll back to the hotel without even the influence to buy a marginally after-hours drink.

By now I've learned to endure the lonely evening as an occupational hazard. The real headbanger is the lonely three days. Especially as, unlike most comedians, I rarely stay in bed after eight o'clock, which leaves twelve whole hours before having to be anywhere at all. In those twelve hours you can learn the true meaning of boredom very quickly. For boredom doesn't arise from having nothing to do, it comes about when there's nothing you have to do.

There's plenty I could do in those twelve hours. I could stay in my hotel room and read a book. I could wander around the town. I could go to the pictures. I could even find a local snooker hall and play myself at snooker. Quite possibly I will do all of these things but still be completely bored because I haven't chosen to do any of them; I'm simply doing them because there's still seven hours left.

So in the morning I'll walk round the shopping centre, stopping first at a record shop to flick through the same records I could flick through in record shops at home. Then I'll stop at a café for a pot of tea. But the great service performed by a pot of tea is to provide a junction between tasks.

Tea is a treat earned by the achievement accomplished. For example, 'We've been round the shops, so now we'll have a cup of tea.' But that doesn't work when the only reason I've gone round the shops in the first place is to have something to do before stopping for a pot of tea.

Besides which, it's amazing how little time tea takes to drink when there's nobody to talk to between slurps, so as an exercise in time-wasting, it's extremely unproductive. The whole business of ordering, receiving, waiting for the correct strength, pouring, drinking and paying, taking no more than seven or eight minutes.

A local museum can provide comfort and a touch of purpose. But again, unless it's quite exceptional (like the Transport Museum in Coventry), it takes up hardly any time at all. For the only reason anybody ever reads those bits on the walls that tell you where in the area somebody dug up a Neolithic chisel is to mention it to the person you're with. ('Ooh, that Neolithic chisel was dug up in Lutterworth.')

Remove that motivation and I can get round the whole place in four minutes flat.

Three or four days like this in a row and madness definitely starts to creep up on you. Maybe it's the uneasy thought that no one knows where you are. There is no one in the world who could trace you, because up until you went in there, you didn't know yourself that you'd be wandering into the library to look at the exhibition of local knitting.

After a while the fact that there's nothing to do for another five hours in a place where I know nobody brings on the madness, and with it comes lethargy. So, by the third day the process of getting to the next town somehow takes all day. A sixty mile drive or forty minute train journey for some reason means there's no time to do the one thing I was supposed to do, like paying the gas bill.

But the worst loneliness of all is the solitude of arriving at a gig to find that there have been only fourteen tickets sold. This means sitting forlornly backstage, in absolute despair but requiring to be even more buoyant and exuberant than normal to breathe life into the sparsely populated event.

The worst thing you can do in this situation is to sit near the door and hope that more people arrive, counting each person that comes in and getting excited when a group of four gets out of a car and then feeling distraught when they walk straight past and into a nearby Pizza Hut. But like scratching a spot, the fact that I know it's the worst thing I can do doesn't stop me from doing it.

Infuriatingly the person who's organised the event will try to make things seem better, either for me by saying, 'Well, they're a small crowd but they're very friendly,' or for himself by saying, 'I can't understand it. We did five thousand leaflets and put an advert in the local paper and a poster in the library,' so that he might as well add, 'So it must be that everyone round here thinks you're shit.'

This sort of dilemma is one of the reasons that so many people mistakenly believe stand-up comedy to be the hardest job in the world. For, unlike most other forms of entertainment, it's all down to you. If I can overcome the disappointment of the tiny audience, the show can still go well. If I can't, it won't.

This thought has crossed my mind while waiting to do difficult 'pressure' gigs, in front of big audiences or on live TV. At the last moment I could decide to completely change my mind about what I'm going to do, so that what everyone watching or listening sees and hears depends entirely on the decision I make. There's nobody to discuss it with, and no advice that can be sought.

On a smaller scale, it must be the same sort of feeling a general gets when he's deciding whether to attack from the left or from the right.

That sort of loneliness is so exciting, it's terrifying.

But...

AT A POINT when I'd virtually given up on getting a programme on radio or television, Radio Five offered me a series of the show that was to become *The Mark Steel Solution*.

The idea was that in each programme I would propose a seemingly ridiculous solution to one of society's problems and create an argument for why it would be thoroughly reasonable. The first *Solutions* we thought of were 'Anyone born in Britain should be deported,' and 'No one should go to school until they're thirty-five.' Pete Sinclair, my co-writer and I were given a producer to work with.

In many ways, the old Radio Five was a wonderful station, providing an ideal setting for new writers to learn by their mistakes, and it was staffed by people who had a tremendous passion for their programmes but who had no chance of achieving fame, fortune or cocaine as a result. Run on a shoestring and launched without a single penny spent on publicity, it survived mostly because of the dedication of those who believed in its purpose. And that was probably why we ended up making a comedy series with a producer who had no sense of humour.

Having no sense of humour, like being a racist or a stingy bastard, is a condition that no one admits to. As such it is one of those phrases which is commonly followed by the word 'but...' For example: I'm not a stingy bastard but I don't see why I should buy a Christmas present for my daughter,' or, 'I'm not a racist but it's time we stopped letting them marry our women'.

And no one bellows more emphatically that they've 'got a sense of humour but...' than those with no sense of humour.

211

An added twist to this peculiarity is that the industry that seems to contain the greatest percentage of people with no sense of humour is the comedy business. Dozens of books with phrases like 'funny old world' and 'ha-ha' in the title have been written in recent years by the sort of person who hears a joke and then says 'But that's impossible' or 'I didn't think there were any dinosaurs still alive'.

Executives in TV comedy are notorious for sitting through a recording and asking everyone in the vicinity: 'Was it funny?'

One of the clues to spotting someone with no sense of humour is that they love analysing what is and what isn't funny. 'I suppose what you do is funny because it combines the enormity of global issues with the absurd minutiae of banal stereotypes,' journalists in charge of comedy will say, getting a blank stare from the comedian in response.

There's no point in trying to explain to these people that without an indefinable love of mischief and the sense of our own ridiculousness that most of us share, there is no such thing as funny. For the problem they have is simply that they don't get it. You might as well try explaining to a psychopath why it's wrong to boil people's heads in a pot.

So every script we presented to this poor producer left him baffled and distraught. Virtually every joke left him either bemused ('but that's impossible'), or in a rage because he disagreed with the literal meaning of the words.

For example a sketch in the 'School' episode about the misery inflicted in games lessons on the fattest kid in class, earned this written response:

'This is language and stereotyping that jars with me. It's not just fat kids that are the last to be picked. It's also the skinny ones who don't go along with the macho bravado of some of the others. A clearer explanation of why the teachers can't accept non-conformity with the absolute average and less clichéd victims are required.'

212

So straight away we were faced with a dilemma. The two possible answers to that criticism were: (a) to point out how the sketch actually sympathised with the not 'absolutely average' fat kid; or, (b) say, 'You're fucking mad, mate.'

In the same script was a sketch in which getting a hiding from a bully was such an accepted part of the school day that the bullies kept a register to make sure that every other kid got a daily belting. Each kid they thumped had to have a reason for being hit, so the sketch went:

BULLY: Name?

KID: Jenkins

BULLY: Abnormality?

KID: Slightly overweight

BULLY: Oy, Pavarotti, (Wallop) take that, my son.

The next boy got belted for being 'Slightly underweight' and the last one for 'Having a girl's middle name'.

So back came: 'I don't like the use of "Abnormality". The sketch would lose little by having "reason for being bullied" instead of abnormality. Similarly I would rather have a list of political surnames than a feminine name which has anti-gay overtones. So maybe the bully beats up the kid for being called Tebbit, Thatcher or Churchill.'

So where do you start? There we were, presented with a list of suggestions that would leave us with a nonsensical sketch about a bunch of left-wing bullies who refused to say 'abnormality' on grounds of liberal politeness, and who attacked other kids for having middle names that corresponded with leading figures from the Conservative Party.

I had noticed before that one of the symptoms of people with no sense of humour is this peculiar inability to distinguish between words said by someone as themselves, and words said by a character in a play or novel. It's quite common for these people to see someone playing the part of a sexist bloke, and complain to the comedian performing it that they were using sexist language. Clearly not grasping the vital piece of information that what they're watching is an act, and that it isn't really happening. I usually tell these people that they should never go to see Shakespeare, because they'd end up running on to the stage screaming, 'You can't do that, that's murder.'

But on this occasion, the person concerned was producing our radio series.

Our problems had hardly begun. A sketch which included a teacher giving an absurd safety lecture about the potential dangers of magnesium sulphate provoked: 'Does magnesium sulphate ignite on heating? If so, we must choose a chemical that doesn't.'

I doubt whether there is such a thing as magnesium sulphate, but if by coincidence our made up name is a real substance what are the chances of: (a) it being dangerous when heated up; and, (b) our sketch encouraging kids to try it?

Then we were advised to include a section about political censorship in schools, eg: 'Why do schools take you to the Imperial War Museum but not Greenham Common on a day trip. Which is the more relevant to today?'

The marvellous thing here was that at this time the Imperial War Museum was showing an anti-war exhibition related to the events in the Gulf, while at Greenham Common, all the cruise missiles and the women's' camp that surrounded them had long since disappeared. So the question being asked was: 'Which is more relevant? An anti war display or an empty field?'

As the series progressed our frustration gave way to fascination in the study of humourlessness. One of the characters in the series recurred each week, and had a catchphrase, 'They could have spent that money hanging people,' which he repeated in every programme. But upon reading the fifth script the producer commented, 'You can't say that, you used that joke once before.'

A line that ended by calling David Icke 'mad' was

stopped because he wasn't, strictly speaking, mad. A sketch that included the phrase 'Fairy Liquid' was rearranged so as not to give publicity to the product, with an addendum of: 'How could you?' written underneath his objection.

And so on and so on. Every joke we thought of created simultaneous feelings within us of 'That should get a good laugh,' and 'Oh Christ, what's he going to say about that one?' The problem was that nothing in the world was, to him funny. He might smile knowledgeably, point a finger and say, 'Hmm, that's funny,' in the way we say, 'That tastes nice' after a spoonful of soup. But nothing genuinely made him laugh at all. So we were reduced to negotiating over every line, sketch and idea with someone who was talking an entirely different language.

'Just because the burglar has a working-class accent, doesn't encourage a stereotypical view of working-class youth as criminals,' we might have to say, adding something like, 'In fact the ingenuity of the burglar challenges notions of intellectual inferiority amongst the deprived,' to stop the whole sketch from being cut. Before saying anything we'd have to try and second guess his reaction so we could calmly forestall a major outburst. I imagine that negotiating with terrorists who've hijacked an aeroplane would involve a similar process.

There was certainly the same constant threat of a tantrum. For just as with a certain type of drunk, you could never be completely relaxed. No matter how cordial the atmosphere appeared to be, just one misplaced word was all it required to provoke a magnificent rage.

'That should get a laugh,' one of us said at one point and regretted it. 'That's it, is it? That's all we care about? Whether or not we get a laugh? I thought you were better than that, but clearly I'm wasting my time. That's what matters to you more than anything else in this world, is it? Whether or not we "get a laugh"?'

But nothing, nothing at all, compared to the argument about the swan. It's quite possible that our 'Incident of the Swan' will go down as the greatest conflict that has ever taken place over a swan in the history of entertainment.

The joke was one that I'd done many times before in my act, about the infuriating bureaucracy that we're forced to endure in Britain, over what should be a simple matter like hiring a car.

'No matter how well you equip yourself with bits of identification,' went the piece, 'they'll always catch you out.'

So it starts off easily enough. 'Can I see your driving licence?'

'Yes.'

'Passport?'

'Yes.'

'Birth certificate?'

'Yep'

'Eventually,' it continued, 'They'll catch you out.'

'Swan?'

'I'm sorry.'

'Have you got a swan with your name and address on, please?'

'Well, of course not.'

'Then I'm afraid I can't let you take the car.'

'Finally,' I would add, 'they make out they're being helpful by saying something like, "Well, have you got a friend who could bring in their swan?"'

This was the one joke we were prepared to battle over. 'It's stupid and childish,' the producer would shout.

'Well of course it is, that's what makes it funny,' we'd reply.

Then he rewrote it on the script, replacing the word 'swan' with 'grandmother's library ticket.'

'But that isn't funny,' we'd yell.

'But it makes sense,' he'd scream.

216

For weeks and weeks the argument raged. But it was all pointless, because basically if someone can't see that a swan is a funny thing to be asked for but a grandmother's library ticket isn't, there's no point in trying to persuade them.

In the event it was agreed that 'swan' would be the word spoken.

Maybe a sense of humour is an over-rated quality. This particular producer had constructed many documentaries, youth programmes and dramas and done them perfectly well. No doubt the whole experience was as difficult for him as it was for us. It can't be easy trying to persuade someone that it's stupid to say 'swan', when they just can't understand you. A Russian who can't speak English is no more stupid than an Englishman who can't speak Russian, so who's to say which of us was right, as we were each talking in different languages.

But if there is a God, he must have a sense of humour. Because the moment I spoke the word 'swan', the whole audience howled and applauded with a vigour that the joke had never remotely caused before. And though I'm aware that smugness is a horrible, conceited and obnoxious emotion, I couldn't help sniggering when the producer came up at the end and said, 'I was wrong about the swan.'

It was a gracious thing to say, but I wonder whether anybody has ever, ever, before been that wrong about a fucking swan.

Their Norman

REBELLION COMES IN many forms, and on one night mine involved wearing a blue suit. The official invite to the Writers' Guild Annual Awards Ceremony at the Dorchester Hotel stated 'black tie', but in the spirit of Lenin, I wore blue.

'Keep an eye on him,' I thought I heard a steward mutter, having noticed my flair for disobedience and considering the chandeliers in jeopardy.

It was the first such ceremony I'd ever been invited to, and it was because the first series of *The Mark Steel Solution* had been shortlisted for an award. My ticket, paid for by the BBC, had cost ninety quid. 'Ladies and gentlemen, Mr Mark Steel,' announced a doorman as I entered, and a few people looked round with an expression that said, 'Who's he? Is it that bloke off *The Bill*?'

The formality of these occasions is so horribly stifling that it's impossible to relax. You've no idea whether or not you've transgressed some rule of etiquette unknowingly, like using an adjective with a 'y' in during dessert. So, although it sounds deliberately loutish, I ended up thinking, 'I wish I was down my local.'

Before the presentations came a toast for The Queen, which was a fascinating social lesson. 'To The Queen,' projected the Master of Ceremonies. One third of the room stood upright, as if by reflex and responded in full voice. 'To The Queen,' they bellowed and raised their glasses.

Another third of the room stayed seated, quite deliberately refusing to participate. But the other third got up, half sat down again, desperately scoured the room to see which way the wind was blowing, muttering, 'To, er, to... Que...' while leaning on the table neither up nor down.

The food was that *nouvelle* muck that leaves you starving and, much as I wish it didn't, I found the whole event starting to bring out the Swanley in me. So, totally beyond self-control, I started complaining that the reason there were no kebab shops in Park Lane was that no one would eat these absurd quaint but tiny dinners, and everyone would piss off round the back for a large shish with chilli sauce.

It was announced that a gentleman from each table should be elected to organise the raffle (£5 a ticket), and four tables proudly revolted and elected a woman.

Award winners ranged from Edna O'Brien to the cast of *Coronation Street*, and everyone agreed that Joanna Lumley looked stunning in her tiara.

The important thing to remember here is that it wasn't the people who were suffocatingly appalling, it was the situation. Most of them were writers, actors and producers who, if they were in a pub or a normal restaurant would have been perfectly pleasant, unbound from the stress and tension of this formal nonsense.

But in the midst of this glamour, who would you imagine was the star of the evening? Who was applauded the most, with those twee claps in which the palms of the hand are never more than a tenth of an inch apart that everybody demonstrated, assuming them to be in keeping with the occasion? Meryl Streep? Emma Thompson, perhaps? No – the star of the show was TUC General Secretary, Norman Willis.

The Writers' Guild, bizarrely enough, is affiliated to the TUC, so guest he was, and he stole the night. Making a speech perfect for the occasion, he began with the witticism, 'The BBC's problems remind me of Shakespeare – to fee or not to fee.'

Then came equally dreadful joke after equally dreadful joke, with only one reference to his other life. 'An important part of writing is a sense of nostalgia. And we certainly have plenty of that at the TUC.' Norman's was probably the least political speech of the evening. Most speakers at least managed a: 'Come on, government, how about a little more support for the arts?' but even that was too radical for Norman.

Some did challenge the sobriety of the occasion. The woman presenting the children's stories award said, 'Let's hope that next year Thomas the Tank Engine wins, for doing Tower Hamlets a favour and running over Derek Beackon.' (Beackon was the British National Party candidate with an alarming chance of being re-elected a councillor in the Isle of Dogs). But Norm preferred to stick to being the darling of the ball. Before I'd always thought of him as a bumbling oaf but this performance changed my mind. For not only was he comfortable in these surroundings, he was the star.

The reason he normally appeared so incompetent is because he was not only awkward with rank and file trade union members, even the official Labour movement made him uncomfortable. But a ninety quid glamour do involving Joanna Lumley and a tiara and he was in his element, with none of the fidgeting and slurring associated with his dreadful incoherent speeches at union conferences.

At least union leaders in the old days would have a northern accent or do their waistcoat buttons up wrong or have gravy down their tie, or something to set them apart from the managers they grovelled to. But for Norman the ambition was never beer and sandwiches at Number Ten, but champagne and *mousse de flétan et rosette de saumon fumé neige raifort* at the Dorchester.

If only, I pondered in my glowing blue suit, Norman Willis had gone through life as an actor, presenter and after dinner speaker. And Joanna Lumley had been leader of the TUC. For the extent of his failure as a workers' leader is probably best summed up by the number of people who, if they were to read this would say: 'Who on earth is Norman Willis, then?'

Programme

6.30 PM
RECEPTION

7.15 PM
DINNER

TOASTS
THE QUEEN

THE WRITERS GUILD
by
ALAN YENTOB
(Controller, BBC 1)

REPLY ON BEHALF OF THE GUILD
by
GERALD KELSEY
(Chairman)

9.30 PM
Presentation of
THE WRITERS' GUILD OF GREAT BRITAIN
AWARDS FOR 1993

Hosts
DENIS NORDEN and JIMMY PERRY

10.30 PM (approx)
Dancing to LAURIE HOLLOWAY and His Orchestra

12.30 AM
CARRIAGES

'It's Only Death, Officer'

DRIVING TO A show in Peckham one night, I was trying to memorise a new piece I'd just written about violence. To help me I would occasionally glance at a pad I'd placed on the passenger seat, on which I'd written:

<u>Violence</u>
dead leg
pub fight
stabbing
death

Near the theatre I took a wrong turning and spun the car round to go back up the road, and at that moment noticed a policeman watching me from his squad car. Flashing his lights, he pulled me over and gave me the sarcastic, 'Lost are we, then?' routine.

Just as he was about to return to his car he looked across at my passenger seat and noticed the pad.

'What's that?' he asked.

'It's, er, a script,' I told him.

'Am I supposed to believe that's a script?' he asked.

'Well, it's a sort of outline of a comedy thing,' I tried to explain, but he wasn't having it and after a few minutes I made the mistake of losing control.

'All right, do you think it's a list of things I was going to do tonight?' I asked him. 'And if I was going to do those things do you think I'd need a list in case I got half way through and forgot. Finding myself stood in a pub with a Stanley knife going, 'Now what did I come in here for?'

He let me go, but that's probably the sort of incident that could lead to eighteen years inside and a half hour special on *Rough Justice*.

The Day I Changed Somebody's Mind – II

'I TELL YER what, mate, I loved that bit about the coppers. That was great that. True 'n' all, that's just what they're like,' said this bloke after a show one night.

It was a particularly vicious bit I'd done about the police, so the fact that this bloke enjoyed it so much was making me believe that what I do on stage can change people's minds.

There is only one reasonable answer when someone asks whether you can change people's minds through comedy? Of course not. For reasons I've already gone into, the Gulf War was an exception, but generally you can only make people feel more positive about something they already agree with, or maybe make them question something they've never thought about before. For instance, if I saw a comedian do a routine about the injustices of gymnastic marking, it might well influence my opinion on the matter, which right now is about zero.

But the most sobering thought for anyone involved in comedy or in any type of theatre or art is that you can write, film or paint something about an issue and be completely satisfied that it expresses exactly what you feel, only for someone else to see it and conclude the opposite —which is, of course, their right.

It's almost certain that someone somewhere has watched *One Flew Over The Cuckoo's Nest* and decided that it portrays the warmth and compassion of mental institutions. I met a hotel owner who said she loved *Fawlty Towers* because it shows how hard it is to run a hotel full of ignorant guests.

And I did a whole ninety minute show about England

being screwed up because we once had an Empire, and it was reviewed in Edinburgh as a show pleading for a return to the good old days when Britain ruled the world.

The bloke who applauded my piece about the police had really got the right idea, though. 'Bloody great, that stuff about the old bill, mate,' he continued. 'Vicious, but great, mind. My brother would love listening to you. He's a copper. He'd love it. Nice geezer. You'd like him.'

Can You Pay Me Less, Please?

'HOW MUCH DO you charge,' I was asked, and I didn't know. I would have probably done it for sixty quid, but this was a big company wanting an act at their Christmas party, and I'd heard that you could sometimes get a fortune for events like this. It crossed my mind to say something ridiculous like, 'A thousand pounds,' just to see what they'd say. Then I decided to ask for five hundred. After all they probably pay out that amount to solicitors and accountants for a day's work, so why not for a comedian? And it would involve at least a day to work out a show that would be relevant, so five hundred could easily be justified.

But I couldn't say the words. I just couldn't bring myself to say the words, 'I charge five hundred quid.' Surely no one was worth five hundred quid a day. It would have taken me ten weeks as a milkman, or twenty weeks when I was unemployed, or four hundred weeks when I was a paper boy to accumulate five hundred quid. So after a couple of 'Ums' and an 'Ah,' which must have sounded like I was working out an estimate the way a builder does with a pencil he's taken from behind his ear, I said the highest figure I could manage to utter.

'Two hundred quid,' I said.

'Oh right, well that's certainly much less than we were expecting, that's marvellous,' said the woman.

The difficulty in these situations is that most of us are brought up with such modest aspirations, both materially and more generally. As a child, I would be told that if I worked hard at school and did my homework instead of mucking about with my mates, I could be like the boy up the road and get a job in a bank. Subtly and unconsciously we're led to believe that there is a 'They' who do all things of importance. 'They' are lawyers, politicians, and people who decide things. For instance '*They* are building a new Tesco's,' or '*They* are closing down the bank where that boy up the road works.'

No one really knows who 'They' are, except that it isn't us. We can only hope to get into a position where 'They' employ and house us in as comfortable manner as possible.

To see which part of the 'They' divide somebody comes from you only have to watch them enter a restaurant. Most of us would stand limply by the entrance before meekly suggesting that it would be very nice if we could sit down please, if that's all right and there isn't anyone more important they have to attend to. 'They' march straight up to the waiter and bellow, 'Table for four, please,' before dumping their coats in his arms and debating a film review.

There can be few professions that rely on confidence more than that of the comedian, so the greatest hurdle most people have to overcome before being capable of taking the stage, is their own sense of intimidation. Most of us are brought up with such low esteem that the first thing said to a comedian after a show is often, 'I don't know how you get up there in front of all those people.'

Sometimes it falls upon a stage hand or someone from the box office to do my introduction. 'What do I say?' they repeat four or five times before writing it down and finally announcing: 'Now would you please welcome our comedian for the evening, Mark Steel.' Later, when I thank this poor makeshift MC, they sometimes tell me they missed the entire show because they were sitting in a storeroom, recovering from the panic.

But so sharp is the divide between those who expect to make decisions and those who expect only to act by the decisions of others, that overcoming the fear of performing to hundreds of people in public is barely a first step towards feeling confident about meeting someone considered important.

When I first started performing, I was amazed by the brazen nature with which Cambridge graduates would demand gigs from comedy promoters, with a 'Look, just give us a booking', the way a car driver might say, 'Look, just give me the map' to a passenger whose navigation isn't working. Then three months after their first gig, they'd be glibly asking for five hundred pounds.

Later they would confidently stroll into media executives' offices to set up lunch meetings, leaving the rest of us to stand watching like a queue of people who've been waiting for twenty minutes to be served at a bank and then seen a strident figure in a suit go straight to the front declaring that he's terribly sorry but must be served immediately, because he's in a hurry.

The media world, like a courtroom, is designed to make the great majority of us feel uneasy. Every time I've attended a media lunch or party I've had to employ maximum concentration to keep up with the language of: 'I hear they do an excellent starter,' and 'Oh, you originate in Kent? We're thinking of purchasing a cottage out that way.' Often you can't get a drink except from a tray held by some poor sod whose job it is to stand still saying, 'Wine sir?' to every idiot that happens to meander past.

It's at these events that deals are struck, acquaintances turned into business friendships and ideas run up flagpoles. If you don't feel at home at them you'll lose out to those who do. I've found that my best move is to stand still, with my hands in my pockets, like a schoolboy in a pub garden with his dad and his dad's mates, all of whom are all talking about car parts and the price of furniture.

Yet rarely does the confidence with which somebody flouts their abilities, coincide with the amount of ability they have to flout. For example I'm certain that there are many people in senior positions in the media who are less talented than Mrs Edmonds. I met her while I was working on a radio programme that required 120 pages of script to be transcribed off a tape, and because of a bureaucratic bungle there was no one at the BBC available to do it.

Mrs Edmond's son is a clerk at the BBC and he told me that his mother used to be a typist, and might be able to help. So I went round to her house to give her the tapes. After a pot of tea and some chocolate cake, she nervously told me how she wasn't very fast, and wasn't very good and was liable to makes lots of mistakes. She hoped she wouldn't ruin the programme, and better check one more time which was the 'on' button on the tape, and was sorry for living so far away. Though she went on to do an excellent job, she asked me several times whether I was sure it wouldn't be better to ask someone else.

'Mrs Edmonds,' I insisted, 'I'm sure you'll be fine. Now one thing we should sort out – this will be two days' work, so how much do you charge?'

'Oh, that's all right, dear,' she said. 'I don't want any money, I'm grateful for the practice.'

Jealousy

WHOEVER INCLUDED 'ENVY' in the Seven Deadly Sins should have added a subsection, for there are two distinct types of envy. One embraces calculating and malicious plotting; gossip-spreading, manoeuvring, dolls, pins and satanic ritual. And then there's the envy you really don't want to feel but just can't help.

Envy is an inevitable part of the occupation of writing and performing (although most of us wishes it weren't), and anyone in this job who tells you otherwise is either lying, or else has had a piss-easy life that involved going straight from Cambridge into a major television contract.

The most distressing part of performer's envy is that the closer you are to someone, the more likely it is that they'll be the person you're envious of. If a comedian who's not generally considered to be very good suddenly appears on television presenting a celebrity gardening panel game called *Whose Bush Am I Pruning?* I don't think: 'Why is he on TV and I'm not?' It doesn't bother me any more than if someone gets promoted to be general manager of a Burger King, because that's not something I want to do.

But if someone started shooting to fame as 'the loud-mouthed south Londoner', I would congratulate them, but think, 'Well, if they get their TV show, there's no chance of me getting one.'

Is this as dreadful as it sounds? When sportsmen are dropped from their team and end up on the TV panel instead, isn't there a bit of them thinking, 'I hope my team gets stuffed'? If two friends go for the same job how are they supposed to feel after the decision is made? Even if you tell your friend that you're delighted they were successful, you'll clearly not be as delighted as if they hadn't been – or else you wouldn't have bothered turning up for the interview.

It's not the selfishness of human beings on display here, as most people don't enjoy these feelings. But just as it's possible to be angry when you know you shouldn't be because the poor bloke holding you up in the supermarket checkout can't help it if he's eighty-five and blind, or you wish you didn't fancy the lollipop lady, envy doesn't need to be invited to turn up.

The occasions when it's easiest to be generous are when someone who's not doing as well as you starts doing better than they were. Just as in a game of Scrabble, if your opponent gets a forty point word when you're a hundred points ahead you'll say, 'Well done,' and mean it. But if they do it right at the end to win the game you're more likely to stomp into the bedroom muttering, 'Cheating git.'

Similarly, if I hear a dreadful comedy show on the radio, I just think, 'Oh dear, that's dreadful.' But that's because I have my own radio series. If I didn't, whenever I heard almost any comedy show on radio, I'd think: 'Well, how is it that gets on and mine was turned down?'

For one of the more infuriating aspects of the entertainment industry is that the decisions about who should or shouldn't be given the breaks are completely arbitrary. Influential media executives regularly take a shine to someone who rarely goes down well with any audience and who annoys everyone they ever meet (except influential media executives). In football it'd be like promoting the club that came ninth. And what is that, if not envy?

The tough part is that in this job there's no escape from the fact that others in the same profession have achieved a status you haven't. If someone is unfairly promoted over you at the office, that affects your day at work. But in entertainment, you wander into a newsagent's shop and there on the covers of magazines is the bloke you saw get booed off-stage six months before. Go for a meal at a friend's house and half way through pudding, the bastard will appear on the telly. Drive up to the shops and their cheeky face will stare back at you, sixty-feet high on a billboard. Sit in a café and the people at the next table might be discussing the programme he's in.

It's easy to see how certain performers find the injustices of the system intolerable and become so consumed with envy that it devours them completely. The only way to deal with it is to recognise it when it appears and stamp on it as quickly as possible – although like certain species of garden weed, you can never eliminate envy, only keep it under control. Especially as unfairness is envy's greatest ally.

If the performer I'm just a shade envious of, gets their own TV show and makes a fine job of it, I do find it genuinely uplifting and take pleasure in congratulating them. But when it turns out to be complete drivel and everyone who's ever seen them live says, 'How did they get on telly, they're complete drivel,' I consider forming the provisional wing of the Comedy Liberation Front.

Despite the enormous disappointment when someone gets the position we wanted, most of us – whatever our profession – do manage to wish others well. Most of us would prefer to be unequivocally delighted about other's success, but are aware that the other side of their success is our failure. Only a world obsessed with competition would organise work this way. Surely comedy, like any other trade, would be of a higher standard if those of us working within it were encouraged to work together instead of scrambling against each other for the few places allotted at the table.

Because, as it stands, the easiest route to what is considered the top, is to develop a malicious, manoeuvring, gossip-spreading dolls-and-pins type of envy; and not even have the decency to feel bad about it.

Oranges Are Not The Only Joke

THE IMPORTANT QUESTION I was pondering on the train up to Middlesborough, the day after a bizarre sex-accident had killed off a Tory MP, was, 'How did anyone discover the sexual qualities of an orange in the first place?' Was he once dangling from a flex, suspenders on, bag on head, thinking: 'Now it just needs something else. An item of fruit perhaps?'

When I arrived at the town's comedy club the compere told me he'd organised a competition for the evening, the prize going to the writer of the best Stephen Milligan joke. He justified it by saying, 'I don't care what they do in their private lives. In fact I reckon if they find something exciting the rest of us don't know about, they've got a duty to tell us so we can all try. But I hate them for being hypocrites.'

In the club was a fair cross-section of north eastern people. Ex-ship-builders, Teeside Poly students, office workers and the unemployed.

At the end of the evening the compere read out the entries. 'The man from Del Monte says yes, YES, YES!' said one.

'Stephen Milligan was an honourable man. Last October he said, "If John Major's still prime minister by February, I'll hang myself from a piece of flex with a bag on my head",' said another.

And then there were the less inventive: 'What do you call a strangled Tory? A good start,' efforts.

And as the jokes were read out, not only did nobody object, the whole place erupted with the fulsome roar of a packed terrace of football supporters cheering an opposing player being sent off.

It could be that these sorts of jokes always flare up after such incidents. But if it had been a Labour MP found dangling, the jokes would only have had an air of mischief, along the lines of: 'The good news about Ayrton Senna is his car's been fixed'. The comedy club's lack of sympathy for Milligan however, was typical of an anti-Tory, rather than anti-weird bloke with a plastic bag reaction.

The signs of hatred for Major's government can easily be missed by those of us who spent the 1980s spitting vitriol about Thatcher. Years of having people reply to a rant with 'off he goes again' have had their affect.

So, on the morning the Milligan story was first in the news, I was in the BBC radio light entertainment corridor. I prepared myself for the task of responding to the inevitable, 'Well, I feel sorry for the family' comments with some gibberish about how although it's a tragedy for this individual, it does show the hypocrisy of the Back to Basics party, etc. Then, a woman producer in her late-thirties, who had never before shown any inclination of being to the left of Roy Hattersley yelled to me: 'Isn't it brilliant about the strangled Tory?'

So it is that the Conservatives hadn't the foggiest idea of how despised they really were. Would Kenneth Clarke ever have claimed, 'Once the economy picks up, our support will return,' if he'd seen the room of perfectly respectable law-abiding, mortgage-paying citizens cheering with delight as the compere read out the words of the winner: 'Ha, ha. Dead Tory.'

Nazis

ACCORDING TO THE likes of the *Daily Telegraph*, the people who attend demonstrations, pickets, lobbies and any event on which it's expected you carry a placard are 'Rent-a-mob'.

'Always the same ones every time,' they complain, like a headmaster arriving at his office to find a line of boys that have been caught smoking in the toilets. And to a certain extent they're right.

But every now and then something sparks off the public imagination to such an extent that those familiar with campaigning are completely taken by surprise. This was not something however, I ever expected to witness among fellow comedians. For comedians aren't bound together like other work-forces who might suddenly perceive a common enemy. There's no common pay scale or agreed tea breaks, and no 'comedy villages' in which whole families have been comedians going back generations.

A group of us attended a demonstration in support of the Health Service, carrying a 'Comedians for the NHS' banner in 1988. And there have been many benefits organised for dozens of causes. But nothing compared to the burst of activity which took place in 1994 to oppose the re-election of a British National Party councillor on the Isle of Dogs.

It was suggested that a special leaflet should be designed and printed, in the name of 'Comedians against the Nazis,' with reasons for not voting for the BNP inside. And that the comedians should then distribute thousands of these leaflets to every household in the area the candidate was standing.

The point at which you can be certain a campaign is developing a sense of momentum is when it erupts into complete chaos. Someone wouldn't go in a group with someone else because they reckoned that a couple of years earlier he'd nicked his material. Someone insisted that they knew Chas and Dave and could get them to come, and half an hour was spent discussing how we could get Roger Moore as well.

Someone wanted to bring down his mates because they: 'Hate the BNP and would love a bundle.' (This wasn't allowed.)

Someone said she wouldn't take part 'Because I'm a lesbian and I think that's political enough.' Someone else said he'd love to come but unfortunately couldn't make Sunday as he always did loads of speed on a Saturday night.

Despite all this, most got on with their jobs, employing military precision and contagious enthusiasm. Unlike so many veteran campaigners, burdened by experiences of organising things that fall to bits, the agitating comics did everything required to get leaflets designed and printed, the press contacted, the benefits organised to pay for the printing, a pub room booked for meeting on the day, cars arranged to get everyone to the starting point, and a posse of comedy leafleters confirmed. Such a momentum was reached that anybody not taking part, stood out more than those who were.

The wonderful thing about someone getting involved in this process for the first time is that they approach their task with such high expectations, unable to believe that there could be anybody less fervent about the issue than they are. Steve Gribbin took the job of telephoning a list of thirty people to ask if they would take part, and began reporting back the following week on how it had gone. Full of rage, he revealed how twenty-seven had agreed to take part (a success rate I'd never come across before), and was therefore magnificently furious about the three who hadn't.

By the time we'd assembled on the day, there were sixty-seven people from the comedy business ready to do the job.

And so singers, promoters and acts who had never done anything more radical than an illusion with three pieces of string, went strutting along the landings of Tower Hamlets, distributing leaflets and trying eagerly to convey to the residents how strongly they felt about rejecting the fascists.

Most of them had never before taken part in any such event before. In fact, many of them had never taken part in a Sunday morning before.

I couldn't help feeling immensely proud when a short, mild-mannered and completely unideological woman insisted with utter indignation that I had no right to miss out that particular flat just because of the Alsatian.

The 'sensible' view of the world is that politics is something that only happens in parliament. Yet activities like anti-Nazi events prove that if something needs changing, you can help change it, even if you're not an MP. No one says, 'If we want the Isle of Dogs leafleted we must get the government to pass a white paper called The Putting of Leaflets Through Doors on the Isle of Dogs Bill.' You just do it.

On days like that it's possible to sense how not sixty-seven but millions could become involved in shaping society. Once they become involved, those who have sneered the most in the past, are the most insistent that everyone's there on time and can't leave before it's finished.

The BNP did lose the vote, and the rise of fascism in London was brought to a halt, at least temporarily, as a result. How much, if any, difference the sixty-seven comics who took part in the 'Comedians against the Nazis' episode made, we'll never know, but at the very least, it dramatically altered the lives of most of the sixty-seven people involved.

William, It Really Is Nothing

IT'S A STRANGE FEATURE of our society that there's a whole industry dedicated to telling us what we're thinking. Experts in consumer trends, politics, theatre and fashion are writing in every magazine, are on every radio chat show and pop up on lunchtime news programmes on days when nothing much has happened, to tell us that we're more reliant on cars, eating less apples and more kiwi fruit, and are less interested in trade unions than ever before.

And yet, and here's the strangest part, the experts whose job it is to inform us about public opinion rarely have the slightest contact with the public. Theatre and TV critics who state with absolute confidence what's in and what's out, spend their evenings at opening nights and gala performances complimenting the host on their choice of catering firm and telling people, 'Hope you had a marvellous time in Hong Kong'.

Political commentators who calculate how everyone will react to certain events, spend their afternoons having lunch in clubs that pride themselves on their collection of eighteenth century brandies, maybe with some old retired minister who last got on a bus as a publicity stunt for the general election of 1931.

Many of the trends that these experts tell us about amount to one idea: that the old class divide no longer makes sense. The boom time for this theory followed the Tory Party's victory in 1992. 'The reason Kinnock lost,' I heard one expert say on the radio, 'was because the nodding of his head, his hand movements and his gritty accent reminded people of a working class that no longer exists.' The man who said this was deputy editor of *The*

Independent, and a living symbol of Islington luvviness. How the fuck would he know what anybody thought about anything other than about delightful little restaurants in Stoke Newington, and very reasonable at £40 a head?

The outcome of the election proved for these people that anything connected to the concept of a working class was dead and buried.

This idea permeated its way through to the world of comedy. So a review of Mark Thomas by William Cook in *The Guardian* in August 1992 complained that the anti-establishment nature of his act was completely out of date because, 'Hasn't he realised after the Tory's fourth election victory that people are no longer interested in these sorts of ideas?'

Elsewhere reviews and articles about comedians in most of the broadsheets and magazines pushed a consistent theme; that the future of comedy was 'classless'. Cook lauds his favourite act for exactly this reason, although the comic he was referring to would be the first to admit that his background is classically middle class. One act who told stories about the awful jobs he'd had was referred to as 'Hidebound by old fashioned notions of class.' Obviously the comedian had remembered his jobs wrongly.

By the time this idea had been repeated enough times by the sort of people who would discuss the colour yellow on *The Late Show*, it was sufficient to have a working-class accent or refer to a normal family background to warrant a tag of '(tut, tut) out of date'. In conjunction with all this comes a recurring rant about the restrictive past, when lefty comedians prevented anybody from doing material that wasn't PC, followed by a relieved sigh that said, 'Thank goodness those days have gone.' That this was the case is now registered in comedy circles as part of history; a fact that can no more be contradicted than the result of the Battle of Hastings or the invention of the steam engine.

But when was this time when the media was overrun by communist comics? True, there was the Jenny Lecoat period in the early 1980s when 'Alternative Cabaret' rose and fell. But that lasted for no more than a year (and was certainly all over by the time the likes of William Cook arrived) and hardly existed outside London. But most importantly, these 'alternative' venues were tiny. To say that they dominated the world of entertainment is like saying that sport is being taken over by Australian Rules Football because Channel 4 shows it on the odd Sunday afternoon.

The liberal trendiness side of comedy made a few small inroads into the mass media, but compared to *Surprise Surprise*, Paul Daniels and Russ Abbott, it can hardly be said to have ruled the airwaves with McCarthyite dogma.

The infuriating thing about the obsession the media hacks have of purging any 'notions of class' from comedy, is that, despite the protestations of experts in every field, notions of class seem more relevant and more popular now than ever before.

There may not be many dockers or miners left, but if these critics stopped for one minute while buying their avocados to chat with the checkout operator at the supermarket, or could be bothered to say a few words to the bloke stuck all day at the petrol station, they would sense what is strikingly obvious to millions of people – none of whom have a regular column in a newspaper. And that is that as the twentieth century grinds away, most people are working longer hours for less money and feeling less secure than they have for years.

There is also a growing anger about the injustices of society, which is something that is potentially explosive. For example, the fury over the rampant greed of top executives who give themselves enormous salary increases would have been inconceivable in the 1970s. The distaste for the royal family, the contempt for privatisation and the automatic approval of anyone who opposes the government is wide-spread and unmissable. Unless, of course, you happen to be paid large sums of money for writing about what we're all supposed to be thinking.

Comedy need not be just a diatribe about personal annoyances. Surely it can be about the lives that most people lead.

In 1994 I invited William Cook to debate these ideas with Jo Brand and myself at a week-long event in London. Hundreds of speakers were there to address thousands of people on a huge number of subjects. Various prominent scientists, academics and politicians were speaking, and nobody was paid for doing so. He told me he'd be delighted to take part, but unfortunately there was something he had to know first. 'Is there, er, I mean, well... is there a payment involved?' he asked.

I told him that there wasn't, but that he would get his expenses. 'Oh dear,' he said. 'Well, you see, I usually demand a fee for something like this.'

Clearly it wasn't going to be possible. It seemed that he was only willing to participate on the basis of it being a professional engagement, rather like an after-dinner speech. I had no idea what the fee for that sort of gig must be, but guessed it must come in at at least two hundred quid.

'Well, if there's no way you'll do it for free it won't be possible,' I explained.

He was clearly disappointed, so I asked him out of interest how much exactly he would charge.

'Well, let's see,' he answered. 'For a speech in a debate I, well... altogether it would be, well, I couldn't do it for less than fifteen pounds.'

And class is supposed to no longer be relevant.

Anyone who 'ums' and 'ahs' that much about fifteen quid is either skint – in which case they're obviously working-class – or else is someone who never does or says anything without putting a price on it – in which case they're utterly and irredeemably as middle class as it's possible to be.

Gypsy Tart

ONE ASPECT OF BEING Slightly Successful is that you get asked to go on the radio about once every three days. The struggling comedian isn't known by the producers, so doesn't often get asked, and successful entertainers are far too busy – unless they've got something to plug. So I'm asked to be on all sorts of programmes, often to comment on matters I know nothing about.

For instance, after my series on the state of English cricket on Radio Five, my name seemed to find its way on to an unofficial list of 'comedians who know about sport'. So one day I arrived at Greater London Radio on a Saturday afternoon thinking I was supposed to be chatting about nothing in particular between the records, and was told that I was there to analyse England's chances against Holland in a soccer world cup qualifying match.

On the day that John Redwood announced he was standing against John Major for the leadership of the Conservative Party, Radio One's *Newsbeat* sent someone to my flat to ask me what I thought. Later that day, my worthless comments were actually part of Radio One's news.

Radio Five in particular often ask for a 'sideways look at the news' from a Slightly Successful Comedian. This is no doubt due to their brief to be 'newsy' and 'youthy' at the same time. Like the time during the South African elections when I heard a presenter say, 'Okay, more news from Cape Town coming up but first a couple more questions from our Inkatha quiz.'

So, on the morning of the FA cup final between Manchester United and Chelsea, I was asked to sit in a radio van outside my flat and talk about the match. Much as I like watching football, I know bugger all about it, so of course I agreed, but two minutes before going on air I was told that for a quirky angle they wanted me to come up with loads of reasons why, as a southerner, I hated the north. Then they told me that there was a northern comic in their Liverpool studio who they'd got to argue with me; who turned out to be my mate Steve who I'd known for ten years. Suddenly we were on the air.

'So Mark, hee hee, tell us then, why will you be supporting Chelsea this afternoon, eh? I expect you've got loads of reasons for hating northerners, so what's the matter with them?'

'Well, nothing really,' I said quite flummoxed. 'What am I supposed to say, that they're all a bunch of whippet-shagging ex-miners with baths full of coal and black pudding? Besides, Manchester United's main player isn't even from the north, he's French.'

The brilliant thing about most young radio presenters is that they're completely unable to think on their feet, so whatever you say, they carry on with their prepared script.

'Well, Steve,' she said. 'What have you got to say to that? Mark thinks you're all a bunch of whippet shagging ex-miners. So let's hear you stick up for the north.'

'Hello, Mark,' said Steve. 'I didn't know you were going to be on this. How are you? Who do you reckon's going to win?'

'Well, Mark,' giggled the presenter, 'Are you going to let a northerner get away with that?'

'I hope Manchester United win,' I said deliberately to make even more of a farce of this stupid interview.

'Well, there we are, hee hee, absolutely mad. Two comedians there fighting the old north-south battles. But what will the players have had for breakfast?' she said moving on to the next daft item.

One of the peculiarities of radio is that it doesn't feel as if anybody's listening. It's so down to earth and run on a shoestring that, after creeping into a tiny studio that looks like the office up the stairs at a car mechanics', you can't help thinking, 'Did anybody hear that?'

Most people, I imagine, listen to the radio with only half an ear, either while they're driving or pottering around the house. So it rarely has anything like the impact of TV. But after one incident, I'm not quite as sure about this as I used to be.

I was a guest on Mark Lamarr's Sunday morning show on GLR and, just before he put a record on, he asked me if there were any phrases I'd known as a kid which I'd since found out were only ever used at my school. On the spot I couldn't think of any.

'Not really' I said, worried that as an answer, this was a little dull.

'I tell you what, though,' I added. 'At Swanley school at least once a week we had a pudding called gypsy tart. Well, a couple of weeks ago I mentioned gypsy tart to my girl-friend and was astonished that she'd never heard of it. To me it was like someone saying they'd never heard of apple pie or bananas and custard. So I don't know if that was just something from Swanley School.'

Within seconds the phone lines were jammed.

'It's Jean from Dartford and I'd like to say that I was a big fan of gypsy tart but it's a traditional gypsy recipe and that's why it's only found in north west Kent.'

Every caller had a recipe, which the following caller would dispute. 'It's *three* parts condensed milk to one brown sugar, not two.'

Caller after caller rang in with stories surrounding the stuff, alternate recipes, theories of its origins, playground rhymes connected with it (eg 'gypsy tart/ makes you fart/cus-tard powder/makes it louder'). A woman rang in and said it could be found in Essex and that all the Kent people had got the recipe wrong, at which point hundreds more Kent people rang up in outrage.

'No more calls about gypsy bloody tart,' begged Mark Lamarr. But it was hopeless. For three solid hours the listeners of London bombarded us with their tales of this obscure Kent (or Essex) pudding.

How many conversations, reminiscences and debates were sparked by this show? How many people were reminded of gypsy tart and as a result made one over the next few days? How many lives were modestly altered following my chance remark? Were the sales figures for condensed milk and brown sugar significantly altered because of it? I want to know.

For months afterwards, people would come up to me at gigs and tell me that they'd heard the gypsy tart show and how much they'd enjoyed it. And do you know? I could never bloody stand the stuff.

The Real Irish Joke

I CALLED PATRICK for the fifth time in two days. 'Do you know which plane I'm coming over on, yet?' I asked again. 'Only I'm supposed to be doing the first gig tomorrow night, so I really ought to have some idea of the ticket you've booked for me.'

'Ah well, to be honest,' he began, which sounded extremely ominous, (every other time he'd just said, 'Can I get back to you in a couple of hours?' and then had not done so) the flight tickets are a little more expensive than we thought, so I'm not really sure we can afford it.

I tried to explain that as I was supposed to be doing five nights around Ireland, the travel to and from the place came not so much under the category of 'luxury' as 'necessity'. 'Well yes, you've got a point there,' he admitted, and said he'd get back to me in a couple of hours.

Fours hour later, I rang again. 'Ah, I've good news,' he said. 'We've managed to get you a cheap ticket,' and he gave me the details. 'Now,' he continued. 'The only thing. When you go to pick the ticket up, you'll need to make yourself look under twenty-one.'

Every trip I'd ever made to Ireland had been a marvellous exercise in shambolic organisation. The first time was about five years earlier, and I was provisionally booked to do three nights in Dublin; the first at a college, the second on a TV chat show and the third at a theatre. They booked me on a plane that left Luton at eight in the morning, so I asked if I could rearrange it for later. 'No problem,' said Tom who told me that Mary would meet me at midday at the airport.

So I arrived at Dublin and Mary was waiting as promised. As we got in her car I asked what time we had to

246

be at the college. 'Oh well,' she said, 'The college gig was for this morning, so we've had to cancel that.'

'Why didn't you tell me it was this morning?' I started to yell until I realised there was no point. 'All right, I've got nothing until tomorrow night then.'

'Er, what's tomorrow night?'

'This television thing.'

'Er, ah, that's cancelled,' she said, as if I should be pleased. And so I was in Dublin to do one night at a theatre, and had arrived two and a half days early.

The show itself wasn't due to begin until half past ten, and I was told that the building had to close at midnight. But just before I was going on, the promoter asked if I'd mind if a local poet did a couple of minutes first. 'No, that'll be fine,' I said at which point the poet went on stage and read his poems for forty-five minutes.

This meant that I had now travelled to a foreign country to wait almost three days to do half an hour, and my patience with the 'organisers' snapped. A member of the audience could hear the furore and came backstage to ask what was the matter. 'It's almost half past bloody eleven now and the building shuts at twelve,' I ranted, and she took me to one side and said, 'No Mark, the building shuts at twelve – Irish time.'

With that one sentence, I suddenly began to understand the workings of the country. It's not a matter of 'the building shuts at twelve o'clock, but (wink, wink) we really stay open until half past two.' For it does shut at twelve o'clock, but at twelve o'clock – Irish time.'

I remembered this as I was asked to make myself look 'under twenty-one'. So I realised that if I turned up with a grey beard, walking stick, First World War medals and a badge saying 'I am 90,' the clerk would just say, 'There's your under twenty-one special price ticket, sir,' for we were talking about twenty-one – in Irish years.

247

This is one of the reasons that many comedians have gone out to Ireland, done gigs that are completely chaotic, at huge inconvenience for very little money. There's something captivating about the place, so that after a few hours you find yourself greeting people with, 'How's the crack?'

What would be infuriating in England becomes part of the charm of Ireland. After a while you find yourself in rhythm with the disorganisation, so that anything which runs smoothly is almost a disappointment. The hour before a show starts is quite likely to be spent travelling around in the promoter's van, knocking on the doors of his mates who he thinks might have a microphone stand. Arriving at a club in Cork I found no one there except a country dancing class, until half an hour before I was due on stage, when the promoter turned up apologising that he'd had to unexpectedly give his mother a lift across town.

Yet somehow these places seem to work incredibly efficiently. Once they get started the shows have a brilliant atmosphere, making me wonder whether all the phoning, faxing and shouting that goes on in England to make sure that events take place without a hitch, isn't a waste of time.

Apart from the chaos, anybody doing a series of shows in Ireland has to be prepared for the unwritten part of the contract which dictates that every night you have to get drunk. Every bar does a lock-in and every town has a late club, and Galway at two in the morning on a weekday becomes a bustling mass of students greeting each other across the road with phrases like, 'Dermot, ya focken wee basterd, hiya doing,' as if they were brothers reunited after twenty years.

On every Irish tour I've done, Galway has been the fourth night, which means I'd been drunk on the previous three.

There are times when you say, 'Tonight I'm not going to have a drink,' when you know that what you mean is you'll have one lemonade, go 'Oh, bollocks,' and buy a pint convinced that you tried your best. But by the time I reached Galway this time, I really meant it.

'So, for a late drink,' began Kieran, 'There's a club where the students go, or another by the Quayside, or they'll do us a lock in here or...'

'Kieran, I'm not having a drink tonight,' I told him. And the look on his face reminded me of a friend who once described how he'd travelled to an African village. Taken in by a wonderful family he was offered cows' lungs as a local delicacy, and he'd had no choice but to eat them, because to refuse would have been an insult to their religion. By saying I wasn't having a drink, I might as well have said, 'I piss on your God and spit on your mother.' I ended up drunk.

As if to add to the charm of the hangover, some days present you with journeys that you're just not used to in England. 'There's Derry,' you mutter as you unfold your map, 'and there's Galway. Well, that doesn't look far.' And it isn't. But it still takes six hours on a bus which leaves the ground every few seconds as it hammers into a bump or hole in the road, so that after twenty minutes the attempt I'd made at doing some writing looked like the sheet of paper a four year old proudly presents you in the hope that you'll stick it on the fridge.

For every minute of the journey, the radio plays the sort of songs that end up on K-Tel compilations, but tuned slightly off the station and with a hint of opera in the background.

And yet during such a tour, you can't help but be struck by the contradictions of the country. This is a nation which for many years would not modernise its roads or its methods, for it was ruled by institutions completely subservient to the thoroughly un-modernist Catholic Church. Divorce was illegal, publications could be closed down for printing telephone numbers of anywhere that even gave advice about abortions and huge numbers became convinced that the spirit of St Mary was moving statues and making them weep. Until the 1970s, gaelic football and hurling matches could only officially be started by a bishop.

Yet the carefree, vibrant nature with which most people go about their business, displays an enthusiasm which is no longer under such an ecclesiastical stranglehold. The first time I ever did a show in Dublin, I was warned to remember that ideas weren't as liberal as in England. On more recent tours, the opposite has been true.

The singer/comedian who toured with me last was a young woman whose act consisted of parodies of standard songs, reworked to contain as many references to sex as she could manage. Sitting there watching her, I wondered if ten years earlier a Galway audience would have understood, let alone applauded, a woman singing 'Smoother Vibrator' (to the tune of 'Smooth Operator'), and 'You Make Me Feel Like a Natural Yoghurt'?

Instead of needing to be warned off touchy subjects, comedians now have to be warned not to ignore them. The more scurrilous somebody is about the Catholic Church the more they're appreciated, for no one is more fervent about an idea than the most recent convert, whether it's to a religion, a political party or a non-smoker. And the cheers of audiences for anyone denigrating the church or the ideas behind it, are signs of a youth that has recently converted away from catholicism to an ideology that incorporates condoms, pills, gays, and having sex without having to beg the Lord for forgiveness.

Most youth in Ireland still adhere to the church to some extent, of course. They still pray, say grace and go to mass more often than their British counterparts. But do they really mean it, as they once did?

After doing a piece in Cork about the Pope which had gone down far better than it ever did in England, I said, 'What I enjoyed about that was that to me it was just a joke, but for laughing at it you're all going to burn in hell for eternity.'

Just about everyone laughed, and a few even clapped. Would they, I wonder have done that if they really thought there was even a one in ten chance that the punishment was an eternity of damnation?

If there is, I only hope that someone like Tom and Mary are in charge, as it would take most of eternity for them to get it together to find the matches.

Belfast

IN DECEMBER 1993, in the week that the possibility of a peace process in Northern Ireland was first mentioned, I was due to do a gig in Belfast and another in Derry. Both venues were thriving comedy clubs with weekly shows featuring an English act and an Irish act. Except for the previous week, when the RUC had cleared the place a few minutes before the show, because of a bomb.

It seems to astonish many people that in a troubled area like Belfast, normal life continues. 'Well, you be careful,' you're warned, as if you're likely to join an Orange march by mistake. (My mother once warned me to be careful when I said I was going to Dublin, and I reminded her that southern Ireland hadn't been at war since 1922. 'Well just be careful,' she repeated and I said, 'Well, I think waiting seventy years after a war's ended before visiting a place is being reasonably cautious'; but I don't think she got the joke).

The 'Situation', as the people of Northern Ireland describe it, is in evidence throughout the towns. The murals, the checkpoints, the armed police. But for the most part, normal life goes on, especially in central Belfast where the population is mixed, and where the University provides much of the clientele for the trendier bars, and the comedy club.

But one of the fascinating things about the place is that a two hundred yard stroll in the wrong direction can lead you into a completely different environment. Suddenly, instead of being surrounded by portraits of James Connolly and Bobby Sands, you're looking up at King William and his horse.

Wandering through one of these unofficial border areas

just before the show, I thought of a joke. 'Graffiti in England is usually just "Chelsea", or "Bethnal Green Boys", but here you've got a whole city of Rolf Harris's; kids running up to walls with a bucket of paint and a brush going, "Gonna give him a balaclava, nice little kalashnikov there, can you see what it is, yet?"'

Done in a vaguely presentable Rolf Harris voice, I was confident it would get a laugh. But while I was waiting to go on I was struck by the danger of starting with this bit. In front of me were over two hundred people, in roughly equal numbers of Catholic and Protestant, who had to live through The Troubles, and they might not appreciate an English comedian striding into the place for a couple of days and flippantly joking about the whole business.

But then Paddy Kealty, the compere began the evening with an impersonation of Ian Paisley singing 'Happy Talks', and followed this with a joint IRA/UVF rap that started, 'Everybody in the house say yo've got five minutes to get out,' and ended, 'Boom, boom, shake the room.'

'But he's known here and he's Irish,' I pondered. What to do? The show was going fine, and after twenty minutes or so I noticed that in this packed, sweaty bar there was an empty table at the front. I pointed this out to the audience and commented that it could only be because people were afraid that they might be picked on. Then I found myself saying something that I just couldn't stop once I'd started. 'You're a strange crowd,' I began. 'You don't mind dodging a shower of shrapnel every time you go out for a pint of milk but you're scared that if you sit down the front the comedian will take the piss.'

Everyone seemed happy with this, so I did the Rolf Harris joke and now the whole thing was in a different gear. The stuff on the Birmingham Six, loyalists and the typical English attitude to Ireland were the most popular parts of the gig. In fact the more scathing about any institution, across the spectrum, the better the act went. And this was no twee arts centre with a pottery exhibition as you walk past the box office. The make up of the crowd was shown by the entries for the joke competition. Virtually every written reply to: 'What's the difference between a Gladiator and a bottle of Jack Daniels?' expressed a wish to do something to Jet of the Gladiators that would be quite tricky with a bottle of whisky.

The enthusiasm for overtly political humour amongst a typical working-class audience was noticeably different from English clubs. But it was also different to how it might have been before.

For none of the Protestants objected to the comments supporting the Birmingham Six. And Paisley seemed to be seen as an oaf by everyone. A previous generation might not have taken so kindly to unionist leaders being lampooned; after all, to them the Orange Lodge could have provided a job and a council flat. Now all they can provide are bowler hats.

And I'm sure that a couple of years earlier, quips about Republicans would have prompted cries of, 'Yer either with us or against us' from the Catholics. But now both sides appeared able to laugh in common at the absurdities of 'The Situation', including laughing at their own leaders in full display of a crowd from the opposite side of the divide.

Can you conclude anything about the possibilities for peace from a comedy club? Well, certainly there is a new desire for peace. Unionists may still be elected by most Protestants, but whereas a few years ago they were revered, now they're thought of as the best of a shabby bunch.

On the Catholic side, Republicanism will continue in various forms, but the most forthright bellowers of 'Boys of the Old Brigade', are now seen by many as ridiculous.

The potential for Catholic and Protestant unity, and the weariness with the old ideas was apparent that night as both sides of the community laughed equally at the nonsense of the 'Situation' from which none of them benefit.

And yet, over the course of the next two years the prime minister of Britain continued to make statements like, 'The thought of talking to terrorists turns my stomach,' although he was happy to have lunch with the rulers of countries like China, Nigeria and Saudi Arabia. For two years he played with the passionate plea for peace that was expressed in a small way in that comedy club; dithering, stalling and demanding ridiculous preconditions. For two years, half the length of the first world war, he sat with the present of talks in his lap, and refused to open it in case it annoyed the likes of Paisley, until the two year long opportunity was wasted and the bombing resumed.

But from my experience of Belfast society, it's clear that 'The Situation', is not hopeless. For there is a genuine and passionate wish by many Irish men and women, disillusioned with the failures of Republicanism and Loyalism, who have come to see that – Catholic or Protestant – they have much in common. Low wages, high unemployment, fear of violence, and all the blokes fancy Jet.

The Great Publicity Trick

EVENTUALLY, WITH MY own tour and radio series, the time arrived for me to make a proper attempt to get properly organised publicity. How many people, this made me wonder, have any idea how much of a fraud the publicity world is? Getting a peek into the machinery that controls this process made me feel like the hero in a film who gets captured by a baddie, who's saying, 'I am going to kill you; but first let me show you how I intend to use this underground cave as my base for taking over the world.'

'You'll never get away with this wicked plan to fool the entire population,' I felt like saying to those in control.

The trickery begins even at the modest level of local newspapers and radio for, as long as the publicity company which sends out the press release is considered reputable, newspapers repeat it word for word, except for the sort of slight changes a schoolchild makes when they copy something from a book and give it in as their homework.

So if there's a mistake on the press release, as there once was on one of mine, saying that I was writing a play which had, in fact, been finished years ago, it gets repeated throughout the country and spreads into thousands of local freebie newspapers with the uncontrollable force of a computer virus.

In fact, as long as you used a publicist the media took notice of, it would be quite simple to invent an act, write that they used to be a monk and taught Woody Allen how to play the clarinet, and this would be printed and announced without question throughout the nation.

For what most of the media is after is a quirky angle, which is why I sometimes find articles about myself in local papers under headlines like, 'Ex-Milkman Delivers the Laughs', and full of lines like, 'But while he was carrying his crate, it was jokes he kept bottled up.'

The alarming part is that not only do newspapers not mind if you make up a string of lies – so long as it sounds interesting and isn't libellous – they positively encourage it. So, it's not the journalists who are conned by a bogus story, but every poor sod who reads it and then assumes that there's an act going round who used to be a monk and who taught Woody Allen how to play the clarinet.

For these reasons, whenever I've had some small successes at getting publicity, in some ways it's actually been quite depressing. Because it only seems to confirm that to get on in the world of entertainment, producing work of a high quality comes a poor second to having a keen sense of business. Which also means that unless you're dedicated to the business of publicity, it's almost impossible to compete with those who are.

Every time you see an article in a Sunday magazine along the lines of 'We asked ten celebrities for their favourite recipes involving gooseberries,' the ten celebrities included are there as a result of publicity agents badgering the relevant editor for an excuse to mention their client.

During the Festival, Edinburgh has become ridiculously full of billboards, sides of buses and taxis covered with huge pictures of comedians in 'I'm a loony me, I never stop' pose. Wars have been fought over areas smaller than the size of some of these posters, which will display a large picture of an act who's probably never done more than a twenty minute gig, underneath a slogan such as: 'Funnier than Billy Connolly.'

And to a certain extent this works, because it creates an impression to anyone who sees it that here is an act who is a legitimate part of professional showbiz and if you haven't heard of them, you should have.

When an unknown character starts popping up regularly as a panelist on daytime TV game shows and as the person judging the best flan on a cooking programme, it's often because their agent has got another act on their books who's become famous and they've said: 'You can only have the big name if you use this other one as well.'

Millions of people will then start to know the name and face of someone, and simply think that they seem to have been on a lot of things lately, as if by accident.

Production companies employ spin doctors to bombard newspapers with invented stories about how someone on a show they're making is getting back with their wife or husband, or is getting married, or is furious with someone else who's famous for saying at a showbiz party that they've got a fat arse. It's easy to see how experts like Liz Hurley arrange with photographers and media hacks that they will turn up at a certain event wearing a 'shocking' dress, so that the photograph will appear in every newspaper, and the event becomes news.

This is the most disturbing part of watching this process at work, because it makes you realise that what we consider news is for the most part a con, whatever the issue. Most of us watch or read the news thinking that those items masquerading as such have become so because they are, well, the most important things that have happened that day or week. But the Liz Hurley safety-pin dress story was only news because it was in the mutual interests of Liz Hurley and the media that it should be.

The thing about seeing some of these tricks at first hand is you start to wonder whether anything at all that appears as news has happened naturally, or whether every single item has been manipulated into place for the benefit of whoever the story involves.

Certainly, when the news concerns what a member of the royal family, a politician or a sportsman has said, this can only be 'news' because it was put on a press release and discussed between a press office and the relevant journalists. When a story starts 'Tributes have been flooding in...' it can only be because the people making them want publicity for themselves. For where do these tributes flood in to? Is there a place where everyone takes their tributes, and then journalists go and find them, saying, 'Aaah, this one's sweet.' Of course not. The press officer of the celebrity or politician making the tribute contacts the relevant news editors and makes a statement which has been carefully worded to show themselves in the best light. Which is why when a world leader dies, no newsreader will ever say: 'The French President said, "To tell you the truth, I never really met him".'

Any story that starts, 'Figures released today...' or, 'A new report...' is probably a publicity company manipulation, and anything whatsoever involving someone in entertainment almost certainly is – unless they've died (though even then you can't be sure). But what about earthquakes, wars and tidal waves? By the time you've taken part in a couple of publicity campaigns you can't help wondering whether even they are the result of a fax from the PR company working for the country they've happened in saying, 'What about an item on Tanzania as you haven't done anything on us for a while?'

Yet no matter how deceitful you find the business of news management, in this job it's impossible to avoid. So I find myself in the most hypocritical of all positions, condemning it as a fraud and then pulling 'I'm a loony me, I never stop' face (see cover).

Nevertheless, the truly wonderful part is that while publicity can make millions of people aware of someone, it can't make anybody like them. So acts with the most ruthless agents and assertive publicists often get articles written about them in dozens of newspapers and journals and then

259

walk out on stage in a thousand-seater venue to see eighteen people looking back at them. Presenters can be hyped into celebrity status and shoved on to TV on an almost daily basis, but if they've no charm or talent, it only means that instead of a few blokes down the pub thinking he's a pain, there's forty million people going, 'Not that wanker again', whenever they see the Daz advert.

Which must be why the entertainment business is constantly littered with the debris of fallen stars. People who've not lost the talent they once had, but who never had any in the first place, and only achieved celebrity status because they played the glossy magazine game to brilliant effect. Many of these characters, having shot to fame originally on the back of a PR drive, can't understand why it can't work again. Maybe they were duped more than anyone else by their own propaganda.

The fact that the machinery of publicity, with all its money and connections, can still only work to a limited extent gives us great hope. For no one can have had more efficient publicity machines than Mussolini, Ceaucescu or Robert Maxwell; and look what happened to them.

A Real Life Banker

NOTHING QUITE PREPARES you for real life experience. So the first time you see the Eiffel Tower, it looks astonishing, even though it should be no surprise that it's tall and Eiffel Tower-shaped. I was amazed in New York when someone leaned over and said 'Hey buddy, you from out of state?' in a New York accent.

And I was astonished to hear the views of a chief economist from National Westminster Bank, from a distance of about four feet. Hearing him in the flesh at a debate organised by Greater London Radio was more educational than studying a year's supply of *FT* supplements.

The debate was one of a series concerning the issues of the day as they affected London, and I had been asked to do a comic introduction and summing up for each one. The topic this day was 'Work in London', and Mr Economist's attitude reminded me of the scene from John Steinbeck's novel *The Grapes of Wrath*, in which Tom returns from prison to find his farming family are being forced off their land. He demands to know who's responsible so that he can deal with them, and can't understand that 'it's the bank', which has no face or name, but is just The Bank.

Mr Economist's arguments were the arguments of The Bank. We can't go on expecting the high living standards we've become used to. We're still paid more than workers in Asia which makes us uncompetitive. To create jobs we've got to raise productivity and tighten our belts and stop being sentimental when a company (eg, NatWest Bank) sacks hundreds of people to make us more efficient, etc, etc.

Yet more striking than the words he mouthed was the manner he in which he spoke them. A frail-looking man, he looked like the obsessed scientist in a B-movie who insists on continuing with his experiment even though he knows it will wipe out Detroit. His eyes were fixed, his hand movements tiny and economical and you could imagine his voice coming at you from a Dalek, telling you that you're about to be exterminated for being surplus to requirements. He looked quite capable of wrecking hopes and plans, without losing a wink of sleep because, to him, people were not living, breathing creatures, but units. Numbers on a graph to be employed, clothed and fed only so long as it's fiscally viable to do so. When you look into his eyes, you understand he sees the entire human race as customers, and anyone who can't afford the ticket, will find out that he and his like are the planet's bouncers, paid to stop you getting in the door.

Also in the room were representatives of trade unions, low pay units, charities and various lobbying groups; after all, this was a debate. So how would they deal with the deadly doctor?

Some responded by ignoring him. Others by accepting that of course we can't expect people to keep their jobs if savings can be made, but pleaded for compassion from the likes of the wrinkled banker. Everyone seemed to agree that if the market tells us we've got to do without jobs, wages, hospitals and buses, we can no more resist it that we can stop the tide. The banker had made his case and no one would do more than try to modify it to include a smidgeon of humanity, please.

It was a depressing spectacle, for it made it obvious how the organisations which once would have proudly opposed the concept that nothing has a right to exist unless it makes a profit, have surrendered. Twenty or thirty years ago there would have been people in that room equipped to refute the banker's callous ideals.

'You could go on forever with the stuff about, "We're

pricing ourselves out of a job",' I said in my summing-up. 'So that if we all lived in cardboard boxes you could say, "But in Taiwan, they're prepared to live in paper ones so we've got to be prepared to make more sacrifices".'

'You say we need to raise productivity to protect jobs,' I added. 'So if we raised it as much as the miners did would that be enough, cos that worked a treat in saving their jobs didn't it?'

Finally I commented that I doubted whether his theory extends to all lines of work, probably not to chief economists, for example. So if were to I discover that Sri Lankan chief economists were chief economising for forty pounds a week, would he be prepared to drop his salary accordingly? Mr Economist sat still and unmoved, no more taking notice of what I was saying than a cat does when you tell it not to bring birds inside. For like the cat, he doesn't understand our language, and is only doing his job.

Most people seemed to appreciate my tirade, which was quite depressing, for it shouldn't have been difficult to oppose Mr Economist's corporate view of the world more coherently than someone who was only there to take the piss.

The most basic socialist, or even liberal, should have been capable of putting up a challenge to a wealthy executive calling for everyone's belts to be tightened except his own. But this 'debate' seemed to prove that the most basic socialist arguments, which once would have been second nature to any member of the Labour Party, have now been forgotten at best, and abandoned at worst.

And yet when the human consequences of the free market are opposed, the challenger is better supported than they ever would have been before. Confirming that while the 1990s are times in which less people call themselves socialists than for many years, more people agree with socialist ideas than at any time in living memory.

Hattersley

USUALLY, WHEN SOMEONE tells you that they feel their age they mean it with a sense of regret. Someone has called them 'pop', or was surprised that they'd heard of Kurt Cobain, maybe.

Once, on Radio Four's *Loose Ends*, I was seated next to Roy Hattersley. Had I been in my twenties I would probably have seized the opportunity to go into a rant about some of the things (like calling for 'exemplary sentences' for anyone found to be involved in the Poll Tax Riot) that he'd annoyed me with in the past. But instead, being in my mellower and reflective thirties, I politely mentioned how I'd once written a column in which I'd parodied his articles in *The Guardian*, which are often full of gratuitous literary references and irrelevant Yorkshire reminiscences, expecting him to see the joke.

'For instance, you might write "the current Northern Ireland Peace Process reminds me of the rambling hills behind Pontefract and the effect they'd have had on Pip from *Great Expectations*",' I told him.

All the guests giggled politely, except Roy who stiffened his back, became frighteningly like his *Spitting Image* puppet and after a few seconds' silence, yelled, 'Well, I hope you never get any work again.' The astonishing result was that several twee Radio Four types witnessed an encounter between an SWP member and Roy Hattersley, and all decided that Hattersley was the loud, stroppy one.

'I really feel my age,' I thought on the way home, 'and it's brilliant.'

The Girlfriend

FOR ME, ONE of the consequences of becoming a comedian at the age of twenty-two was a string of chaotic relationships. This only ended when, after ten years of enduring almost every conceivable strand of fiasco, I was forced to admit that the evidence leaned in favour of the blame being, at least partly, mine.

For men are at their most dangerous, to others and to themselves, during their mid-twenties. Much of this stems from the trauma we suffer as fifteen to eighteen year-olds, when it's assumed by everybody that we're having sex on an hourly basis. The sad truth is that most of us are too shy and insecure to say 'thank you' to the girl in the bakers without going purple with embarrassment.

When I was sixteen-years-old and working in an office, everybody else in the building would taunt me on a daily basis with comments like, 'What's her name then?' and 'Are you going out with a young lady this weekend?' Until eventually I became so fed up of timidly admitting that I hadn't got a girlfriend, that it seemed easier to make one up.

The trouble then was that within minutes I was embroiled in a web of deceit, as questions were fired at me with the rapidity of a House Un-American Activities investigation.

'What does she do?'
'Have you met her parents?'
'Is it serious?'
'What are you getting her for Christmas?'
'Where did you meet her?'
'Are you bringing her to the office party?'
For three weeks I spent every moment dreading that I'd

be found out, having created an entirely fictitious girlfriend who by now had a favourite band, a middle name and a dislike for boiled eggs. Eventually I announced that I'd chucked her, and the whole office made 'Aaah, what a pity' type noises, while I, on the other hand, have never been so relieved about the ending of a relationship.

For most teenage boys, the task of asking someone out is a tortuous, agonising process in which the dread of being refused is only exceeded by the dread of being accepted. And yet at the same time, they're assumed to be strutting their way through the female population at a rate of dozens per week. And on top of that, they are unable to see as much as a grapefruit or an accounts ledger without in some way being reminded of rampant sex. (Though no one warns you that this part of the predicament remains with you for at least twenty years.)

By the time that heterosexual men have reached their twenties they have mostly, though not always, (by a combination of trial and error, and luck) managed the occasional sexual encounter. If that person happens to then become a comedian, they are forced to become more confident, to be able to relate to women and to be in situations where they will meet potential partners.

The trouble can be that the sexual deprivation of your teenage years can lead to the complications that follow in your twenties. I remember feeling obliged to pursue every opportunity to ask someone out that there was. Like these people who can't bear to leave food on their plate because they remember the 1930s when, 'We were grateful for every cabbage,' I just felt that to turn a semi-chance down was morally wrong. A sort of: 'There are people in this world who'd be grateful for that semi-chance,' attitude.

The state of my warped frame of mind at that time became clear to me quite recently when I was sent a tape of a gig I'd done in 1985. In one piece I was talking about how the first time you go to bed with somebody you nervously concentrate on getting everything right. But after three months with the same person you could be half way through and think, 'Oh, *The Sweeney* is on tonight.'

Three months! I remembered doing that material but was sure that it had been, 'but after two years with the same person'. But three months! As if anything that's lasted that long has become such a ridiculously old fashioned, long term commitment that it's not surprising that everything's gone stale and bitter.

Maybe these attitudes apply to most blokes in their early twenties, but the world of the comedy clubs complicates things further. So I did make an attempt at 'settling down', but was confronted by reconciling this with an environment where it was expected that I would stay up drinking until four in the morning at least three nights a week.

Anyone in the comedy fraternity who didn't take part in the whip-rounds for crates of beer and spontaneous parties that followed were considered weird, the way eight year olds think of someone who never comes out to play.

Just as when I was seven I couldn't even imagine a time when I wouldn't be interested in toy cars and comics, at twenty-five I couldn't even imagine a time when I wouldn't relish the idea of staying up all night with some dope and a bottle of tequila.

Of course I would justify this to the woman I was living with. 'Well, I don't finish work until half past eleven at night so to go to bed at half past four is just like you going to bed at ten o'clock.' But this was rubbish.

Similarly, when I was asked what I'd done all day, I would state that I'd been thinking about tomorrow night's show, jotting down ideas, making calls about gigs and so on. When she said that it didn't look as if I'd been doing anything at all, I would be appalled at the injustice of this accusation.

'You've no idea about how much work goes into a gig,' I'd yell.

But when I look back on it now, I think, 'Well, what did I do all day?'

There must be thousands of blokes at this age who've ruined relationships in this way, but for a struggling comedian it serves a purpose. For when you're a struggling comedian at a comedian's party at a comedy club you are nonetheless a comedian. Once you go home you are just another bloke in a council flat, and are reminded only of the struggling.

This is probably why so many performers take the distressing course of ditching their partners within months of becoming famous. For, as they do so, they are shedding the one thing that can remind them of what they were.

Whatever the reason, most male comedians in their twenties seem to alternate between eighteen month relationships that end up going haywire, and eighteen months of being in a 'well, I'm sort of still seeing her, but it's sort of on and off and there's this woman I met in Sunderland who's down for the weekend and I've started seeing the girl who works at that new venue...' situation.

Now, shacked up in alarmingly cheerful and stable domesticity, I wonder how anyone could tolerate that constant chaos and yet at the time, it seemed quite exciting.

My girlfriend is the one who has to deal with the completely unavoidable problems of living with a comedian. She has to accept that it's impossible to have a social life that fits in with the rest of the world; that I'm liable to launch into a rant, delivered in a silly voice at least twice a day; that I demand to be left alone in the half-hour before going on stage; and then demand to be left alone for six hours at a time while I'm writing, before insisting that she reads what I've done, the second I finish it.

There are probably many more drawbacks I'm not even

aware of. And yet, one of the reasons it can work, is the same reason why every attempt at stability failed ten years ago. Back then, if I was asked to pick up some shopping on the way to a gig, I would think 'I'm doing a show, I haven't got time to worry about shopping.' Now, if I say 'I've got to go to Broadcasting House tomorrow to do a live interview,' I find it quite comforting to be asked, 'Well, can you get some sausages on the way back?'

It's marvellously therapeutic to come home after doing a two hour show to two hundred people that's gone brilliantly and be told as you come in that the plumber rang and won't be round until Tuesday.

It's probably just that it takes this long to get the job into perspective, and to realise that no matter how much or how little acclaim you attract, there are other things that are just as important.

The Horny-Handed Sons of Entertainment

'I COULDN'T BELIEVE my first day here,' a woman working as a researcher for Granada Television in Manchester, told me. 'At five o'clock I started to put my things into my bag and the others said "What are you doing?"'

'I said, "I'm putting my things into my bag," and they all said, "But we haven't finished sorting out this problem".'

'"Well, can't we do it tomorrow?" I said, and they all looked at me as if I was mad.'

'"You can't just go, just like that," they said.'

'"But it's five o'clock. Our hours are nine to five and it's five o'clock," I said, but they all just kept saying, "But we haven't finished."'

The woman was in her thirties and her colleagues were in their twenties, and she was experiencing the culture shock that those who started work in the 1970s come across when they mix with those that started work in the 1980s.

Of all the workforces whose wages and conditions worsened in the 1980s you'd be hard pressed to find one that was as battered as those who staff the entertainments industry.

Partly this was because of the rise of the production company. Instead of broadcasters like the BBC, London Weekend or Central making all their own programmes, many are now made by independent companies, which rely on selling their ideas, one at a time, to the TV stations. As such they are run in a hand-to-mouth fashion and have hardly any permanent staff, and certainly no trade unions.

For example, when I was working on a weekly programme made by a production company for BBC2, the producer, researchers, clerical staff, van drivers, stage designers and crew in charge of setting up the lights were all employed on short-term contracts, covering the eight weeks of the show and little more.

On recording days they would do a day's work at the office, drive up to Nottingham or wherever the show was being recorded that week and continue working until midnight when the studio was cleared. Then they'd have to be back in the London office for work in the morning.

They were all impressively cheerful in the midst of the agonising from comedians, producers and writers that erupts in these situations and, at the end of the eight weeks would all have to start touting for work again.

Nowadays, whenever I turn up at a commercial radio station, I'm greeted by a chirpy employee who offers me tea or coffee, takes my coat, enthuses about their work and then tells me that they hope at the end of six months to be offered a job there, because at the moment they're on work experience, which pays them dole money plus travel to the job. The deal at many of these companies is that in return for these uncertain conditions, there's a 'Hey, but this is such a cool, laid-back *Happy Days* atmosphere'.

At one of these stations I was taken through to the 'chill-out room' to wait to go on air. The chill-out room, I was informed by a woman on work experience was the idea of the go-ahead management. There was a Sega megadrive computer games machine, a fridge full of beers, a pinball machine, a coffee machine and a couple of huge bean-bag armchairs that once you've sat on you have no idea what to do with your legs. 'Any time you feel a little stressed out,' they'd been told by the bosses, 'you just chill-out in the chill-out room.' Except, she told me, behind the huge glass panel at the end of the chill out room was the director's office, so that any Kung-Fu Combat chilling-out had to be done in full view of the people who could sack you at any moment.

Far from standing apart from the new working conditions, the old companies, including the BBC, have desperately tried to copy them. They've also copied the 'trendy management' methods, having courses at every opportunity, believing that these things boost morale. One employee I know – a man so mild-mannered that if he caught a burglar in his house he'd apologise for having an out-of-date record collection – went into a fit of rage after one such course, saying, 'It was a blatant propaganda exercise and sapped out the last ounce of morale anyone had left,' and, 'the only person who enjoyed it was the accountant.'

'Now, tell us what you really think about the company,' the presenter had begun. As if anyone was likely to tell the truth and say, 'I think you're all wankers, mate.'

For no amount of beanbag armchairs or sitting in circles could disguise the fact that virtually every producer or secretary in BBC Radio is now on a short term contract of between six months and two years. Or that offices are continually being shut down so that the staff can be moved into smaller ones, or that since the canteen was privatised the food has been horrible, and that you're now charged 1p for a cup, whilst everyone knows that the management have spent hundreds of thousand of pounds on a new escalator whose main purpose is purely aesthetic.

One employee told me how they'd been involved in organising the arrangements for a speech by John Birt to a business conference. Just before he began he decided that the seats in the concert hall weren't luxurious enough for businessmen to sit on, so at huge expense, they had to hire dozens of special chairs that would be of a quality deemed suitable for a businessman's arse. Then the water jugs were judged to be too down-market for such a select gathering and they had to go out again to buy a new lot. Eventually Birt made the speech, and a whole row of comfy businessmen with splendid water jugs by their side, slept through the whole thing.

There's a story the staff tell of how the loyal and thorough security guards (who could spot you trying to pinch a BBC biro from eighty paces) were replaced by a private company to save money, and the following week thousands of pounds worth of sound equipment went straight out the back door. I've no idea whether the story's true, but what I do know is that everyone wants it to be.

The argument put forward by the trimmers and downsizers in modern business is that cost-cutting means the public get better services. But is that true?

'Producer Choice', the BBC's own version of an internal market means that each producer has an allotted budget, and must pay each department they use, the going rate for the slightest job. For example, when I was working on a topical show and rang up the news desk for the name of someone who'd been in the news that week I was asked for my chargecard number. Then the clerk gave me the answer and charged the programme I was working on, like the kid at school you pay to do your maths homework for you.

There are now fewer rehearsals, as paying the actors to do them would take the programme over-budget. Even sandwiches are no longer provided on the day of the recording, so half an hour before they are due to begin, the performers can be found anxiously queuing up at Burger King.

With television it seems to be even more true that the first requirement of most programmes is that they should be made cheaply. The opening shots in any discussion about a potential TV idea involve a producer grimacing that there just isn't very much money. Which all amounts to one possible conclusion: if the employees are being paid less and are on worse contracts at the same time as the money spent on programmes is less, then someone somewhere is making more money at everybody else's expense. And that someone can only be shareholders.

The cut-throat practices of the 1980s are assumed to be

273

out of date, superseded by the caring 1990s. But the world of entertainment is just one area in which the accumulation of vast fortunes by a tiny minority has continued unabated, the difference now being that hardly anyone agrees that it can be justified. And there's a pinball machine.

'There's a programme being made for Granada,' my agent told me. 'And they want to do a feature on you; follow you up to a gig, film the show, do an interview, it'll be about fifteen minutes of their show.'

We discussed whether it would be a good show to do, and after a while I asked him how much money they were offering.

'Er, not good,' he said.

'Oh Christ, is it one of these fifty quid things?' I asked.

'No, it's worse than that,' he said. 'It's nothing. They say it will be good publicity.'

As I was about to go on tour I decided to do it anyway, but the day before the show they rang up.

'Can you give the cameraman a lift home?' they asked, 'Only we can't afford to pay his fare.'

The cameraman, an enthusiastic and conscientious lad from East Anglia was on work experience, and was sleeping on the office floor during the week, as he couldn't afford to rent anywhere.

The day before filming started, the directors of Granada (who I imagine can go home at five o'clock, if they want to), bought the company which controls Forte hotels for £3.8 billion.

Something to Look Forward to

ONE OF THE most enjoyable panel games I've done was a Radio Four programme called *A Look Forward to the Past*, in which guests have to answer a series of questions about history, whilst keeping it 'topical and relevant'.

It was recorded in a studio with no audience and the presenter was Paul Boateng, black Labour MP for Brent. My only previous memory of the man was watching him drape a garland of flowers around his neck when he won his parliamentary seat in the 1987 election, proclaiming, 'Yesterday, Soweto; today, Brent.'

When I arrived at the studio, it was clear he had lost none of his previously-displayed pomposity; every handshake and sip of wine exuded the kind of aloofness any West End actress would have been proud of.

The other guests on the show were a middle-aged professor of history called Lisa Jardine; *Times* columnist and Nigel Lawson's son-in-law, John Diamond; and Loyd Grossman.

'In the first round,' began Paul, 'I ask my guests where and when in history they would have liked to have been in charge.'

Someone mentioned being with an artist and someone else mentioned a character I'd never heard of, and then it was my turn: 'I'd like to have been the boss of The Grand Hotel in 1984; so I could have said to the IRA, "About two feet to the left should do it."'

'Okay, cut, cut, *cut*!' screamed Paul. 'Oh for goodness sake,' he howled and threw up his arms. 'I mean if we're not going to take it seriously.'

He then turned to the other guests with a sort of 'who invited him?' demeanour, and had to spend a couple of minutes recovering. After the recording resumed, he enjoyed long conversations about Erasmus and Martin Luther and the legal implications of something or other, in which I took very little part.

The final round was a question about which of two characters in history we would rather have been, and my choice was Lenin or Stalin.

'Well, many people judge one to have been a continuation of the other,' I replied, 'but in fact there are one or two differences. For example, Lenin believed the factories, villages and army should be run by the workers, peasants and soldiers whereas Stalin believed they should be run by Stalin. Lenin believed in freeing the nationalities whereas Stalin believed in invading them. Lenin encouraged debate but Stalin's debating method was to have his opponents shot, and Lenin wrote volumes whereas Stalin commissioned people to write volumes about himself along the lines of *The Sun Shines For But Half a Day, Whereas You, Comrade Stalin, Shine All Night As Well*. So my answer is Lenin.'

Boateng looked a little puzzled, and then turned to the other guests. 'Well, weren't Lenin and Stalin really exactly the same?' he asked the academic, the son-in-law and the cook, confident that such an esteemed gathering would share his revulsion for all matters Bolshevik.

'No,' yelled all three at once.

'You can't blame Lenin for crimes perpetrated after his death,' said the professor.

'Stalin was a brute but Lenin was extremely principled,' said John Diamond.

'I think I'd like to have been Lenin,' said Loyd Grossman.

Ah, yesterday, St Petersburg; tomorrow, Brent.

Please Allow Me To Introduce Myself

AFTER THE HUBBUB of doing a few TV shows during my 'this is someone new' phase, my appearances became quite infrequent. But every time I found myself in a television studio, I was struck by its atmosphere of urgency, seriousness and importance.

Especially *importance*, which is practically emblazoned across the maze of brightly-lit sets, cables, cameras with seats that go up and down like dentists' chairs, women running across the floor with powder puffs and combs in case someone's eyebrow gets ruffled, countless lights, blokes with clipboards, blokes with headphones and someone with one hand up your shirt and another down the back of your trousers trying to fit a radio microphone.

A radio audience sits in a radio theatre, hears a brief introduction from the producer, witnesses the recording, at most ten minutes of re-takes and then goes to a nearby pub with the performers. A TV audience is bundled through the corridors of a television centre into a studio with plastic raked seating, sits through forty minutes of a warm-up act who gets interrupted before each of his punchlines by a floor manager who wants to know if a blue shirt will clash with a green chair. Eventually they see the first part of the show on monitors above their heads, then a sketch performed in front of them which is repeated three times, after which an angry director tells them that they really must try and laugh a little louder, and you wonder whether he's going to burst into tears and say, 'Right, get out – the lot of you, the whole audience is sacked.'

One word which rarely applies to a TV studio is 'fun', for

they're such arenas of tension that the slightest task becomes a huge palaver. For example:

Barry Cryer was the compere for a TV stand-up comedy programme I was on, and part of his introduction of me was to say 'You may have heard his Radio One series, *The Mark Steel Solution*.

Later, a woman with a clipboard told me that we would have to re-film the introductions. 'In that case,' I asked, 'would it be possible to get Barry to say Radio Four, instead of Radio One, because the series goes out on Radio Four.'

'Oh,' she said, clearly troubled. 'You mean you're not happy with your introduction.'

'No, it's not that,' I said, trying to reassure her, as she seemed *most* perturbed, 'The introduction's fine except for the word "One", which would be better as "Four."'

'Well, I wish you'd let me know earlier,' she said beginning to fret. 'I mean, if you'd let me know earlier, we may have been able to do something, but ...'

'No, the introduction was fine. Honestly. It was a really good introduction. And it doesn't really matter, but I just thought that as it has to be filmed again anyway we might as well ask Barry to say "Four," that's all.'

'Oh. I don't know,' she said, adding the odd grunt, evidently now under a good deal of stress. 'I just don't know what we can do.'

'No, don't worry,' I interrupted, concerned that the price of having the right radio station broadcast would be a nervous breakdown and a broken clipboard.

'I'm sorry,' she said suddenly indignant. 'There's nothing I can do to change it now. All the writers have gone home.'

Maybe it would have been simpler just to arrange for the whole radio series to go out on Radio Four, instead.

Bosses

IN MOST JOBS you'll find people who'll tell you that the further up the ladder you go, the less people know about their job. Well, I was at a dinner organised by a production company, and the head of the firm, who can probably be counted amongst the dozen most powerful people in British comedy, told me what he thought about the film *Pulp Fiction*.

'What I loved about it,' he enthused, 'is that in one scene John Travolta gets killed and then in the next scene he's sort of back alive again, as if by magic and that's such a great idea.'

If a ten-year-old child were to misunderstand such a simple concept as the cinematic flashback, wouldn't you put his or her name down for special classes at once?

Flo

'BUT HE'S A comedian,' a British producer is likely to say if a comedian is suggested for an acting role, in much the same way you might say, 'But he's a maths teacher' if someone suggested getting a maths teacher to rewire your electrics. Perhaps that's why there was a ten year gap between my first and second TV acting roles.

The second of these, in 1995, was doubly compelling simply because it was the first time for years that I'd done anything like a normal job, working alongside a group of people I'd been randomly thrown together with.

Contrary to their perceived image, most actors seem endearingly down to earth, although some manage to live up beautifully to their stereotype.

'There is an extremely famous picture of me in a celebrated version of *Mother Courage*,' one actress blurted out suddenly during a moment of silence in the queue for breakfast.

Another woman, called Flo, walked twenty yards across the car park to tell a group of us who were waiting to be called into the costumes van how much she enjoyed working with Leslie Phillips. 'Clive Dunn, he's another lovely chap,' she'd say, sparing no time between 'guess who I've met?' stories. Each one would conclude with a little piece of information that would confirm how well acquainted she was with the particular celebrity, like: 'And he's very fond of rabbits, you know.'

After running through Ian Carmichael, Frank Windsor, Terry-Thomas and a few more that were just a blur, I tried to get her to talk about something else. (Keeping her quiet was clearly not an option.)

'What's that in your bag?' I asked, having noticed a peculiar metal framed object sticking out of it.

'Oh, that's my portable seat,' she said. 'You don't go anywhere without one of these when you've been in the business as long as I have. Four or five hours standing around on set can be pretty trying at my age, let me tell you. I think it was Prunella Scales who first advised me to get one…'

The strangest part of this scene was that she had already got changed and was dressed as a canteen lady in a blue pinafore with a hairnet and dirty apron. She was in her early sixties and looked perfect for the role she was going to play, and yet she was speaking in this classic BBC accent about Leslie Grantham's garden.

'I'll tell you who is an absolute beast,' she went on. 'Ronnie Corbett. Now he and I were working together on an episode of *Sorry*, and I cracked a joke…'

Suddenly the wardrobe woman arrived. 'Okay, all those who haven't changed, if you could go to the costume van, please, and we'll need you on set in fifteen minutes,' she said with authority, thus wrecking the Ronnie Corbett story.

Fifteen minutes later, having changed, we went across to the set. Flo marched confidently across to us and said: 'And Ronnie turned straight round saying, "I crack the jokes around here, if you don't mind",' as if the time lag since the interruption had never existed. Unable to feign interest any longer, I walked away.

I'm sure there's a character like Flo on almost every set, but to someone who doesn't often see filming at first hand, she was fascinating; as was every camera and shout of 'Running up', 'Action', and 'That's a wrap.' Everything was exciting, the way a chip shop or a bookmakers is exciting when you're three and you see one for the first time. But for the camera crew, runners, wardrobe, make-up and catering staff, a film-set is nothing more than a travelling factory – particularly for the extras.

One of the few times I'd previously witnessed the paraphernalia of film was as an extra for a scene set in a First World War trench, in which I'd played a soldier. Every five minutes or so, a woman from make-up with a bark like an inner city pub landlady at closing time, would yell: 'More mud!' at which her assistants would slap more mud over our faces with the elegance of moonlighting plasterers.

Now that I was a bona fide actor, I recalled that day when I heard the director whisper to his assistant: 'What about that one? No, the second from the left.'

We were about to act out a scene in which three of us were sitting chatting at a table, and an extra was needed to bring us some tea and say, 'Here you are.' So the second extra from the left was asked to do this. Suddenly his whole day was different. From then on the director would call him by his first name instead of 'you', and as his mates continued their conversations in the background, he had to listen to where he was supposed to be. And, on top of that, he'd have been paid at least double the extras' rate.

As we waited to begin the scene, Flo approached us again. 'The thing is,' she told us, 'I'm remarkably good at accents. You see a lot of people try to do a Cornish accent but end up with Devon. But I'm from Cornwall and I know the difference. So that's very handy when it comes to parts that require a Cornish accent. I've got a lot of work that way over the years, I can tell you. Not long ago I played the role of a Cornish woman in an art college. Not a lot of money in doing shows at an art college, but you meet a lot of people and make a lot of contacts. And that's what's important in this job: contacts.'

As we waited for the film crew to adjust the lighting, she went relentlessly on and on.

Trying desperately to get a conversation going which would have enough life in it to drown her out, someone asked a young actress who had recently left drama school how many of her fellow students had given up on account of not getting much work.

'What they say,' answered the actress, 'is that a lot give up after two years but if people stick it out beyond that, the next stage is ten years.'

'Oh, I've often considered giving it all up,' said Flo apparently out of character. 'But every time I think about it, another part comes along and I think, "Well, maybe this is the one that will lead to something big." Thirty years I've been thinking that now. I nearly gave up this year but then this came along and I thought, "Oh well, you never know what might come of it."'

'Okay,' yelled the director and clapped his hands. 'Everyone get in position.'

'Right, here we go then,' said Flo.

'That's strange,' I thought. 'I didn't know there was a canteen lady in this scene.'

And she wandered over to the back of the set, where she was to hand a tray of tea to the recently-promoted extra whose job it was to bring the tray to the table and say, 'Here you are.'

'I wouldn't worry too much about the way Alan collects the tray,' I heard the director whisper. 'I mean that bit's not going to be in shot anyway.'

Mortality

MOST PEOPLE WOULD imagine that if a TV producer tells you that he'd really like to make a series from your idea, it'd be reason to celebrate. In fact, you'd be better off crawling immediately into bed, covering your head with the duvet and trying to imagine waves breaking gently on a deserted beach.

For this producer will probably set in motion a process that will cover many years, and succeed only in getting you to ponder your own mortality.

If TV executives decide that a certain type of show – like a quiz show hosted by a particular presenter, or a costume drama starring a favourite actor – would fit their schedules, a series can be decided upon, made and put on the screen. It's a very different task to get an idea which has originated with the writer or performer on screen.

The first stage in the process will be lunch, quite possibly with someone who's currently working with Noel Edmonds. The purpose of this lunch is 'just to sound out a few ideas', and takes place in a brasserie with menus two feet high, describing dishes like *sausage portions with potato mashettes served on a traditional bed of fresh baked beans, £14.95.* I'm introduced by the producer to someone in a suit and braces who is described as 'our projects and developments officer,' but who barely says a word and who I never hear of again.

The proposed programme is hardly mentioned at the lunch and I start to think, 'I wonder when we're going to sound out these ideas,' and then the lunch ends with everyone thanking me enormously for coming, and saying how it was very useful to meet me, and that they'll be in touch.

The next stage is to draw up what's known as the Treatment. This is the laborious task of summarising the whole project on two sides of paper, using phrases like, 'The show will be innovative with instantly identifiable characters and yet personable and intimate.' As a guide to whether a programme is going to be any good or not, these things have got to be absolutely useless. The Treatment for *Fawlty Towers* must have been full of stuff like, 'The humour will derive from the debunking of the snobbish Englishness conveyed by the manic hotel proprietor.'

This Treatment will then go backwards and forwards between the producer and the performer four or five times, with odd sentences being removed and lines like 'Much of the show will take place in the launderette itself' added.

Between each exchange, five or six weeks will pass, although occasionally there will be a burst of apparent progress. 'Could you fax me a copy of the revised Treatment, your CV and a couple of pages about what you're working on at the moment, and get it to me in the next hour,' I might well be asked.

'But I'm just off to Gloucester.'

'Look, can't you cancel it? Only there's a meeting this afternoon with the head of In-House Laughter-Based Entertainment and I want to pitch our idea at him.'

So I'll rapidly put something together, rush down the printers to fax the stuff through and get to Gloucester late. The next day I think, 'I wonder when I'll hear about that meeting.' Then another six weeks goes by and it's never mentioned again.

The concept of the meeting in the media world is in itself a fascinating process. 'I'm in a meeting,' a producer said to his secretary once when he was chatting to me about the England cricket team.

'I'm afraid he's in a meeting at the moment,' I heard the secretary say to whoever was on the phone.

It should really have made me feel important, but instead I just recalled the hundreds of occasions I'd rung someone in the media and been told, 'He's in a meeting.'

There must be many naïve people who try to contact media executives and are told, 'He's in a meeting,' and therefore believe that he can't be disturbed because he really is in a meeting. Possibly they imagine he's among a group of businessmen surrounding a table, banging their fists and yelling things like, 'I'm telling you, if we go with McCluskey it'll screw up the whole operation.'

But they're more likely to be saying, 'I've always said that in test cricket you can't be without a specialist wicket-keeper.'

Now, whenever I'm told, 'He's in a meeting', I'm fascinated to know what sort of bizarre unmeeting-like activity this person is actually performing at that moment. No doubt people have been informed, 'He's in a meeting,' when the 'he' in question has been asleep, arranging for the car to be serviced, playing clock patience, or possibly even masturbating. Yet the desired affect is achieved, which is that the caller goes away feeling less important than they did before they picked up the phone.

The trick is to eventually be part of a meeting that prevents anybody else getting through. And this is the aim of the producer who you're working with; to get a meeting with someone from the inner circle of the media's decision-making process. Should you succeed in getting this far, you will then find that the meeting will be arranged for a ridiculous time in the future. A secretary will contact you at 10.40am on July 11th, and say, without a hint of humour in her voice, 'So, could we make it 12.30pm on October 19th?'

How busy, I wonder, is the President of the United States? Is he so busy that he can't find half an hour in the next three months? Because if not, that makes him less busy than whoever's third in command of the Comedy section of the Light

Entertainment department of the New Ideas division of BBC2.

This meeting will almost certainly be cancelled. Normally this happens on the morning the meeting should take place, with a phone call from a secretary saying how dreadfully sorry her boss is, but he's had to go to Finland.

So then it's back to meetings with the producer at six weekly intervals. Throughout this process I never have the slightest idea what's happening. A producer will enthuse about a forthcoming meeting with someone important at Manchester, but then at the next meeting it turns out that there never was anyone at Manchester, but apparently there *is* someone in Birmingham, who has just been appointed head of something which has just received money from somewhere, and the producer is scheduled to meet with them a month from now. Once I sat and listened while a producer told me in earnest excitement, hands wringing with anticipation, that he'd organised a meeting with the religious affairs department of the BBC and was very confident that they would want to make our comedy programme.

After the treatment has been with a particular department for a year, the person nominally in charge of it leaves their job and is replaced by someone who asks you to rewrite it to fit in with their new brief for the channel, which is to include more of something this programme hasn't got.

Even getting this far depends largely on status. At one point I never got further than, 'He's in a meeting.' Then I started getting to the stage of the booked but cancelled meeting with the executive. These days, I sometimes get to actually have the meeting with the executive, which seems to go one of two ways.

The meeting can end with a discussion about an 'offers' meeting. An 'offers' meeting is where various heads of department 'offer' their ideas to the controller of the whole channel, who at that point either agrees that the programme should be made or rejects it as unsuitable. The first time I went through this stage, I spent the day of the offers meeting anxiously wondering how it was going. Had they got to my programme yet? What was the weather like; would that affect their mood? What was the final verdict?

After two days had gone by, I assumed that as no one had been in touch, I should be reconciled to rejection, but after a week I found out why I hadn't heard – the meeting had been cancelled.

Once however, I experienced the second type of outcome, whereby a senior executive enthusiastically endorses the show and tells the producer that he'll be in touch to start discussing a budget and a schedule for making the show.

This was in 1987 and I never heard from him again.

And on and on and on it goes. Nothing ever seemingly gets accepted, but neither does anything ever get rejected. In some ways it would be easier if all this was just a comment on me personally, and was their polite way of saying, 'Look, we don't want your bloody show, now leave us alone.' But every other writer and performer, including those who have finally succeeded in getting things on, are treated the same way. Indeed, as with any creaking bureaucracy, even the bureaucrats themselves recognise it as crazy but are completely unable to do anything about it. So it's not even anyone in particular's fault.

There are people I used to scream about who have titles like 'Head of Development', and 'Assistant Programme Commissioner', who most people assume are extremely influential, but who I now know are as frustrated as anyone about how powerless they are to get anything they approve of on air. Like Frankenstein's monster, the system has developed a will of its own and has assumed total control.

On top of this, even when a show is finally commissioned there is often a two year time lag before it makes its way on to the box. So that even when new programmes do eventually arrive on to the screen, it's usually taken between five and seven years for them to make the trip.

Meaning that the whole of the Second World War, from Chamberlain's announcement, through Dunkirk, the Battle of Britain, Pearl Harbour, the siege of Stalingrad, the Normandy landings and the fall of Mussolini, to VE day, was a quicker process than that of getting a comedy show on the telly.

Which is why the whole business has made me quite aware of my own mortality.

When a producer says, 'I think we've got a good chance of getting your radio series on the box,' my first thought is, 'Well, I hope I stay alive long enough.' For how do any of us know what we'll be doing in seven years' time? If we're not dead we might be deaf or blind or have become born-again christians or peace protesters stuck up a tree. A scientist can work on a long term project in the knowledge that his work can be continued when he's no longer there. But once a performer's dead, he's fucked.

Any comedian in their seventies approached by a producer must, in all seriousness think 'I might as well apply for a mortgage'.

There must have been programme ideas which have bobbled around for years before finally being commissioned, only for the network to discover that the proposed presenter of the show has died.

If that happened I wonder whether in their dying breath the comedian thought: 'Ha, ha – this'll serve the buggers right.'

A Message in Malvern

DRIVING WITH AN open sun-roof through the classically English country villages of Worcestershire on a sunny day in April, I felt the way you're supposed to imagine the driver in an American road movie feeling, as he steams through Arizona in an open-top cadillac, with Chuck Berry belting away on the soundtrack.

Malvern is the most beautiful of all these villages, built on the side of the sort of hill Londoners call a mountain. And, although the weather wasn't as hot as an average day in July, it seemed hotter because only a couple of weeks before it had been freezing.

The show was in a school which had been converted into a theatre for the duration of the Malvern Festival, and the staff were exceptionally friendly. I was shown into the headmaster's office, which for the night doubled as a dressing room.

What, I wondered, could I start the show with, as I knew very little about Malvern that'd be of use?

Then the phone rang. Playing the role of the headmaster I thought I'd answer it. 'Er, hello, man, er, right, is Steve there?' I was asked.

'No, I'm afraid he's not,' I told him.

'Oh right, well, like, who am I, like, speaking to?'

'Mark, this is Mark.'

'Oh, is that Mark Steel?'

'Well, yes,' I told him, quite flattered to be identified.

'Yeah, I recognise your voice off the radio. Look, Mark, er, did you notice whether there was a group of hippies playing drums outside the room you're in?'

'Er, no. No, there isn't.'

'Are you sure, man, cos it's important.'

'Well, I'm sure I'd have noticed a group of hippies playing drums. Hang on, I'll ask if anyone's seen them,' I offered, intrigued by the surrealism of the situation.

I went out to the makeshift box office and asked if anyone had seen a group of hippies playing drums.

'Oh yes,' I was told. 'They're down by the river.

'They're down by the river,' I told my new friend.

'Well, like, could you take them a message?' he asked.

'Well, I can't personally,' I told him, 'I'm just about to go on stage, but I can try to get someone else to do it. Hang on.'

So I went back to the box office and said 'Could someone nip down to the hippies playing drums by the river and take a message?'

'No problem,' said the box office woman.

'So what is the message?' I asked the bloke on the phone.

'Could you tell Carl that Bryn's arrived and he's ready to have his nipple pierced?'

I repeated the message to the box office woman and without looking up from the magazine she was flicking through, she called out: 'Yeah, that's fine,' as if it was a routine message.

Perhaps it is in Malvern.

Are You Talking to Me?

ONE OF THE joys of being a regular guest on radio programmes is that many stations arrange cabs to take you to the studio and back.

The drivers work for companies who have accounts with the station, so unlike most cabbies, they have beautifully warm and comfortable cars without a length of dented chrome panelling hanging off the wing, and instead of playing Shabba Ranks at top volume, they love sharing their opinions and experiences.

Some of my favourites have been:

Robin Day
I'd just finished a Sunday morning show on Greater London Radio and met the MP Tony Banks as I was coming out. He was going to be taking part in a debate about whether MPs should appear on programmes as celebrities, and apparently Robin Day would be on the phone.

'I tell you what mate, could you put GLR on for me, please,' I asked as I got in the cab.

He put it on, and after a while sure enough there was Robin Day.

'Who's that?' he said.

'Robin Day.'

'I thought it was. I fucking thought it was. Do you know I was taking him from here one day and he's sat there right there where you are now. Anyway he's sniffing and sneezing like I don't know what and I said: "I tell you what, you don't want to be out on a day when you're sniffing and sneezing and breathing your germs all over London".

'He says: "Do you know who I am? I'm Robin Day."

'I says: "I don't give a fuck who you are, you shouldn't be breathing germs all over London, you cunt." That told him.'

Good day for Birds
Travelling up to a station called Heart FM in west London, on a steamy sweltering day.

'I tell you what,' began the bald and tubby cabbie, about fifty years old, 'Today is what I call a good day for birds. Especially them city birds. I get a job going up the city and I think "Oo, my Christ, I don't want to go up there, I'll end up driving up the pavement." Now, I tell you what I mean by a good day for birds. Not just a baking hot day, oh no. See that's all right but you want a little bit of wind. A little bit of a breeze, yer see, and then every now again *wooof!* and the old skirt goes up in the air. That's what I call a good day for birds.'

The Roadworks
As we were leaving the house I pointed out that it was best to turn right because they had the road dug up on the left.

'Oh they've mucked up the road have they? Like this government, they're mucked up. Don't yer reckon? They muck up everything this lot. Mind you, Labour aren't much better. John Smith? No, you need a revolution, that's what you need in this country. Like Karl Marx said in *The Communist Manifesto*: "The world is becoming ever more divided into two great classes, bourgeois and proletarian," and that's true, when you think about it.'

By now we were just turning right, it was 6.15 am and he'd gone from the roadworks to Marx in under a minute. My sort of cabbie.

The Present
Most of these cabbies, when asked, reveal that they've ended up in the job because they were made redundant from their

last one. One, with an unfeasibly posh accent told of how he'd worked for a company which traded in futures (I've never quite understood what that means). The son of the managing director was put in charge of a huge budget and made some terrible investments, the company went bankrupt and there he was driving cars.

Another time, returning from a morning show just after Christmas, I asked the driver if he enjoyed his job.

'Well, you've got to work,' he said. 'I mean, this doesn't really pay the mortgage but it's better than rotting away at home. I was a salesman before this; selling cars instead of driving them. Still, there's plenty worse off. I mean some of the blokes who were laid off at my place haven't found anything, so I shouldn't complain. And you can have quite a laugh with some of the passengers so it's not so bad.'

We carried on chatting until we reached my road.

'Just down here on the left please,' I said.

'Here, you on that morning show every week, are yer?' he asked. 'Only you might be able to help me out. See, a few weeks ago I won a competition on there and they were supposed to send me a mug and a T-shirt, and it hasn't arrived. I mean, I wouldn't normally be bothered only with me being so skint I was relying on that for me daughter's Christmas present. So if you could have a word.'

The French

Going up to GLR one Sunday, a couple of days after the IRA bomb that broke the cease-fire, the driver stopped at a newsagents so that I could get a paper.

'Well, you might not agree with me, but I'm a fan of John Major. I know most people don't like him but I think he's done a good job. But this Ireland business, he's only got himself to blame. They should have been talking to Sinn Féin as soon as they called that cease-fire.'

Over the next half an hour he revealed himself as remarkably well informed about Ireland. Then, as we were approaching the radio station he said: 'Now the funny thing is, I never go over the Docklands as a rule, but on the day the bomb went off over there I'd been there twice. Took a French bloke over there to that City airport first time. I don't know why he wanted to do that, it's quicker on the Eurostar.'

'Well, it should be,' I said 'But when I went on it, it whizzed through France at 180 miles an hour, got through the tunnel no problem and then got stuck in Kent and we sat there for two hours not moving.'

'Well, that's cos we don't like ripping up our countryside, but the French don't give a shit about things like that,' he said.

'Well no, it's cos they've invested public money and we haven't,' I answered.

'I suppose you like that French food an' all,' he said suddenly.

'Er, well, yeah, I don't mind it,' I said.

'I thought you did. I thought you fucking did. Have you been eating garlic?'

'Well, last night I had a meal that had garlic in it.'

'I thought so. I fucking thought so. Cos I hope you don't mind me saying, Mr Steel but you stink. You fucking stink. I said to myself as soon as you got in the car, *Coor fucking hell*, I'm not gonna be able to have anyone else in here today after that smelly fucker, he fucking reeks of the stuff. I mean, no offence, Mr Steel, but you stink like a fucking polecat.'

And the amazing thing was that when he said 'No offence,' I honestly believe he meant it.

Who's in Control Here?

AFTER THIRTEEN YEARS in the job, what's the point?

Standing in the wings of a theatre in Portsmouth a couple of years ago, I pondered this very question. The double act that was on before me were stripping down to their g-strings and tipping custard over each other. Amidst the screeching 'Yeeeugh' noises of the audience, one of them, covered in gunk walked up to the microphone to announce, 'And now, the main act of the evening, Mark Steel,' and I made my way on to the stage, circumnavigating the splodges of custard in the style of someone avoiding puddles in a car park when wearing new shoes.

To start with, the aim of almost anyone who goes into writing or performing, whether comedy, poetry, prose or playwriting is to have control over what you're doing, so that you can express something you feel strongly about, to make it worth sitting studiously over a blank piece of paper for.

Most people at some point have a crack at putting down their ideas and thoughts, whether in the form of a diary, a poem, story, song or joke. The most unlikely characters – next door neighbours, Avon ladies or street-fighting blokes who look like they'd kick your head in for knowing who Wordsworth was – might ask you one day if you know anyone who could publish their poems. I've been asked by builders, market traders and fishmongers if I could use the influence they imagine I wield to get their sketches to the right producer or their prose to whoever it is in the BBC who reads prose.

What very few people realise is that even if you can make a living from writing or performing, your work will probably end up totally different to what you intended in the first place. Because the moment entertainment becomes a profession, the control starts slipping away. When I appeared at Wrexham Polytechnic and at the worst of the miners' benefits, far from doing what I felt was my funniest material, I was restricted to doing whatever was most likely to keep order.

Later, in the regular clubs I would censor myself, with the need to get quick laughs that offended nobody. Once I started doing longer sets I would often find myself going on after a joke competition to which the winning joke was something like, 'The difference is you can't stick your knob in a rainbow.'

The further up the ladder you go, the worse it seems to get. The chiefs of light entertainment are remarkably consistent in their lack of ideas or opinions. If you offer a fervent view on almost any social issue to people whose title is Head of Comedy, they will invariably stand there with the uncomfortable look of someone trapped at a party by a bloke who knows all about computers.

Say you think that something in the news is outrageous and they'll reply, 'Yes, er, well, my word, hmmm, you certainly seem to know a lot about it,' when in fact all you've read is the front page of the *Daily Mirror*.

The minute someone approaches the job from an angle of wanting to make a point that matters to them, the majority of executives, journalists, promoters and producers go into a gormless trance that makes you wonder whether you asked if you could have oral sex with their grandmother by mistake.

And the tragedy of most people who are unable to get angry about social issues is that without anger there can be little passion. How can you love Mozart, Otis Redding and The Clash without despising Cliff Richard and Mr Blobby?

Without vitriol there can be little warmth and humanity.

For how can you respect the girl at the supermarket check-out, or the lad who has to sleep in the production company office, without having contempt for the wealthy people who employ them and treat them so abominably?

Occasionally wonderful programmes, plays and shows do make it on to the screen or into the West End, but it's usually not because of the people who run the business, but despite them. The entertainer has to have not only the passion to create the work in the first place but the inexhaustible tenacity to battle their way through a system which is dedicated to the bland and inoffensive.

Which is why, at times, every entertainer finds him- or herself doing gigs, writing scripts, or performing in radio and TV slots that they are in no sense proud of, but which they think might be good for their career.

At this point it's essential to stop and try to remember why you started in the first place, and ask whether all those people who would love to scratch a living expressing their ideas do so because 'One day I want to be seen by twenty million people on a toilet roll advert, up to my neck in Andrex.'

I'm fortunate enough to be able to do my own live show, which reminds me what the point is with every performance. For the marvellous thing about being a stand-up comedian is that if you have your own audience, you have complete control.

One day during the Edinburgh Festival, I asked the owner of a petrol station if I could borrow his pen to write a cheque. 'No!' he screamed, telling me he would sell me one but he was sick and tired of people coming in without their own pens. So every night of the Festival I would recount the tale and take my revenge as the audience laughed at his rudeness.

That tiny power seems all the more valuable when it's used against more powerful foes than grumpy garage owners. And there's no one to tell you to water it down, be careful, or not be libellous, or 'Really have a go at the Tories,' or say that they can't change the introduction, because the writers have gone home.

To make a living and still retain that degree of control is the reason I started in comedy, and it's the reason most people start. Every writer and performer's ambition should be to get into a position where, if you end up doing something that's a pile of shit, you have no one to blame but yourself.

Funny

I WAS IN a hotel room in Norwich, ironing my shirt, before heading off to do the show at the theatre, watching the local news programme, *Look East*. One of the quirky items they have on these shows, about cub scouts who keep crocodiles or vicars who do handstands, came to an end and, in that special important-sounding local news link man voice, the presenter said, 'Now; we've all heard of the Bayeux Tapestry, but how many of us have heard of South Waltham Junior School tapestry?'

This, it struck me, was funny. That night I mentioned it in the show and everyone laughed. And yet tens of thousands of people must have seen the programme, but probably very few realised until it was pointed out to them, that they'd seen something funny.

In a sense, that is exactly the job of the comedian. Simply to point out that the people and situations that we come across in the course of our normal business are funny.

Which is why it completely misses the point to ask, as often happens when comedians are interviewed, about the subjects that are considered too serious to joke about. For this misunderstands the most important thing about what's funny, which is that things are funny because they're serious. Relationships are funny, school is funny, work and being skint and burglaries and people who annoy you are funny, because they matter. Primroses, the chemical symbol for lead or the shape of lettuces aren't funny, because they don't matter and are therefore not serious in any way.

No one would ask a playwright, musician or novelist whether there are subjects they would never tackle because they're just too serious. But comedy is thought of in this way; it's assumed that it can't deal with matters any more urgent than how difficult it is finding the end of a roll of Sellotape.

Journalists write things like, 'Why doesn't he stop trying to tell us what's wrong with the world and stick to making us laugh?' But the answer must be that there's nothing funnier than what's wrong with the world. In a peculiar way, another group that shares this view is the irritating band of pseudo-lefties whose political activity consists of watching anti-establishment comedians and then haranguing them after the show for doing a line which they consider sexist or anti-Greek or some such thing.

For what they are saying is that something is only funny if it's directed against something or someone *they* don't like. 'I like a joke as much as the rest of us,' they often begin, reminding me of the teacher who'd say the same thing before explaining that it wasn't funny for Micky Tillman to make a farting noise every time the room went quiet. Like anyone else who begins a sentence with these words, what the teacher meant was that she liked a joke as long as the butt of it was somebody else. This is clearly nonsense, because it *was* funny when Micky Tillman made his farting noise.

Just as it was funny the day after the 1992 election when someone said to me, 'Have you heard the good news? Labour are still two per cent ahead in the polls.'

'How could you laugh at something as serious as that?' I can imagine people saying. But then how can you laugh at something as serious as some poor bastard having to spend all day serving coffees on a train to such an extent that he believes in Sandwich of the Month? To find that situation funny is not to take pleasure from the plight of the poor sod, but to find the condition of the whole human race extremely funny and extremely serious. Very few of us can escape the world in which important businessmen with control over vast amounts of wealth sit round tables and announce excitedly, 'Gentlemen, we have a new sales drive on sandwiches. I give you – Sandwich of the Month.'

The entertainer can entertain by trying to get their audience to escape the problems of the world, if only for the period of their performance. Or they can try to reach into the pit of misery that surrounds us and, without sparing the reality, find something positive to share.

Isn't it extremely serious and extremely funny that a Scotsman pretends in a poetry group that he wrote a poem written two hundred years ago by Robbie Burns; or that hundreds of people feel strongly enough about preserving gypsy tart that they ring up a radio station with the recipe; that stoned musicians scream, 'Hiya doin' everybodyyyyy?' to twenty students in Dudley; or that even more stoned people will drive a van down the motorway at thirty miles an hour giving a lift to a complete stranger?

And what could be more positive than the humour and resilience of the bed and breakfast family in Hull; the compassion of the miners and their supporters at the benefits; the vigour of the table-thumping Owen Dudley-Edwards and the enthusiasm of the erstwhile apolitical comedians in campaigning against fascism; the forthright passion of the cabbies and the determination of the lad up the tree trying to catch roses; the considered professionalism of a presenter on *Look East*; the realisation that most people, even racist Geordies, name-dropping actresses and desperate impressionists are only as they are because society's values have made them like that; and that wherever there is injustice there are people who will cheer on the comedians who make themselves part of the opposition to those injustices?

But finally, how can it be anything but positive to experience at close hand so many people and so many situations that can be inspiring, depressing, passionate, bland, arrogant, perverse or mad, and yet are all – above everything else – funny.

Also published by THE DO-NOT PRESS

Down & Out in Shoreditch & Hoxton
by Stewart Home

A slice-and-dice splatter novel in which time-travelling streetwalkers hump their way from the trendy east London of today back to the skid row mutilations of the Jack the Ripper era. Amid the psychological dislocations, warm blood isn't the only thing that gets sucked by the night creatures who haunt Home's anti-narrative. This is without doubt the weirdest book ever written, the illegitimate offspring of the Marquis de Sade balling a post-modern literary extremist at at ladies of gangster rap convention.

'A repellent, sick psychodrama that is sadistic, morally reprehensible and has no redeeming features whatsoever. I loved it.'
– Kathy Acker

A Dysfunctional Success – The Wreckless Eric Manual
by Eric Goulden

Wreckless Eric first found fame in the 1970s when he signed to the emergent Stiff Records label. His label-mates included Ian Dury, Elvis Costello and Nick Lowe. Much more than a biography, 'A Dysfunctional Success' spans most of an eventful life, telling of Eric's time at art college and at work (including quality control at a lemonade bottling plant and as a bus-boy in a department store), his start in the music business and of his battle with alcoholism.

'Magnificent.' – *The Guardian.*
'*A Dysfunctional Success* is very possibly the most entertaining read of this or indeed any other year.' – *Mojo*

Judas Pig
by 'Horace Silver'

Billy Abrahams is a career criminal who makes a very good living from violence, armed robbery, operating sex shops and stealing from other criminals. But he becomes increasingly haunted by childhood ghosts and by the ever-growing influence of Danny, his psychopathic partner in crime.

Billy finds himself starting to look beyond the violence and the scams, slowly descending into a drug-fuelled netherworld that affects his judgment and his perceptions. He is finally tipped over the edge when Danny commits an act even Billy cannot stomach. And that's when things really start to go wrong...

Judas Pig is the real deal. This explosive first novel from a reformed career criminal comes with authenticity stamped all the way through. Dark and vivid, bleak yet often funny and beautifully written, this is a book that will stay with you long after you turn the final page.